ROCHDALE

PAST AND PRESENT

A

HISTORY AND GUIDE

BY

WILLIAM ROBERTSON,

REPORTER.

"Go, little book, from this my solitude!
I cast thee on the waters—go thy ways!
And if, as I believe, thy vein be good,
The world will find thee after many days."

ROCHDALE:
PRINTED AND PUBLISHED BY SCHOFIELD AND HOBLYN.

1875.

THE TOWN HALL, ROCHDALE.

PREFACE.

THIS work has been written for the purpose of supplying a want which has been long felt, and contains a variety of information which has never before appeared in print.

It would have been easy, with the materials at hand, to have largely extended the work, and the task of condensing the matter at disposal has not been unattended with difficulty.

Our information has been derived from sources which we believe to be trustworthy, and we have endeavoured to be correct in our statements of fact. Probably, however, some inaccuracies may be discovered, and this is perhaps inseparable from a work of the kind. Any errors or omissions that may be pointed out will be carefully noted, and corrected or supplied in a future edition, should such be necessary.

If in any instance our remarks tend to give pain to individuals we can safely aver that we have not "set down aught in malice," and have simply endeavoured to be just. Our lighter sallies we hope may create some amusement, and may possibly relieve the work from any tediousness of detail that may be apparent.

That the book will be found useful we have little doubt, and if the public should honour it with their approval, we shall be most happy to publish a new and greatly enlarged edition. Any information that may be supplied for future use we shall be glad to receive, and we trust our readers will kindly bear this in mind.

We cannot conclude without sincerely thanking our friends and coadjutors for the assistance they have rendered to us in the compilation of the work, and we gratefully acknowledge the obligations under which they have thus placed us. Information has been most readily supplied in every instance, and it is pleasant to recall to mind and record here the favour which has been shown to us by many influential persons in the town. But for their aid we should have been comparatively helpless, and if the work possesses any merit, it is mainly owing to the kind offices of many valued friends and fellow-workers.

ROCHDALE, *February*, 1875.

CONTENTS.

INTRODUCTORY.

"The Norman shall tread on the Saxon's heel,
And the stranger shall rule o'er England's weal;
Through castle or hall, by night or by day,
The stranger shall thrive for ever and aye;
But in Rached, above the rest,
The stranger shall thrive best."

ROCHDALE is of great antiquity, and is, no doubt, of Saxon origin. The name, "Rochdale," has been the subject of some little controversy, and various derivations have been suggested as being alone correct. In the Norman survey the name is spelt "Recedham;" and "Gamel," a Saxon thane, appears at that time to have been lord of the place. At or soon after the Norman Conquest the river was named the "Rach," whence we have "Rached," and "Recedham," the latter signifying the habitation on the "Rached." Then we have, subsequently, "Racheham," "Ratchdale," "Rotchdale," and, finally, as at the present day, "Rochdale." Clearly, the river flowing through the town gives the name to the town itself; and, so, we have "Roch" from the river, and "dale" from the valley or low-lying land through which the river flows. That a castle existed in Rochdale, prior to the Conquest, seems to be established if tradition may be relied on; nevertheless, there is no mention of such an erection in the survey we have

referred to. In our day the site of this castle is pointed
out with some degree of assurance; but we think this
must be regarded as simply conjectural. "Castleton,"
one of the townships within the municipal borough, is
said to derive its name from the fact that in this division
was situated the *castle* of Gamel, the thane or lord, and
this locality is supposed to have formed the town of
ancient times which has, in the course of many generations, spread itself and become the important and
wealthy town of Rochdale in which we have the happiness to live at the present day. "Castlehill," the
late residence of Mr. Samuel Lomax, deceased, is
pointed out as the site of the ancient castle of Gamel,
and in the valley immediately below a spot is known as
"Killdanes," in memory, as tradition asserts, of warlike
encounters between the Saxons and Danes, in which, by
all accounts, the Danes suffered immense slaughter.

It is an undoubted fact that the Church of St. Chad's
was in existence previously to 1193, as an ancient
record proves this to have been the case, Geoffry,
Dean of Whalley, being in possession of the Church
prior to that period, as rector. Indeed, the year 1180
has been assigned as the time when the Church was
erected. The glebe lands of St. Chad's are of considerable value, and are now vested in the Ecclesiastical
Commissioners for England, under an Act of Parliament
passed in 1866. In that year it was stated that the
value of the living was £5,000 per annum. The parish
is of very great extent, and is situated in the Hundred
of Salford. It is one of the largest parishes in the
kingdom; but it is of the town that we have more
particularly to speak. The municipal divisions of the

borough, which are the same as the Parliamentary, are the following :—Castleton Ward, North; Castleton Ward, East ; Castleton Ward, West ; Castleton Ward, South ; Spotland Ward, East ; Spotland Ward, West ; Wardleworth Ward, East ; Wardleworth Ward, West ; Wardleworth Ward, South ; and Wuerdle Ward. According to the census of 1871 the population of the respective townships forming the parish was as follows :— Blatchinworth and Calderbrook, 6,691 ; Butterworth, 7,923 ; Castleton, 31,331 ; Spotland, 35,596 ; Wardleworth, 19,300 ; and Wuerdle and Wardle, 8,988 ; and the total population of the parish (including Todmorden and Walsden, 9,332), according to the same census, was 119,161. The population of the municipal borough is estimated 65,458, and the number of voters is 12,891. A comparison of these figures with those of the immediately preceding census shows an immense and rapid increase in the numbers which the town and parish now contain ; and reference to other statistical returns proves that the wealth of Rochdale has kept pace with the increasing population. A single glance around us will give indubitable evidence of the immense wealth of which Rochdale is the centre ; its warehouses, mills, foundries, and manufactories of various kinds meeting the eye in almost every direction. The Rochdale of the present day can bear but little resemblance to the Rochdale of only fifty years ago ; and as our increase in wealth and population is so immense and rapid, the Rochdale of our time will, in like manner, bear but little resemblance to the Rochdale which will show itself to the gaze of our posterity fifty years hence, when we who are now so proud of our

good old town are slumbering beneath the clods of the
valley. It may be, and it is no poetic dream to imagine
so, that the Roach will in that day have become
a clear and unpolluted stream in which the trout and
other delicate denizens of fresh water streams will
disport themselves; and when the angler, standing on
its tree-embowered banks, may find excellent sport to
repay him for his patient labours, or it may be that

> " The river then shall boast its pigmy boat,
> Urged on by pains, half-grounded, half afloat,
> While at her stern an angler takes his stand,
> And marks the fish he purposes to land;
> From that clear space, where in the cheerful ray
> Of the warm sun the scaly people play."

Rochdale was enfranchised under the Reform Act
of 1832, and returns one member to the Imperial
Parliament, the present member, Mr. Thomas Bayley
Potter, son of the late Sir John Potter, having
held the seat since the year 1865. He succeeded
the late Mr. Richard Cobden, on the lamented death
of that honourable gentleman. The number of
electors on the Parliamentary list is 10,566; and there
are 10 polling places provided for voters. The principal
manufactures of the town and neighbourhood consist
of cotton and woollen fabrics, and cotton spinning, and
Rochdale may be considered as the seat of the woollen
manufacture for the kingdom. A considerable trade is
carried on in these branches of industry, giving
employment to vast numbers of men, women, and
children. Carpets are also manufactured, and there are
dyeing, bleaching, and silk spinning works. Rochdale
is famed for its machinery, and there are several large
establishments devoted to this important manufacture

as well as large iron and other foundries, and steam engine and boiler making works.

In the neighbourhood of Rochdale there is a large number of valuable coal mines, affording an abundant supply of that important product. The stone quarries of the locality are also numerous, and the supply of stone is abundant, and the quality good.

The public improvements which have been made in the town in the course of the last forty or fifty years have been numerous and advantageous to the inhabitants. Our streets present a marked improvement in every respect, and the general appearance of the town is far more pleasing than it used to be in years gone by. These changes have been effected by the local authorities under powers conferred on them by Parliament; and although the expenditure upon these objects has been necessarily heavy, few persons can complain that the outlay has not been judicious, and, for the most part, absolutely necessary in the general interests of the people. The opening up of new and important thoroughfares in several parts of the borough has conduced to the public welfare; and perhaps no improvements of late years are more to be commended than the new and handsome thoroughfare from the Manchester-road along the street past the Town Hall, and the wonderful change which has been effected by the formation of the Bury New Road. These are only samples of the good work which has been accomplished by the Corporation, and for which we are of opinion the burgesses ought to be grateful. The sanitary condition of the town has been materially benefited by the changes which have been effected; and in the course of

a few years more we hope that still further alterations
in the same direction may be carried out.   Of late years
the sewering of the town has received special attention,
and it need scarcely be added that this particular subject
is well worthy the closest consideration and care on
the part of those who have the health of the inhabitants
at heart.   It must be ' obvious that whatever tends to
improve the health of a town is in strict keeping with
the spirit of the times, and nothing reflects greater
credit upon the governing powers of a great centre of
commercial industry such as ours, than clean, spacious,
and well-lighted streets, and a complete and efficient
system of drains and sewers.   In sanitary matters, at
any rate, we are clearly in advance of our forefathers,
for their notions on such subjects were of the
narrowest and most unpractical kind; but then we live
in more enlightened days, and it would be sad indeed
if the lessons which time and experience have taught us
did not result in material and satisfactory progress in
the path of improvement.

The churches and chapels in Rochdale are numerous,
and many of the former are of great beauty.   In the
succeeding pages, the various places of worship are
noticed, and detailed particulars given respecting many
of them, which may be interesting and useful.

We have quoted at the head of these observations a
few lines which allude to the proverb " that the stranger
shall thrive best in Rached," but we have done so only
for the purpose of remarking that we distinctly object
to any such ridiculous notion being entitled to the
slightest consideration or belief.   Such a statement is
no more true of Rochdale than of any other town in the

kingdom. Here, as elsewhere, industry and integrity
win the day; and if the proverb, or whatever it may be
called, were in any sense peculiar to Rochdale, we
should be in a sorry plight at the present day; and we
should not be able to point to our modern magnates who
are "native here and to the manner born," who flourish
among us so honourably, and who are so deservedly
respected and esteemed. So

> Despite the old proverb which folks oft rehearse,
> And which some one has turned into excellent verse,
> The natives take issue on subject so grim,
> And regard the assertion as moonshine or whim.
> For the truth is that here, as in places elsewhere,
> The man must succeed who does things "on the square;"
> And nor native nor stranger can hope to win fame,
> If patient endeavour surround not his name.
> Heaven's blessing on good, honest work must prevail,
> Whilst inaction and fraud must as certainly fail;
> And if natives and strangers together unite,
> The name of old Rached will grow still in might.

Of the families of the worthy men we have been
alluding to, it was our intention to have spoken at
length in a later part of the present little work, if our
space had permitted; and we could then have shown
how, from small means, aided by untiring effort and
honourable conduct, the heads of many of these families
built up patiently, and little by little, the substantial
structure of wealth and consequence which their descendants possess at the present time. We have no
doubt that sufficient materials for such a purpose would
have been readily supplied to us; for what can be more
creditable to any man than that he should have made
his way in the world by his own exertions, and left
behind him a good name and honestly-acquired wealth

for those who succeeded him ? We feel that none of
these families can look back at their, in some cases,
humble origin, without feelings of a pride which does
them honour ; and the wealth which has been acquired
for them, and which they have been able to increase by
"following the same rule and minding the same things,"
enables them to find employment and the means of
livelihood for thousands upon thousands of their fellow
men who throng their busy mills and manufactories,
and who thus help to develop the wealth and commerce
of their native land.

With reference to the public improvements of recent
years, we may mention the magnificent Town Hall
of which Rochdale can boast. Externally the building
attracts attention from its great beauty, and, internally,
its completeness and exquisite adornments must be
closely inspected in order to be appreciated. Within it
is a perfect study, and in all respects it is a building
which has not many equals. Local critics, now and
then, find fault and complain of the needless expenditure which has been incurred in what is sometimes
termed a merely ornamental edifice ; but remarks of
this kind are not now very frequent, and there seems
to be a sort of quiet pride that we have in Rochdale a
hall for the conduct of the public business of the town
which is worthy of the attention alike of the connoisseur
and of the man of practical ideas. A full description of
this building will be found in the ensuing pages.

THE GOVERNMENT OF THE TOWN.

THE town of Rochdale had not a defined boundary until the year 1825, when an Act was obtained by which it was enacted that a circle with a radius of three-fourths of a mile, measured from the Old Market Place, should constitute the town of Rochdale; and all those householders, owners or occupiers of any messuage of the value of £35 per annum, except licensed victuallers, were appointed and declared to be Commissioners for the purpose of lighting, cleansing, watching, and regulating the town, and to make certain improvements. The authorities, previous to this date, were the County Magistrates, who held Petit Sessions to dispose of civil and criminal cases, and, with the Overseers and Churchwardens, carried out the Poor Laws, and appointed the Parish Constables; the Lord of the Manor, who held a Court Leet, and regulated market tolls, &c., and the Highway Surveyors, who managed the streets. In each of the townships of Castleton, Spotland, and Wardleworth, there was, also, a select vestry, which joined in the management of Parish affairs.

From 1825 to 1844, the Commissioners of Police managed the town's affairs with considerable credit. For some years they held their meetings at the Welling-

2

ton Hotel, but in 1839 they erected the Commissioners'
Rooms, in Smith Street, and from that period until the
erection of the Town Hall, of which more anon, these
Rooms were the seat of government.

Amongst the leading Commissioners at this period
were Messrs. Samuel Taylor, Jacob Bright, James
Butterworth, Abraham Brierley, Thomas Chadwick,
Benjamin Heape, Robert Leach, Joseph Butterworth,
Lawrence Hardman, William Whittle Barton, George
Ashworth, John Howard, Joseph Wood, James Gibson,
Thomas Booth, Charles Butterworth, Wm. Chadwick,
John Chadwick, Samuel Lomax, John Roby, Matthew
Greenlees, Thos. Robinson, Joseph Sellers, John Petrie,
Wm. Littlewood, John Whitaker, and James Leach.

The first elected Commissioners who made the
declaration under the Act of 1844, were Messrs. James
Leach, Thomas Booth, Richard Ashworth, Joseph
Bottomley, Edward Taylor, James Erving, John Hoyle,
Thomas Livsey, John Mason, John Petrie, Wm.
Brown, James Grinyer, William Pilling, Richard
Simpson, William Warburton Whitley, Wm. Bartlemore,
Thomas Fisher, Robert Heap, Jesse Hall, Robert
Pagan, John Dania, Benjamin Greenhalgh, John
Turner Littlewood, Thomas Leach, Joshua Radcliffe,
Edmund Barrow, Wm. Crawshaw, Wm. Holt (Mardyke),
Wm. Standring, James Thompson, George Adamson,
William Whittle Barton, William Holt (Roche House),
Thomas Howarth, Robert Kelsall, John Milnes,
William Petrie, George Proctor, Joseph Sugden,
John Tempest, Charles Walker, John Whitaker,
Thomas Robinson, Samuel Holland, James Gibson,
Thomas Shaw, Thomas Turner, Richard Whitworth,

W. M. Dunhill, T. Ashworth, G. Mansell, J. Howard, Robert Taylor Heape, Benjamin Bright, and Jas Booth.

The chairman of the commissioners was styled, for convenience or courtesy, the chief-constable. There was also a treasurer and a law clerk, the latter only receiving a salary of twelve guineas per annum for his attendance at the monthly meetings. The constabulary of the town consisted of a head-constable and two assistants, and some half-dozen night watchmen. The scavenging of the town was done by contract for some time, but it was soon found needful to alter this method and employ a scavenging staff. The commissioners contracted for the lighting of the town with the gas company, which had been formed in 1823. The charge for each public lamp was a constant source of dispute betwixt the gas company and the commissioners. The lowest price was 42s. per lamp to burn 1,500 hours.

The defects of the Act, and the absence of power to manufacture gas, wherewith to light the town, led the commissioners and the ratepayers to apply for another Act, which was obtained in 1844. By this Act, the £35 qualification was continued, and the commissioners were elected by the £10 householders who were on the Parliamentary Register, and were limited in number to 60; Wardleworth electing 27, Castleton 21, and Spotland 12. The authority of the commissioners was considerably extended; the power to pave and sewer being granted. An effort to procure power to form baths and recreation grounds was defeated by the strenuous opposition of several wealthy ratepayers.

The power to make and sell gas was, however, conferred, and this may be said to have been an

important turning point in the history of the town. A
dispute of some three years' continuance, between the
commissioners and the gas company, culminated in the
decision by the commissioners not to light the public
lamps for one season, and for the next year to light
them with oil instead of gas.   Connected with this
dispute, the gas company professed inability to supply
certain ratepayers with gas, and also some public lamps,
and applied to Parliament for increased powers.   Thus,
the gas company and the commissioners were seeking
the same power.   At the suggestion of the Committee
of the House of Commons, an offer to sell the gas
works to the commissioners was made.   The price
asked was £24,000, this being double the subscribed
capital.

At a commissioners' meeting, it was moved by Mr. W.
W. Barton, and seconded by Mr. T. Livsey, "That the
gas works be not purchased, and that new works be
erected."   An amendment was moved by Mr. Edward
Taylor, and seconded by Mr. Robert Kelsall, "That
the gas works be purchased for £21,000," which
amendment, after an exciting discussion, was carried
by a majority of three, and the works were accordingly
bought by the Town;   the purchase being completed
in November, 1844, by the ceremony of delivering a
sod and the key, which was done by Mr. Samuel
Lomax, of Townhead, manufacturer, the chairman
of the company, and Mr. J. S. Lancashire, manager
to Mr. W. W. Barton, who had been appointed to take
possession on behalf of the commissioners.

The progress of the gas works since that day will be
learnt elsewhere, but it may be proper here to state

that at a very large public meeting of the ratepayers, held in 1843, before application was made to Parliament that it was resolved that all the profits derived from the manufacture of gas should be appropriated to the improvement of the town; such as widening streets, the erection of bridges, building a town hall, &c. Several important improvements, namely, the widening of Toad Lane, Blackwater Street, and the Old Market Place were named in the Act.

The improvement of Toad Lane was not carried out, but the others were accomplished within five years, the time allowed by the Act, and have been paid for entirely by the profits of gas. These widenings of the streets of Blackwater, part of which is now called Lord Street, and the Old Market Place, now a continuance of Yorkshire Street, completely altered the characteristic of the centre of the town.

Scarcely had the projected improvements been completed, and the attention of the commissioners given to the requirements of a rapidly increasing population, when it was found that the Act was defective in giving the required powers to a body disposed to secure the health and comfort of the inhabitants it governed. In the year 1848, Parliament passed the 'Public Health Act,' and the discussions and enlightenment consequent on the passing of this measure, gave the commissioners to see the defects of the Act of 1844—and accordingly in 1850, it was resolved to apply for increased powers to pave, sewer, and cleanse the town, to regulate the buildings and remove nuisances. This effort was subsequently opposed by a majority of the commissioners, and the application was deferred till 1853, when an Act was procured with larger scope, including the erection of baths, the formation of recreation grounds, and the con-construction of a cemetery; and it also conferred on every householder the right to vote in the election of com-missioners. The Rate Book was the Register of Voters, and the inhabitants of houses of less than £10 yearly value had the power to pay the rates and deduct the amount from the rent, if the owner did not pay the rate, so as to secure their votes. There was not known in England so complete an enfranchisement as in this Act. But there was also a power for owners to vote under what is known as Sturges Bourne's Act.

The number of commissioners was reduced to 42, of which Wardleworth returned 18 commissioners, Castleton 15, and Spotland 9.

The borrowing powers were limited by the Act of 1825, to £2,000; by that of 1844, to £48,500; and by the 1853 Act, to £80,000.

Though it will be seen that the improvement com-missioners had practically all the means required for well regulating the town's affairs, so far as related to the health, comfort, and convenience of the inhabitants; yet it was agreed that there was a deficient power, namely:—that the commissioners did not, as a corpora-tion, possess political power, nor govern the town completely, as a corporation created by Royal Charter. Thus the constabulary was directed and controlled by the county magistracy. The chairman of the commis-sioners had not the same prestige or political influence possessed by a mayor in the eye or ear of Parliament, a mayor being at once recognised whilst a chairman was not. That the returning officer for borough elections would be the mayor. That a mayor could at any time call a public meeting of the inhabitants. That the power to vote under Sturges Bourne's Act was not as equitable a mode as that of the Municipal Corporations Act. These reasons were doubtless influential in inducing the inhabitant householders to petition Her Majesty for a charter of incorporation. There were, however, other causes at work which assisted in bringing about the conclusion to petition. Thus, in carrying out the Act of 1853, the necessary cost incurred began to cause complaints against the commissioners, and against, more especially, the surveyor, Mr. W. W. Barton, and there was some floating notion that a change of government might be advantageous. This idea was carefully fanned by those who had failed in causing the surveyor to swerve from what he believed to be right to the public. The agitation for a charter of incorporation was carried on with vigour, and the town became divided into two parties; one party strongly advocated that the borough should consist of eight wards, and the other that it should have only three wards as under the commissioners. The latter party was successful, and accordingly Castleton, Spotland, and Wardleworth were declared to be the wards. The charter of incorporation was granted by Her Majesty on the 9th of September, 1856, and it directed that her trusty and well-beloved subject, Zachary Mellor, and failing him, her equally trusty and well-beloved William Whittle Barton, should prepare the first register of voters. The first council met on December 19th, 1856, in the Commissioners Rooms, Smith-street, by permission of the commissioners and elected the mayor and aldermen and town clerk.

The first council consisted of Mr. Jacob Bright, mayor; Aldermen John Tatham, Thos. Livsey, G. L. Ashworth, Joseph Brierley, R. T. Heape, John Schofield, A. H. Royds, Jas. Pilling, jun., A. Stewart, George Healey. Councillors John Whitaker, Joseph Wood, Thos. Robinson, George Mansell, Edward Taylor, John Thomas Pagan, Edmund Ashworth, John Chadwick, Thos. Ladyman, Robert Jewison, Jonathan Nield, Wm. Todd, Wm. Simpson, John Holland Butterworth, Henry Whitehead, Robert Taylor, Peter Johnson, John Nuttall, Jesse Barrow, James Holt, James Edsforth, James Atkinson, Charles Milne, Samuel Taylor, jun., Edmund Lupton, John Cropper Brierley, Samuel Stott, William Boothman, Edward Clegg.   Mr. Zachary Mellor, was appointed town clerk.

The council appointed a Watch Committee, and decided to have the control of the constabulary, and therefore the county constabulary were withdrawn from the borough. The inconvenience attending the existence of two corporate bodies in the same borough was soon felt, as fully one-half the members of the council were also commissioners, and it was decided to apply to Parliament for power to transfer the government of the commissioners to the corporation, and an Act, 20 and 21 Victoria, cap. 50, was passed, to which the Royal assent was given on August 17th, 1857, and the transfer to the corporation of the powers of the commissioners and the authority to put in force the Act of 1853, took place on the 13th of January, 1858, in the Commissioners' Rooms in the presence of both bodies. The Town Council met in the Commissioners' Rooms until 1871, when the Council met for the first time in the

Town Hall, the mayor, G. L. Ashworth, Esq., presiding.
The municipal boundary and the parliamentary boundary
of the borough were the same until 1868, when the
parliamentary was extended. It soon became apparent
how desirable it was that the municipal boundary
should be coterminous with the parliamentary; and
it was so, too, because of the large population adjoining and bordering on the borough boundary; whose
dwellings and surroundings were not in a condition
of sufficient healthiness—and there was no power
existing to improve them. These populations were
also supplied with gas and water by the corporation,
and there was no good reason why the two populations
should not in all things be one community.

It was decided in 1871, to apply to Parliament for
an Act to extend the borough, and also to amend the
Act of 1853. There was also a petition to the Chancellor
of the Duchy of Lancaster, to appoint a borough
bench, which was granted on 20th September, 1872.
"The Rochdale Improvement Act" became law on
July 25th, 1872, and amongst other matters, enacted
that the municipal borough should be coterminous with
the parliamentary borough, and should consist of ten
wards, and that the council should be dissolved on the
1st of November next ensuing, and that at the first
election each ward should send three councillors, out of
whom ten aldermen were to be chosen. It is perhaps
without precedent that an entire council should have
been obliged to be re-elected. The contest which arose
was fought chiefly on political grounds; the chief cry,
however, being the cost and alleged extravagance in the
expenditure on the town hall—the fight was a fierce

one. The burgesses returned 35 Liberal councillors, who had been charged with extravagance, and 5 Conservative councillors who were supposed to be economical. As it may show the severity of the contest it will be interesting to state the numbers who voted for the elected councillors as well as the names :—William Tuer Shawcross, mayor, 479; Aldermen George Leach Ashworth, 589; Edward Taylor, 599; James Booth, 595; George Mansell, 568; Robert Taylor Heape, 609; John Tatham; Charles Whitaker, 468; T. B. Willans, 432; William Simpson. Councillors Samuel Tweedale, 585 ; Thomas Schofield, 439; Robert Adamson, 558; Thomas Reid, 467; John Dearden, 363; James Webster, 477 ; John Hoyle, Wardleworth, 468; Joshua Lord, 414 ; Joshua Stott, 421; F. T. Phillippi, 428; William Baron, 473; Robert Brierley, 421; Henry Fishwick, 415; Wm. Lord, 551; John Tweedale, 582; Thomas Watson, 540; W. J. Petrie, 562; J. S. Hudson, 563; James Tweedale, 539; J. S. Littlewood, 595; Charles Preston, 574; Joshua Heap, 911; Joseph Handley, 490; J. T. Booth, 505; Benjamin Butterworth, 501; Peter Johnson, 559; James Sharrocks, 596; John Leach, 594; John Robinson, 498; and Robert Leach, 529.

THE MAYORS.

The following have filled the office of mayor since the incorporation of the borough :—

Jacob Bright	1856-7	Samuel Stott	1865-6
Robert Taylor Heape	1857-8	John Robinson	1866-7
Andrew Stewart	1858-9	Charles Whitaker	1867-8
Thomas Ashworth	1859-60	George Mansell	1868-9
JosephHamiltonMoore	1860-1	T. B. Willans	1869-70
John Thompson Pagan	1861-2	G. L. Ashworth	1870-1
Geo. Leach Ashworth	1862-3	W. T. Shawcross	1871-2
Samuel Stott	1863-4	W. T. Shawcross	1872-3
John Tatham	1864-5	Charles Whitaker	1173-4

The corporation had Arms granted by the Herald's College in 1857—of which we here give an imprint :—

The heraldic description is—"Argent, woolpack, encircled by two branches of the cotton tree flowered and conjoint proper : a bordure sable charged with 8 martlets of the field, and for the Crest Or, a wreath of the colours a millrind sable, and above, a Fleece Argent banded Or."

THE MEMBERS FOR ROCHDALE.

Rochdale was enfranchised by the Reform Act of 1832, and privileged to send one member, the number of the inhabitants then being 19,041. The right to vote was limited by that Act to householders who occupied dwellings of not less than £10 yearly value. The number of voters was 687, the extent of the borough being a radius of three-fourths of a mile from the old market place. In 1868 the borough was enlarged and the number of voters was 9,280, the right to vote having been extended to all inhabitant householders. In 1871 the Ballot Act was passed. The number of votes on the Register for 1875, is 10,560.

The following are the elections since the Reform Act
of 1832 :—

1832 Dec.   John Fenton (L)   277
    ,,   John Entwisle (C)   246
    ,,   James Taylor (L)   109

1835 June   John Entwisle (C)....   369
    ,,   John Fenton (L)   326

1837 April John Fenton (L)   383
    ,,   Clement Royds (C) ....   339 ·

1837 July   John Fenton (L)   374
    ,,   Capt. Alex. Ramsay (C) 349

1841 July   W. S. Crawford (L)....   399
    ,,   James Fenton (C)   338

1847 June   W. S. Crawford (L)..No contest

1852 July   Edward Miall (L)   529
    ,,   Capt. A. Ramsay (C) ..   375

1857 Mar.   Sir A. Ramsay (C)   534
    ,,   Edward Miall (L)   486

1859 April Richard Cobden (L) No contest

1865 April T. B. Potter (L)   646
    ,,   W. B. Brett (C)   496

1865 July   Thos. B. Potter (L)..No contest

1868 Nov.   T. B. Potter (L) 4455
    ,,   W. W. Schofield (C) .. 3270

1874 Feb.   T. B. Potter (L) 4498
    ,,   R. W. Gamble (C) ..·.. 3998

THE TOWN HALL.

ROCHDALE has few buildings with any pretensions to architectural beauty, and it is therefore no difficult task for the stranger to find his way to the Town Hall. It is a handsome Gothic edifice, so richly ornamented as not inappropriately to have been compared to a cathedral. It stands upon a site round which, as years roll on, it is more than probable a large number of banking houses and government and commercial offices will group themselves; and, erected as it is upon a portion of ground which has been newly laid out for building purposes, and which is so rapidly improving that it promises to become the modern division of the town, it may be considered as already occupying a central position. Not only is this the case as to its situation—it also represents the concentrated business of the town; and besides its Council and other Chambers and its Hall of Justice, it can boast of a Free Public Library, which offers to the inhabitants every facility for the study of literature. And it is a palace of art, as a visit will unmistakably show. Admirably adapted for municipal buildings, a Gothic style has enabled the architect to display a beauty and harmony of detail most pleasing to the æsthetic taste. Full advantage has been taken of the ample scope it invariably affords for outside decorations ; while the interior has been fitted up so magnificently in every respect that there are few municipal structures in the country to be compared with it. It was opened by the mayor, George Leach Ashworth, Esq., with great pomp, amid general rejoicings, on September 27th, 1871.

The building is 88 yards in length, its extreme width being 41 yards. One of its most remarkable features is its imposing tower, which stands 134 feet high at the north-east corner, and is surmounted by a beautiful spire, 106 feet in height, making altogether 240 feet. The spire, which is crocketted and panelled, and richly gilded, is finished with a figure of St. George and the Dragon. The tower rises in five stages, in the upper-most of which is the clock, enclosed in a square gilt cast-iron frame work, the bells being in the lower stages of the octagonal spire. These bells chime the hours and quarters as at Westminster, and there is a carillon apparatus which plays fourteen tunes on twelve bells—the public having each day the benefit of a new tune, which is repeated three times every three hours, though of course the programme is exhausted once a fortnight and has to be revived. This the apparatus itself effects, the tunes being successively taken up at midnight. It has been suggested that 14 more tunes might be provided at a cost of only £50, and by these means, as the music would recur only once a month, sameness would be avoided, and the conse-quent satiety. We place the suggestion at the disposal of some musical member of the corporation, trusting that under his ægis it will be carried out long before a second edition of the present guide is called for.

Standing in front of the Hall we cannot help noticing over the entrance tower thirteen niches, which in course of time will be adorned with the sculptured figures of eminent statesmen and men of science. Just above these niches the canopies are brought into prominent notice by a series of beautifully carved animals in miniature, and in the position of gargoyles, a shield being placed under each niche. Between these we see a row of angels holding a continuous riband, and, suspended from a smaller foliated string course, a little below the other, are two large shields, on which are very skilfully wrought the arms of the county and borough. A graceful running foliage pattern between the columns embellishes the doorway, the caps being carved into oak and maple leaves, while heads of Her Majesty Queen Victoria and the late Prince Consort form the terminations to the labels.

The main portico, with its handsome buttresses and parapet, is in the centre of the front, the principal carving about it being the crockets, gargoyles, and finials. The intersections of the buttresses, with a string course under the parapet, are filled in each case by two fierce looking animals, while on the top of the parapet, above each of the four buttresses, is a large gilded stone lion, the two outside lions holding a shield with the borough arms carved out upon it, while the two middle shields display the arms of the county and the Salford Hundred. The roof of the great hall above, the magnificent interior of which we shall describe as we proceed, is said to be only excelled, so far as regards its span, by the roof of Westminster Hall itself. It is executed in deal and is of excellent workmanship and durability. Conspicuous in its centre is a ventilating spire, reflecting as it were the light of the large one; and it is capped by a nice vane. Between the two entrances we have mentioned is an arcade spanned by two arches, the centre pier of which has a splendid groined and carved canopy. This arcade is in front of the mayor's rooms, on the ground floor. Above it is a passage leading from the tower staircase to another which gives access to all the roofs; and this staircase is surmounted by a beautifully carved spire. Outside the Free Public Library, and over the Refreshment Rooms, which are situated above the mayor's rooms, is an elegantly traced and carved balcony, supported on moulded stone corbels. On the other side of the main portico is the magistrates' private staircase, entered from the corridor in front of the public parade room, and giving access to the grand hall, the borough court, and the magistrates' retiring room at the west end, there being a handsome balcony over the police parade room, similar to that over the mayor's rooms. A stone battlement, a pointed roof, and gilded vane, surmount the magistrates' staircase. The chief constable's house stands at the south-west corner, and is a handsome dwelling, five storeys high. Its main staircase is of octagon plan, and is surmounted by a pointed roof and gilded vane. At the west end of the Town Hall is also an octagon staircase precisely similar to that at the east end. At the back of the Hall appears in bold relief the grand staircase, with its magnificent stained glass, while next to it are the entrances to the large vaults stretching under the entire building. The fire engine station is on the ground floor, a little further to the south-west.

Altogether, the stone work of the Town Hall appears to advantage under the Gothic style, which has been faithfully adhered to throughout, and its otherwise cold grey aspect has been not a little relieved by the charming effect of the gilded spires. A general *coup d'oeil* of what we venture to call "this unique specimen of municipal architecture" may be obtained from the engraving which forms a frontispiece to this guide; and if our readers in glancing at its proportions, thus reduced to a focus, are prepossessed with its external beauties, we feel convinced their surprise and delight would be heightened could we present to their vision an equally faithful portrait of the interior. The eye becomes not only dazzled with its gorgeous appearance, but charmed as it peers by day into the life-like pictures in its coloured windows and it has been said again and again that by gas light the great hall assumes the aspect of some magnificent oriental temple.

From an inspection of the exterior we go back to the base of the tower, and enter through the porch into the vestibule, which may be regarded as an epitome in itself of the style of the whole building. The labels of the inner porch, for instance, are remarkable for two heads, one representing a young swell, and the other a "girl of the period," and this idea is enlarged upon in other portions of the hall, where at almost every step we meet with different illustrations of the style of head dress of various periods, whether monarchical, knightly, ecclesiastical, or civil. Then, again, on entering this porch we are reminded by a broad frieze of the clothing in vogue before the invention of spinning and weaving; for we see figures of the bear, the beaver, the lion,

3

the tiger, the panther, the goat, the fox, the stag, and
the tailor bird.   The panels in the ceiling illustrate the
handicraft trades, beginning with the baker and butcher,
and successively enumerating twenty-seven, such as
the tailor, carpenter, mason, candle maker, collier, &c.,
&c.   The windows are filled with the shields of
England, Ireland, Scotland, and Wales; and in the
tracery appear the crosses of St. George, St. Patrick,
St Andrew, and the badge of Wales.   The windows
of the staircase adjoining the porch are filled with
stained glass, of square quarry pattern, arranged in
horizontal lines, with quarries of golden fleece, and
others of the shuttle.   The crest of the borough is a
fleece argent, and is frequently emblazoned throughout
the hall.   The three large tracery pieces in the staircase
windows just mentioned are set off with the plough,
the sower, and the fleece, all relating to the woollen
manufacture of the town.   There are similar windows
at the other end of the building, having reference to
cotton spinning; the quarries are adorned with cotton
pods and leaves, while the tracery shows the cotton
plant, and the machinery used in the manufacture.
We must not, however, "anticipate," for we are still
in the vestibule at the north-east end of the building.
The carving in the vestibule is very elegant, and we
notice two miniature lions holding up the shield of
Rochdale. All these things give us, as we have said
before, a general though faint idea of what is to be
seen in the main portion of the interior.

   We enter the mayor's reception room, the ceiling of
which has a light turquoise blue ground, ornamented
with clusters of gilt stars, and gold swallows and

butterflies. The sides of the beams, which are beautifully painted, have splendid illustrations, on gold ground, of seven well-known fables of Æsop. The frieze is filled with branches of English forest trees, and amongst some very effective designs, which give employment to both the eye and the mind, is a representation of Day, by an owl worried by small birds, and of Night, by small birds getting punished in return. The walls are diapered with a handsome pine pattern, in sage green and gold toned down. Some very light stained glass is seen along the top of the windows, English fruits being introduced into the lights, while the tracery portrays morning, noon, evening, and night. The story of Jack and the Bean-stalk adorns the quoins of the windows; and, in fact, in this apartment, as in all others, every bit of space has been more or less beautified by the decorator's art. Supporting, as it were, the beams where they join the walls, are four sculptured figures, which were intended for grotesque likenesses of the then mayor (Alderman Geo. L. Ashworth), with the Town Hall in his hand; Mr. W. H. Crossland, the architect; an Alderman in his gown (Mr. E. Taylor); and a Councillor (Mr. W. A. Scott). Amongst the portraits suspended in this room, we may mention a capital likeness of Bright and Cobden, by Fagnani: the former is reading a pamphlet, and his friend appears to be listening attentively. There is also a life-size portrait of Alderman T. Livsey. It was presented with an address to Mrs. Livsey by the Alderman's friends "as a testimony of their esteem for his public services, 1852," and was presented to the corporation in 1874, by his daughter, Mary Livsey.

In the mayor's parlour, which we enter from the apartment just described, we see running along the ceiling a tree of the fabled orchard of the Hesperides, producing golden fruit, guarded by dragons. The peacock, the bird of paradise, the humming bird, and other beautiful birds are perched in its branches, which spread all over the ceiling. In medallions on a frieze of magnolias are several English songsters, and some others on the walls are conventionally treated. Some vine branches grace the beams; with storks in various attitudes. The windows have some exceedingly good imagery of the months of the year, and the four seasons. The sculpture represents the praise of wine. The furniture in the mayor's rooms is of Dantzic oak elaborately carved, the chairs being covered with blue morocco, with the borough arms embossed in gold on the back. The window curtains are made of French tournay. The carpets, which are of a chaste design, are the best Turkey. The portraits here exhibited are those of Jacob Bright, the first mayor of the town, painted by W. Percy, and presented by the members of the Council in 1856; and of Alderman Geo. Leach Ashworth, chairman of the Town Hall Building Committee, painted by Ph. Westcott, and presented to the corporation by public subscription.

The council chamber adjoins the mayor's rooms. It occupies the whole width of the building from front to back, and measures 60 feet in length, by 24 in width. It has four handsome arches in Bath stone, the mouldings of which are adorned with carved pateras, the spandrels being worked into a beautiful foliage. The illustrated subjects which run round the walls near the ceiling represent the great inventions which have given an impetus to the manufacture of woollen, silk, and cotton fabrics, the great staple trades of the town. They are quite a study in themselves, illustrating the progress made from the simplest handwork to the almost perfect machinery of the present day. The names of the inventors and their likenesses, when these could be procured, are given. A rich frieze, with a wreath of cotton foliage, and beautiful designs of the plough, the shuttle, and the spindle, grace the ceiling. The diaper of the wall is suggested by the cotton plant and teazle. The stained glass in the windows is very light, and the subjects introduced are the arms of the Duke of Bridgewater, Sir Richard Arkwright, Sir Robert Peel, and Sir Titus Salt, as men who, though not inventors, have materially assisted—by their intelligence and active influence—the progress made in the textile manufactures. The furniture is very sumptuous, and upholstered in crimson morocco.

Stepping out of the council chamber we reach the exchange, which is just within the grand central entrance. It is 72 feet in length by 39 in width. It is remarkable for its beautifully groined roof, supported by pillars of Aberdeen, Peterhead, and other granites; its richly carved Bath stone caps and bosses; its tiled floor, and its stained-glass windows. The carving is especially effective, both as regards design and execution, the foliage of the Bath stone caps being as perfect an imitation of oak, ivy, and maple as it is possible to conceive, intermingled with the leaves being some native animals and birds, such as the squirrel, owl, hawk, &c. The label mouldings over the doorways leading to the council chamber on the left, and the ladies' cloak room and the lecturer's retiring room on the right, are terminated in easily recognised heads of celebrated men and women. Alternating each other over the tiled floor are the arms of the Duchy of Lancaster and the arms of the borough (surrounded by cotton plant foliage), and the arms of England. In the stained windows, looking upon the main road, are the arms of the continental nations who are regarded as the best customers of the manufacturers of Rochdale, viz.: Sweden and Norway, Prussia, France, Switzerland, Spain, Denmark, Austria, Greece, Turkey, Belgium, Russia, and Portugal. Above these are the principal plants used in commerce : wheat, tobacco, tea, coffee, pimento, indiarubber, indigo, orange, hop, flax, hemp, jute, &c. The windows at the further end are filled with square quarries, stained in various devices.

The grand staircase leading from the exchange to the great hall has a very noble appearance ; indeed, it has been stated on good authority that there is no other in England which can be considered its equal. There is an artistic effect about its lofty groined ceiling, its marble hand-rail, and shafts, and its traceried Bath stone balustrading which can only be realised by personal inspection; and, as we ascend, the eye is dazzled with the resplendent rays streaming in through the large stained window before us, its nine lights being entirely filled with the full blazon of the royal arms of England, and, as we look, they seem to rest upon red and white roses entwined with the arms, supporters, crests, and well-known badges of Great Britain. This is brought out into stronger relief by the windows on either side being merely filled in some centre openings, the one displaying the blazon of the county arms, and the other the arms and the crest of the corporation. In some of the lights above and below, and in the other windows of the staircase, are the arms of the corporate towns in the Duchy of Lancaster, the principal manufacturing towns of Yorkshire, the ports from whence our manufactures are shipped to other ports, the countries that supply us with materials for textile fabrics, and finally, those of the Levant Merchants, the West India Merchants, and the East India Company. All these arms are beautifully coloured, and in every respect will bear minute inspection. A tribute is also paid, in the tracery of the side windows, to the great services rendered to modern progress by the ship, the steamer, the railway, and the telegraph. And the sculptor, to crown the beauty of the more solid portions of the stone-work on which the eye finally rests, has chiselled out, with cunning art, some running foliage upon the sprandrel heads to the traceried balustrading, and the carving here and in connection with the bosses is somewhat akin to that in the exchange. The four seasons of life are beautifully symbolised at each side of the two doors leading from the staircase into the great hall. The busts of John Fenton (the first M.P. for Rochdale) and Cobden stand on the first landing; and they are life-like portraits.

The great hall is one of the handsomest rooms in England. Its extreme length, exclusive of the orchestra, is 30 yards; its breadth 20 yards; and its height, from floor to apex, 68 feet. It will seat twelve hundred persons; and though generally used for public meetings,

concerts, and banquets, it has been found extremely
well adapted for bazaars and balls.   The principal
feature of the hall is the series of stained windows
filled with the kings and queens of England, including
Oliver Cromwell.   Such sumptuous decoration has only
been attempted in one previous instance—that of the
House of Lords.   The figures are under canopies, on
quarry grounds, the quarries being painted with the
initials and badges of the sovereigns.   The first king is
William the Conqueror, the series ending with William
IV.   Cromwell appears in subdued colours, between
Charles I. and Charles II.   The figures of Henry VIII.
and Queen Elizabeth have been pronounced as excep-
tionally fine, and the difficult treatment of the four
Georges has been thoroughly well surmounted.   The
armorial bearings of the sovereigns fill the lights above
the figures, the first being the generally received two-
lion shield of William I., the next one calling for notice
being that of Henry II., who has the three lions; and
this has been the shield of England up to the present
time.   Those who are familiar with the subject will
remember that upon his marriage with Eleanor of
Aquitaine, who wore but one lion on her shield, Henry
II. added it to the two lions he had previously borne,
and thus the two shields merged into one of three lions.
The badges of the royal houses are shown in the tracery
of the windows.   First in order come the carbuncle and
broom plant of the Plantagenets; then the red rose,
antelope, and chained swan of Lancaster; next the
white rose, falcon, and fetterlock of York; and the
badge of red and white rose and portcullis of the Tudors,
which follows, is succeeded by the red and white rose,

shamrock, and thistle of the present day. The figure
of our gracious sovereign, Queen Victoria, has been
reserved for the centre of the circular window over the
organ chamber. She is faithfully represented; and, as
the fountain of honour, is surrounded by the collars and
badges of the orders of knighthood. Opposite, is a
similar window, with the portrait of Prince Albert.
Surrounding the prince, in the quailefoils, are emblems
of painting, sculpture, science, architecture, commerce,
manufacture, and agriculture. Underneath this window
is the large subject of Magna Charta, by Mr. Holiday,
of London. It is quite a study in itself. The attitude
of the insurgent barons appears to be that of a dignified
firmness, without violence, while the king, who is compelled to sign everything, yields the various points with
an appearance of good grace, though secretly determined
to recall those privileges on the first opportunity.
Still he must not be supposed to display too amiable an
acquiescence, as this might have revealed his real
feelings; he is, therefore, granting them their rights
sullenly, his manner betraying an effort to brave out
the situation as best he can. The most noteworthy
feature about the carving in the great hall is that of
sixteen large size angels, magnificently executed,
holding gas pendants. Animals appear in the corbels
and the base, and the labels round the hall are terminated
in heads of prominent male and female celebrities
of the fourteenth century. The roof timbers and
panels are elaborately adorned in gold, and the
colouring is exceedingly rich, the several arms, badges,
and legends of Great Britain being painted in black,
red, and white in the panels, while the red rose

tree of the House of Lancaster sets off the seven principals. The gold soffits of the latter are especially noteworthy for the brilliance and lightness they impart to the roof. Most sucessful has been the treatment of the splendid diaper covering of the walls and the rich mouldings and jambs of the windows in a sort of pine pattern, the colours being black and Indian red. The arcade at the west end of the hall is enriched by some delicate running foliage, consisting of vine, thorn, and oak leaves. The gas fittings are most elaborate, the grand room being lighted with sixteen chandeliers, each composed of two tiers with a large number of burners, the effect being very brilliant at night, when the most salient features of the hall are brought out very prominently.

The refreshment room adjoining the east end of the great hall is large and commodious, being 40 feet by 20 feet; the six corbels in this apartment are appropriately carved into designs of game, wild ducks, pheasants, &c. The sun, moon, stars, and the signs of the zodiac form the ground work for the decoration of the ceiling, and the adornment throughout is as effective as elsewhere. There is a hoist, which is used for bringing things up from the kitchen below, which, by the way, is fitted up with every apparatus required in the culinary art.

Next to the refreshment room is another apartment of the same size, devoted to the meetings of the various committees. Its corbels represent the various passions of human nature; three of the carved illustrations appearing on the one side and three on the other. Pain, for instance, is depicted as a victim to the pangs and horrors of the toothache, while Pleasure is the same individual enjoying his porridge after the cursed masticator has been extracted, which has been effected by a Tim Bobbin doctor, with pincers; the fun being evident. Greed is illustrated by a miser and his money-bags; Avarice by the man who would like to get them, and is determined to carry out his object by deception or murder. Law is seen as a watchman of the olden time, keeping his eye upon the intending robber. The designs are captivating from their very grotesqueness.

The town clerk's, the borough treasurer's, and other public offices, are in this part of the building, and the public enter by the door at the extreme east end. There are mezzanine rooms provided, on the ground floor, for the use of the hall-keeper.

JUDICIAL DEPARTMENT.

This department is entered at the west end of the town hall. The public offices, and the chief-constable's, and watch committee's rooms, are on the ground floor, and from the passage leading thereto we enter a large room, where the police may parade in wet weather. Ranged along two sides of this room are eight cells and one bath-room for the prisoners. Ascending by the staircase, above the west end porch, we reach the borough court, which adjoins the great hall, and is immediately over the parade room, from which the prisoners are brought into the dock by a circular iron staircase, so that they do not come in contact with the public. The court is 51 feet in length and 34 feet wide, There are seats on each side of the dock from the

passage into the gallery above. The walls of the court
are of a greenish grey colour, with a broad frieze in
devices of the Duchy of Lancaster, the ceiling being
enriched with the shields of the county and borough,
and the *rose-en-soleil* of England. Over the oak dado
are figures of greyhounds (which support the arms of
the chancellor of the Duchy) and crowned Lancaster
roses. The three three-light windows in front are filled
with figures of eminent men. The three central ones
are Somers, Mansfield, and Ellenborough, three of
our ablest administrators of law in the three great courts.
On the dexter side are the three great jurists, Jeremy
Bentham, Lord Bacon, and Sir Edward Coke ; while on
the sinister side are the three great defenders of our
rights, King Alfred, Pym (who has given us the best
definition of law), and Hampden. The windows at the
back of the gallery, opposite, are filled with grisaille
glass, rose pattern, with the borough arms in the centre
in cotton foliage.

Leading out of the court is the magistrates' room,
which is one of the most pleasant apartments in the
hall. It overlooks the pleasure grounds. The panels
of the ceiling are partially filled with the armorial
bearings of former mayors, the first being the arms of
Mr. Jacob Bright ; and as there are more panels than
there have been mayors, they display, for the time being,
the arms of the borough and duchy. The walls, as far as
the dado, are hung with embossed leather, with a
beautiful pattern of the pomegranate. The furniture
here, as elsewhere, is made of the best Dantzic oak ;
and the utmost care has been taken in the adaptation of
the woodwork to the rich decorations, the carving being

splendidly executed. The magistrates have a private staircase, which takes them right up to court, or they may enter their room by a gallery before going into court.

Next to the magistrates' room is an office for the magistrates' clerk.

THE FREE PUBLIC LIBRARY.

This library, which was opened on September 18th, 1872, is on the second floor, and is approached by the staircase at the east end of the town hall. It occupies a room 52 feet by 40 feet. The two windows display figures of Guttenberg, the inventor of printing, and Cadmus, of writing. The papyrus plant is appropriately taken for the subject of the grisaille work in one of the lights below, and geometrical and ornamental lines in the other. Here are three niches with elaborately carved bosses, crockets, and pendants in Bath stone, and some elegant spandrels. In the library there are 16,669 volumes.

The total cost of the Town Hall is estimated at £155,000. The principal work in the erection of the building was carried out under the superintendence of the architect, Mr. W. H. Crossland, of Leeds, by the following principal contractors :—Messrs. Warburton Bros., of Harpurhey, the shell and foundation of the building; Messrs. Heaton, Butler, & Bayne, of Garrick-street, London, the decoration of the large hall, borough-court, magistrates' room, mayor's parlour and reception room, council chamber and vestibule, and also the whole of the stained glass; Mr. W. H. Best, of Rochdale, the decoration of all the other rooms; Mr. Thos. Earp, of London, the whole of the carving; Messrs. Wirth, Bros., of Regent-street, London, the joinery; Mr. W. Snowdon, of Rochdale, the furniture; Messrs. Smith & Sons, of Birmingham, the locks; Mr. H. J. King, of Rochdale, the ironmongery; Messrs. Gillett & Bland, of Croydon, the clock and chimes; Mr. Taylor, of Loughborough, the bells; Mr. W. Lott, of London, the gilding of the exterior; and Messrs. Hodkinson, Leicester, & Poynton, of Coventry, the gas fittings.

THE BELLS AND CHIMES.

There are thirteen bells in the tower, of which the largest, the tenor, weighs two and a half tons.

The chimes are struck on the first, second, third, and sixth bells, and the hour on the tenor bell. The tunes, which number fourteen, require the whole of the bells. Indeed, one or two more would add much to the beauty of the melodies; notwithstanding, the tunes are played most effectively, and their names show that they are representative. The order in which they are played is— "The Easter Hymn," "Rule Britannia," "St. Patrick's Day," "Auld Lang Syne," "Partant Pour la Syrié," "Yankee Doodle," "The German Watchman's Song," "104th Psalm," "God Bless the Prince of Wales," "Caller Herring," "God save the Emperor," "Russian National Hymn," "Swiss Boy," and "Home, Sweet Home."

It will be seen that not only our own national tunes are given, but those of the chief nations of Europe, our colonies ("Home, Sweet Home"), and the United

States. The words to most of the tunes are known; there may, perhaps, be one exception in the German Watchman's Song, which might be confounded with the War Song, but it is the song commencing :—

> " Hark! ye neighbours and hear me tell,
> Ten now strikes on the belfry bell,
> Ten are the Holy Commandments given
> To man on earth, by God in heaven." &c.

THE PLEASURE GROUNDS.

"Here the fine setting of well-shaded trees,
The walks there mounting up by small degrees,
The gravel and the green so equal lie,
It, with the rest, draws on your ling'ring eye.
Here the sweet smells that do perfume the air,
So please the smelling sense, that you are fain
Where last you walk'd, to turn and walk again."

A PUBLIC park in the midst of a manufacturing town, such as Rochdale, is a privilege of the highest value, for here not only the children of the rich may pass joyful hours of recreation, but those of the poor may here, for a time, forget the miseries and privations of their crowded and ill-ventilated cottages, and without feeling themselves trespassing, gambol and frolic, or sit at their leisure, enjoying the open air of heaven.

Here the convalescent may stroll about, or may rest on the seats so numerously and thoughtfully provided; and while that sweet scene around cheers his reviving spirits, may, in a grateful mood, thank the Creator who has raised him up from his bed of sickness to feel once more the exhilarating breeze play on his pale and sunken cheek. Here we also see

"The hawthorn bush with seats beneath the shade,"

which do not require a great stretch of the imagination to suppose are

"For talking age and whispering lovers made."

THE PARK, GRAMMAR & SPARROW HILL SCHOOLS.

Here the aged may repair and while away their time; and, perchance, the frolics of the children call to mind the delightful rambles which their native fields and meadows afforded to their earlier years, review their past lives with complacency and an approving conscience, and reflect on their "eternal home." Here the unfortunate artizan, wandering from town to town in search of employment, may find a short respite for his aching brain and limbs ere he "plods his weary way" to another town; and here the spendthrift and drunkard may, in seclusion, brood over their self-inflicted troubles, and resolve on a more creditable course of life for the future. With these reflections, which seem to rise naturally from a contemplation of the beautiful scene, which is here spread out before us, we will proceed to give such a description of the park and pleasure grounds as we hope will prove interesting to our readers. And we think it must be evident that few of the recent improvements made by the corporation of Rochdale reflect more credit on that body than the change which has been effected in the Sparrow Hill and Broadfield.

The corporation wisely determined to secure this property, and employed competent persons to prepare designs as to the laying out and arrangement of the ground. The designs sent in by Messrs. A. Stansfield and Son, of Todmorden, were adopted, and the result is now as presented to the eye of the visitor. The conclusion to which the corporation came was, at the time, somewhat severely criticised, and not without some show of reason. It was stated, over and over again, that vegetation of any kind could, under no circumstances,

4

be expected to flourish or even survive in the middle of the town; and that such an outlay as the completion of the scheme would require would be nothing less than a sheer waste of public money.

The result, however, has proved unmistakeably the propriety of the course adopted by the corporation, and, we think, it may be said that the town of Rochdale is in possession of a privilege which it is in no way disposed to underrate.

On leaving the Town Hall a spacious boulevard of some 900 feet length opens out to Manchester-road, and is now the most deservedly popular and beautiful approach to the town. A row of elm trees is planted on each side the boulevard, and so placed on the outer side of the footpath as eventually to give grateful shelter to foot passengers in hot sunny weather. Each side is bounded by slopes planted with evergreens and other shrubs and trees. By a broad flight of steps and somewhat steep winding walks, in the first Sparrow Hill, the visitor may reach some points of vantage for distant views well worth the trouble it may involve. The same remark applies to the second Sparrow Hill, with this exception that the gradients of the roads are much more easy, and are accessible from two points— one from the thoroughfare up the Sparrow Hill, and the other from the westerly end of the boulevard.

The Park, commonly known as "Broadfield," is an irregular plot of ground some sixteen acres in extent. By a considerable and judicious outlay it has been enclosed with substantial boundary walls, surmounted with handsome palisading. The laying out of the park may be said to embrace two distinct styles of gardening

—the natural and the artificial. The lower and more
irregularly formed portion being better adapted for the
former, and the flat or table land for the latter. This
course has been adopted mainly in deference to the
wishes of the General Purposes Committee, in order to
produce a greater amount of variety in the limited space
at disposal, and so please the various tastes of the
burgesses.

Entering the park from the westerly side of the
boulevard, in front of the handsome Presbyterian
Church, the first object which meets the eye is the small
sheet of water, supplied partly by the drainage of the
ground above, and partly from a source previously
existing. The supply of water is abundant and good,
as the health of the various waterfowl with which the
lake is stocked testifies. A small island of rhododen-
drons in the centre is introduced, so as to break the line
of sight and increase the apparent extent of the water.
Passing up to the higher ground, between luxuriant
banks of evergreens, interspersed only by bright glades
of verdant lawn, the visitor leaves on the right the
boys' play-ground, more than half an acre in extent.
In the extreme west corner is the portion set apart for
the gymnasium. Both this and the play-ground are so
screened by dense shrubberies and raised mounds as to
shut them out from the sight of the visitor who comes
with quieter views of enjoyment. The new schools near
to the west entrance are objects of interest in this
particular portion of the park, and seem to form most
fitting and appropriate surroundings. A principal
road leads from this point along the south-westerly
margin, the terrace of houses being well screened by a
wide border of shrubs and trees.

Passing from this point in the direction of Sparrow Hill Schools, the visitor reaches "Flagstaff Hill," the highest portion of the park. From this eminence a fine view of the surrounding country can be obtained. The spires and towers of no less than nine churches and chapels are visible from one point, and, as objects of interest in the immediate neighbourhood, St. Alban's and Castle Hill are prominent. In the distance is also seen the thriving town of Heywood, and the horizontal outline on the north-westerly side is bounded by Rooley Moor, with its silvery line of sinuous road leading to the ancient Forest of Rossendale. A little to the west of Rooley Moor is plainly visible a cottage which is said to be exactly four miles from Rochdale. On the same side but more to the north are Rushy Hill, Brown Wardle Hill, and Middle Hill, and still more conspicuous, the well-known and picturesque "white house" on Blackstone Edge. While in the lower part of the park the visitor must not omit to notice "Cant Hill" well, where there is an almost unvarying and abundant supply of pure spring water. The well is approached from the thoroughfare in front of Sparrow Hill Schools. Cant Hill has often given rise to little disputation as to its etymology. Some contend that it is owing to the well being a gossiping or tattling place; some that the water of the well had some famous curative powers for those who came regularly to drink its waters; whilst others, and with certainly more show of reason on their side, say that Cant Hill is the "recovery" or strengthening hill, as it was and we hope will continue to be the custom for convalescents to take a walk to the top of the hill for the sake of the refreshing and invigorating breeze. In the year 1845, the Rev. Dr. Molesworth erected the present stonework over the well, and dedicated it "for the use of the poor," and warns the mischievous "for their sake do no damage." Over it he inscribed a scriptural passage:—"Whosoever drinketh of this water shall thirst again : but whosoever drinketh of the water that I shall give him shall never thirst : but the water that I shall give him shall be in him a well of water springing up into everlasting life." Formerly Cant Hill water had a great reputation as making better tea than that from any other source, and even now, it is not uncommon to see the people fetch it for this purpose, from even the most remote parts of the town.

Passing towards the more formal part of the park, we have on the right the girls' play-ground, a large and almost circular plot, snugly enclosed with high mounds, grassy banks, and dense shrubberies, and though within but a few yards of the main thoroughfare through the park, it will eventually have the appearance of as much privacy as the croquet lawn of a private family.

We now come to the more level or geometrical portion of the park, which is approached by two entrances, both opening out of the Broadfield walk.

One of the main features in this portion is the sunk panel on the north-westerly side which is intended to serve as a bowling green, &c. It is entered on the north and south sides by two flights of steps. A broad grass terrace margins the panel, with scroll-work and small circular and other beds for spring bulbs and summer bedding plants. Each side of the terrace is bounded by broad walks in lines parallel, and these

again are flanked by broad bands of shrubberies on
their outer margin.   There are two other entrances
besides those previously named : the principal one
opposite the vicarage gates, and the other from Park-
street, off Drake-street.

For the mind of the botanist, the gardener, and the
educated public, there is another form of interest
attaching to the pleasure grounds, and that is the
native habitat of the plants.   Our world-wide commerce,
and the enterprise of our countrymen, have been the
means of bringing to this land almost everything
that is beautiful and interesting in the vegetable
kingdom ; and, owing to the moderation of our climate,
we can place side by side in our gardens and pleasure
grounds choice specimens from various latitudes.   To
take a few instances only, we have the curious
monkey puzzle or *Araucaria imbricata*, with its rope-
like prickly branches, from the Chilian Andes mountains
in South America, where it bears an edible cone
the size of a child's head ; there is the *Pinus Austriaca*,
the thick and sombre branches of which wave
on the slopes of the Tyrol ; we have also the Rhododendron, of the Swiss Alps, the *Rhododendron ponticum*
and *Azalea*, from the Caucasus ; the *Privet* and the
Aucuba, with its yellow-spotted leaves, from Japan ;
the *Berberis Darwinii*, from South America (named
after the great biologist), struggles for an existence in
our smoky atmosphere ; the hardy little *Pernettia* comes
from the wilds of Terra del Fuego ; the *Ledum*, with its
small leathery leaves, which have been used as tea,
flourishes in the swamps of Canada ; the *Liriodendron*
or Tulip tree also comes to us from North America,

and, finally, there is a young specimen of the big Pine trees of California, the *Wellingtonia Gigantea*, which attains in its native land a height of over three hundred feet.

" Flowers are scattered with a generous profusion in every part of the habitable world; in the snowy arctic regions, and in the sunny lands of the south; on the hoary Nile, and in the sparkling rivulets of our own loved land; on the sandy plains of Africa, and in our quiet fields and woods; in the lonely isles of ocean, and. on the shattered ruins of our halls and towers, nay, on the very walls and roofs of our cottage dwellings; beneath the foot of the laughing child, and round the grave of the grey-haired man."

" In all places, then, and in all seasons,
  Flowers expand their light and soul-like wings,
Teaching us, by the most persuasive reasons
  How akin they are to human things.

And with child-like, credulous affection,
  We behold their tender buds expand;
Emblems of our own great resurrection,
  Ebmlems of the bright and better land."

THE PUBLIC BATHS.

ROCHDALE is not celebrated as a place of resort for valetudinarians seeking bathing facilities; and, indeed, since the fouling of the rivers Roach and Spodden, and the increase of population on the banks of the canal, the natural bathing places have been destroyed, but through the exertions of the late Mr. Alderman Moore, and Mr. Alderman Taylor, and other gentlemen, public baths were erected in Smith Street, in the year 1868, in which the inhabitants may now have the full advantage resulting from bathing. The practice of bathing undoubtedly reaches back to the earliest times, and the most ancient historical accounts, as well as the popular myths, make mention of it, but there is no trace in Rochdale of ancient baths. Bathing is a very important agent in the preservation and restoration of health. Besides promoting cleanliness, the refreshing and invigorating effects of cold bathing, in its various forms, have always been acknowledged, as have, also, the soothing effects of the warm bath, but the virtues of water, as a curative agent, have been more fully developed in modern times. The baths were designed by Mr. E. N. Macdougall, the contractors being Messrs. J. Parker and Son, and have cost £9,500. They are built, in the Italian style of architecture, of brick, and stone dressings, having a façade of 113 feet long, of two storeys, the principal entrance being of stone, with plain moulded heads.

The baths appropriated to the ladies are on the left, and those to the gentlemen on the right of the entrance. There are two large swimming baths, 65 feet 6 inches by 39 feet, and 38 feet high. The water is kept tepid by means of steam. In the galleries surrounding the swimming baths there are slipper baths. In addition to the above, there are excellent and peculiar Turkish baths, which were made after a plan arranged by Mr. Milligan, the manager of the baths. The peculiarity of these baths is that the bather can breathe a cool atmosphere whilst the body is enclosed in hot-air, so that the most susceptible may take the baths without danger. In the year 1868, the total number of bathers visiting the Rochdale Baths amounted to 33,849; in 1869, the number increased to 35,266; in 1870, the number decreased to 31,832; in 1871, to 31,435; but increased, in 1872, to 34,114; in 1873, decreased to 33,016, but at the end of September, 1874, being six months from April 1st, they numbered 32,437.

THE GAS WORKS.

THE works are situate at the foot of Castle Hill, on a part of a space known as Kill Danes, and were erected in the year 1824, by John Malam, gas engineer. The directors were John Roby (chairman), Thomas Booth, Samuel Lomax (Townhead), Joseph Wood (Bank), John Eccroyd (nail maker), Abraham Brierley, and John Chadwick. J. S. Lancashire, was appointed manager.

The works were constructed for the manufacture of gas and coke, the coke ovens being similar to those in use at coal pits. The separate manufacture of coke was soon discontinued. At first the works were equal to a make of about 20,000 cubic feet per day. At that time there was no such thing as a station meter, and there are no reliable figures, but it is supposed that not more than 15,000 cubic feet of gas were consumed per twenty-four hours in the depth of winter, whilst about this quantity is *now* turned out in five minutes. The works cost about £11,000. The opening was celebrated by a grand balloon ascent by Mr. Sadler, who was accompanied by Mr. Roby; and the day was made a general holiday in the town. The balloon descended near Bacup.

From the year 1823 to 1844, the works continued in the hands of the gas company; and, in the latter year, they were purchased by the corporation for the sum of £27,700.

The following statement shows a marvellous increase in the consumption of gas :—

In the year ending March	1844	1854	1864	1874
The money amount of gas sold to private consumers	5,683	8,014	14,159	34,495
The No. of feet of gas made	27,919,000	52,386,000	94,343,000	223,086,000
The No. of Consumers	904	2,650	10,756	16,959
The No. of street Lamps	263	501	677	1,420
The length of main pipes laid in Miles	10	24	43	65
The Mortgage Debt	27,700	31,450	53,349	132,115
The profits paid towards the Town Improvements have been £78,774, being in each of the ten years	......	12,995	21,297	44,482
The average selling price of gas in the years ending	5s. 2¼d.	3s. 10½d.	3s. 10½d.	3s. 9¾d.
The average cost per ton for coal ...	9s. 4¼d.	8s. 9d.	6s. 10d.	17s. 7¾d.
„ „ „ cannel...	17s. 0d.	12s. 8d.	17s. 4d.	25s. 4d.

These figures naturally lead the mind to investigate the extent of the works at their commencement and at the present period. In 1824, there were eighteen retorts and two gas holders, with a capacity or storage room for 36,000 cubic feet. In 1844, the retorts numbered fifty-seven, and there was a storage room for 118,000 feet. At the present date, there is a retort house 100 yards long by 45 yards broad, containing 341 retorts; on each side of the beds of retorts is a coal store, where 6,000 tons of material may be stacked ready for a winter's consumption. A purifying house 35 by 21 yards, a fine massive stone building of two storeys, containing six purifiers, each 24 feet square by 4½ feet deep. The ground floor being used as a revivifying floor.

There is also another purifying house, oxide shed, two large gas holders, tar and ammoniacal liquor tanks, station meters, condensors, &c.

A splendid stack of buildings used for engines, exhausters, boilers, workshops for blacksmiths, fitters.

joiners, meter makers, stores for meters, pipes, and all other materials.

In other buildings are similar appliances required in the manufacture of gas, all being of the most approved construction.

Conspicuous amongst the erections are the scrubbers, like two massive towers, with houses on top of each, standing 50 feet high, 12 feet diameter, used for the purpose of cleansing the gas from ammonia and other impurities.

The room for storage consists of three holders, the largest of which was completed last year, and is a telescopic gasholder 126 feet diameter and 52 feet high, the tank being 26 feet 6 inches deep. The holder has a capacity of 632,000 cubic feet. The total storage room is 1,150,000 cubic feet.

The whole works now cover nearly seven acres, and have been not only extended but remodelled, chiefly since the year 1871, and they are allowed by eminent gas engineers to be equal if not superior to any of a similar size in the United Kingdom. The alterations, extensions, and improvements have been designed by the present manager, Mr. Samuel Hunter, C.E.

The works are now equal to a supply of $1\frac{3}{4}$ millions cubic feet each twenty-four hours, and the increase in the consumption of gas being so rapid it is expected that further extension will be required within a very short time.

THE WATER WORKS.

BEFORE the year 1760, the inhabitants of Rochdale had to rely on pumps and wells for the supply of water. The chief of these were situated at Leyland's Brow, better known as "Packer Spout;" at the "Wet Rake," near the junction of Oldham and Milnrow Roads; the pump in the Lowergates, opposite to the Amen Corner; the pump at the Bishop, near Temple-street; the well or spout supplied by a stream on the east of Blackwater, near Barrack Yard; Kitchen pump, at the end of Bury Road; the spout at Coldwall Brow; Wardleworth Wells; and Cant Hill Well, but nearly all are now gone; the sewerage of the town, and the increase of buildings having destroyed them.

The first reservoir was constructed about the year 1760, by Messrs. Ralph and Samuel Taylor, and John Clegg. It is situated in Leyland's Brow, near the church steps, 25 feet above the centre of the town. Its low level confined the supply only to the inhabitants who resided in the lower parts of the town. However, its value in giving a supply of water inside the house led to the formation of a Water Works Company, who purchased it for an annuity of £80 per annum; and, in the year 1809, an application was made to Parliament and power obtained to use the Noon Sun Spring on Cronkeyshaw, and to make large reservoirs to supply

the town. The Acts of 1816, 1839, and 1847, gave power
to enlarge and form Jepheys, Buckley Wood, Hamer
Pasture, and Brown House Wham reservoirs; and
mains were extended in all directions. In 1866, the
Town Council purchased the Water Works, giving the
shareholders an annuity of £5 12s. on £56 paid stock,
there being in all 1,332 shares, and Parliament
authorised the Corporation to borrow £200,000, and to
purchase land for the making of new reservoirs, one at
Spring Mill, another at Cowm, and small service
reservoirs at Knot Hill, Shawforth, and at Buersil Head.
The construction of Cowm reservoir was commenced in
the year 1867, and is very near completion at a cost
of £189,567. The Spring Mill reservoir is in course of
construction, and the cost up to the present time
amounts to £24,162. The gathering ground of the
Water Works Company was 700 acres, and the capacity
of the reservoirs 147 millions of gallons. The Cowm
reservoir will have a gathering ground of 955 acres,
and a capacity of 228 millions of gallons. The gathering ground of Spring Mill reservoir will be 558 acres,
and its capacity 133 millions of gallons. The whole works
are estimated to give a supply of 20 gallons per head
to 104,500 of a population; Cowm being able to supply
42,500; Spring Mill 24,500; and the old works 37,500.
The whole reservoirs will hold 250 days' supply at the
rate of 20 gallons per head per day, but in practice,
this supply will be diminished by the compensation,
and cannot be reckoned at more than 160 days available
supply. These conclusions are arrived at by the calcu-
lations that one acre will supply forty-four persons,
the rainfall being estimated at 42 inches, the compen-

sation to the owners on the stream at 10 inches, and the evaporation and loss by flood at 24 inches.

The construction of Cowm reservoir was a most expensive affair, caused by unexpected difficulties. Treacherous ground was found in sinking the trench on the westerly side, and the work had to be carried on by night as well as by day for several months. However, at last, the difficulty was surmounted, but then a second presented itself in the shape of a fissured rock in the bed of the reservoir, and under the embankment. A large portion of the rock had to be removed and replaced with concrete. This caused another delay and increased expenditure, but at last it has been made a very fine reservoir, and the four filtering ponds have been constructed on the improved system of fine sand and gravel, resting on layers of boulders, the whole being 3 feet 6 inches thick. Pretty cascades will be formed by the water as it leaves the reservoirs, and can be seen to advantage from the three stone bridges which span the bye-wash and compensation channel. These works have been designed by Messrs. T. & C. Hawksley, consulting engineers, and carried out by Mr. H. Rofe, the resident engineer and manager of the works.

THE MANURE WORKS.

IKE other towns in Lancashire and Yorkshire, Rochdale has undergone great changes, and has experienced great difficulties in being relieved from its sewerage and refuse matter. Some fifty years ago, it was a source of profit to property owners, as it was common with the neighbouring farmers to give a liberal sum per annum for the privilege of removing the midden-steads. Soon after the passing of the police Act of 1825, the rapidly extending population made the ownership of the midden-stead less profitable, and the town had to undertake the duty of removal, which was done by contract. The contractors found no doubt, for some years, it was profitable to sell the manure. The last contract by the town was for £1,300 a year. The neglected and ill-conditioned state of the midden-steads was such that it led to a low state of habit, and was a lively cause of the spread of disease through the town. In 1864, Mr Alderman Taylor (chemist), wrote at the request of Mr. Alderman Mansell, who had the management of this department, to the Scavenging Committee, detailing a method by which, in his view, that which was a nuisance, and expensive, might be turned into a profit, and so arranged as not to be a cause of the spread of disease. This proposition was not at once received; indeed not until

three years after was it seriously entertained. The
growing difficulties were such, that the committee
resolved that a trial should be made of the scheme
proposed, and also of any other plan that might be
suggested. A twelve month's trial was then made, and
the scheme which is now in general use was adopted.
This plan, which has received the name of "the
Rochdale system," we shall now briefly describe. Its
first principle is, that all excreta and refuse of the house
shall be removed at least weekly; that the refuse be
separated into its constituents of ash, cinders, vegetable
matter, iron, glass, pots, &c. The ash and excreta are
then manufactured into manure by a special method
devised by Mr. Alderman Taylor, and the other refuse
used or sold; so that the great nuisance of modern
towns called the "tip," is not required, and that which
has been hitherto a great cost to towns, will become a
source of profit. Repulsive as it might seem, yet, it is
nevertheless a most interesting sight, especially to
farmers, and all persons interested in the sanitary
questions of the day, to see the method of dealing with
this refuse of towns. The works are situated at the
junction of Entwisle-street and Smith-street, and are
well worthy of inspection. From every part of England
eminent visitors have expressed their surprise and
appreciation at the effectiveness and completeness of
the scheme; and, amongst official visitors, the special
Inspector of the Local Government Board of England,
and the special Inspector of the American Government
have declared it to be the best in England or America.
This manure, which was at first used with some doubt
and fear by the farmers, is now bought in large quan-

5

tities, and there are most abundant testimonials of its great value.

On the date we write, October 28th, 1874—in the week previous there were removed 84 tons of excreta and 143 tons of refuse, from 4,434 closets and ash-places. The quantity of manure made was 74 tons. The number of houses thus relieved from the refuse was 7,995, and 116 mills.

The work is accomplished by twelve horses and twenty-four men; twelve horses and eight carts in collecting, and sixteen men in the manufacture.

THE FIRE BRIGADE.

Valour and strength are the Fireman's need,
   And to carry his life in his hand;
In the hour of peril to toil or bleed
   In the midst of a noble band.
To gaze on the flames with undazzled eye,
   As the eagle glares on the sun;
To spare no pains, and to heave no sigh,
   'Till he knows that his work is done.

Where shall we find him? Oh, such men, I ween,
Are found in the ranks of our valiant Sixteen.
      Then honour the Fire Brigade,
      May Heav'n all their efforts aid,
Bold and undaunted and gallant Sixteen!

OUR good old jog-trot ancestors were not, we should imagine, much troubled with great destruction of property by fire in their quiet days, and it is well they were not. We have no desire to throw cold water on our forefathers, but, in truth, their apparatus for extinguishing fires was of a touchingly simple and primitive kind. And this is how they acted:—When a fire was discovered the watchman (usually a slow-going and asthmatic ancient), gave the alarm with his rattle, with all the intensity which his feeble strength allowed, and the captain of the watch, heading his troop, which he picked up here and there as quickly as possible (which was not very quickly), waddled to the scene of the conflagration, armed with buckets, which, by the way, were not always water-tight. There were no mains in those days, but pumps, *some-*

times containing water, were scattered all over the town, and their rusty and ungreased handle joints kept up a chorus of the most creaky and unmelodious music. As the march of improvement continued its course, a couple of miniature fire engines, known as box-engines, were provided by the authorities, but they barely met the requirements of even those days, on account of their positive feebleness. Over fifty years ago, the Commissioners of that time, formed a fire brigade, and Mr. Frank Wynn was appointed the captain. Mr. Samuel Taylor followed, and about thirty-seven years ago Mr. John Eccles was placed at the head of that department as engineer. Two large fire engines were purchased from Messrs. Walker & Co., of Bury, but they were re-sold, as they were found to be too heavy to be satisfactorily worked. Thirty-six years ago, Mr. Eccles made two new engines, "Niagara," and "Extinguisher," and twenty years after, he made a more powerful engine, "Thetis;" and in the same year, a fire escape was purchased from Messrs. Joy & Dearden, of Manchester. In 1874, a steam fire engine, made by Messrs. Merryweather & Son, of London, was bought for the sum of £750, and this engine is capable of throwing water 220 feet high with four three-quarter jets.

The corporation has now at its command "Niagara,' " Extinguisher," " Thetis," and the steam fire engine mentioned. Possessing, therefore, a fall so powerful (as the "Niagara,") the presence of a sea deity " Thetis," and an engine of the greatest motive power— steam—available, surely Mr. Eccles and his able associates could put an " extinguisher " on Mount Etna if it should be considered desirable to try the experiment.

Like Mahomet and his mountain, if Etna will not come to Rochdale to have a "damper" put on, then, in the case supposed, the fire brigade will have to pay a visit to Etna.

Returning to patent facts, however, we must state that the pressure of water in the mains is not equal to that in surrounding towns, as in some it can be thrown 200 feet high, whereas in Rochdale, in the highest part of the town, it can be thrown but 30 feet high, and in the lowest, only 100 feet. The present brigade numbers sixteen. Mr. John Eccles is the head engineer, and Mr. Alfred Eccles assistant engineer. In the Town Hall tower there is a self-acting fire alarm bell, erected by Mr. Henry Butterworth, of Lord-street, which can be heard a distance of four miles, the alarm apparatus being worked by a lever fixed in the police office.

The maintenance of a well-trained and efficient fire brigade, with engines and other apparatus of the most recent and approved kinds, cannot be over estimated in the midst of a wealthy community like Rochdale, and we are glad to observe that the Council has made such provision (water excepted) as should, we think, be sufficient to cope with any emergency that may arise. The requisite pressure from the mains is certainly a matter that calls for prompt attention; for, without a powerful and plentiful supply of water, the utmost exertions of the brigade, energetic as they are at all times, and the most scientifically constructed engines, will avail but little. *Verbum sap.*

THE DISTRICT CORONERSHIP.

THE Rochdale Coroner's District formerly comprised an area of 114,564 statute acres, and at the census in 1861 contained a population of 295,736 persons; but in 1870, when a revision of the districts took place, it was considerably reduced, and it would be a work of great difficulty to approximate its present extent in acres and number of inhabitants. It may be briefly stated that the towns of Rochdale, Oldham, Middleton, Heywood, and the adjacent villages, and also the towns of Bacup, Todmorden, and the intermediate places from Rochdale are comprised in the "Rochdale District."

The honourable office of coroner is one of the most ancient of our institutions, dating even from time immemorial. Coroners were known in the reign of King Alfred, and were officers of high dignity, of which they were, however, considerably shorn by the provisions of Magna Charta and subsequent legislation. Still, at the present time, in addition to their judicial functions, coroners have ministerial authority analogous to that of the high sheriff of the county, in whose stead they can execute processes if required.

Formerly, coroners were paid by fees and mileage, and were often censured for holding inquests unnecessarily to increase the emoluments of the office;

and by 23 and 24 Vict., c. 116, it is provided that they
should be paid by salaries in lieu of fees; the salaries
being subject to quinquennial revision. This provision
would appear to have failed in its purpose of settling
the causes of former differences between the county
justices and the coroners, inasmuch as for many years
past strong efforts have been made by the former to get
the office abolished, and the latter have been somewhat
harassed by persistent enquiries into cases of inquests
alleged to have been unnecessarily held. There can be
no doubt that the existence of coroners' enquiries
acts as a safeguard of our personal safety, and to a
great extent as a powerful deterrent to crime. So it
must have been regarded by a select Committee of the
House of Commons, as, when considering a Bill for the
abolition of coroners' enquiries, they asserted that it
was not advisable to interfere with the discretion which
had been vested in coroners' from time immemorial.

The appointment of county coroners is by an election
at which freeholders of the county alone can vote. The
present coroner, John Molesworth, Esq., was appointed
on January 26th, 1870, at the Lyceum, Baillie Street,
and there being no other candidate, the nomination and
election occupied but a few minutes. This was not,
however, the case with his predecessor, Thos. fferrand
Dearden, Esq., as he had to contest the election, and at
tremendous expense, if the statement be correct that
the cost of the election amounted to a sum equal to
Mr. Dearden's income from the office during the first 15
years! The office had been held by members of his
family for upwards of a century at Mr. Dearden's death,
which occurred on Jan. 2, 1870, his uncle, Thomas

Ferrand, having been appointed in 1795, and his (Mr. Dearden's) great-uncle in, or about, 1767. There is no record at hand to show who were the preceding coroners of the district.

INTERESTING RECORDS.

Upwards of thirty years ago, there were, in proportion to the inhabitants fully as many cases of murder, suicide, and infanticide as there are in the present day. The latter crime seems to have been then of more frequent occurrence than latterly; certainly, a greater proportion of such cases were detected at that period than is now the case.

A few remarks, based on extracts from the Coroners' Court Roll, may not be unacceptable at this point. In former times, the nomenclature of persons was, as may be supposed, considerably varied, and Christian (?) names now seldom heard of were formerly to be met with, as for instance, Gamaliel, Hippolite, Avarinah, Jebazy, Isaacan, Issachar, Halcamus, Lancelot, Dianus, Sylva, Enniel, Lois, Maroner,— to say nothing of the whole run of scriptural appelations. In 1782, a boy of twelve years, named *Sir* Andrew Chadwick Taylor, met with his death accidentally; as, likewise, in 1800, did *Duke* Haigh, aged six years. The name of "Captain" is often given to a child never designed for either army or navy, and that of "Doctor" to others, in no view of their becoming learned in the clerical, legal, or medical professions.

The variety in verdicts affords some little matter for remark. "Died by the Visitation of God." Were "twelve good and lawful men" of this Borough to meet by the coroner's summons to enquire into the cause of a sudden death, and the above verdict were to be returned, the outside public would hold it to be inconclusive of the cause of the death, even if not broaching on irreverence. Still, in cases of sudden death, the cause being perfectly natural, the above verdict was almost invariably returned, and its use was not entirely discontinued till the year 1863, when the present expression, "Died from natural causes," was substituted. The verdict referred to was not confined to sudden mishaps, for it was returned in the cases of death from fighting and wrestling.

In cases of suicide, a verdict of *felo de se* was very rare indeed in past years, and is never returned in the present day, owing, no doubt, to the Christian view that no man can in his proper senses take away his own life. Still, there are a few instances where *felo de se* has been the finding of the jury — the dead being interred at midnight, without the Christian rites of burial, but without the former barbarity of driving a stake through the body, before its interment in four cross roads. Deaths by boiler explosions, machinery, and colliery accidents have been much less frequent of late years than formerly, and, in respect to the latter class of accidents, this district has been amongst the most favoured, for a long period, in its immunity from such serious losses of life as have occurred in other districts. A peculiar usage, formerly attaching to deaths by accident, is worthy of mention, viz., the levying of deodands. Formerly, every personal chattel causing the death of a person was forfeited to the king, or its value assessed, and applied to pious uses and distributed in alms, but by the Statute 9 and 10 Vict., c. 62, deodands were abolished. The formation of the Manchester and Leeds Railway (and especially the Summit Tunnel) was very productive of fatalities to the workmen employed. From February, 1838, to September, 1840, no less than 41 fatal accidents occurred in and about the tunnel, and in ten of these cases deodands amounting altogether to £35 16s. 0d. were levied.

Deaths by Justifiable Homicide were, and still are, of rare occurrence. In November, 1836, a man named Thomas Dronsfield, in attempting violence upon one Thomas Bottomley, was killed by the latter, and his act was considered a case of justifiable homicide. An earlier instance occurs where two of the Scotch rebels, on entering this neighbourhood, made a demand upon a farmer, who threatened to shoot them if they did not leave his premises, and on their refusing he carried out his threat to the fullest extent. Other cases (though very few) are on record, of deaths caused by persons in self-defence. In 1795 (August 4), two men were shot at Rochdale whilst rioting, and a verdict was returned that they were "killed of necessity, and in defence of His Majesty's subjects."

It has been said that Fate bears some mysterious connection with figures, and that a fatality attaches itself especially to the number *three*. Whether this statement be true or not we are unprepared to say; but, in tracing events coming within the coroner's jurisdiction for upwards of a century, we find many strange occurrences which would seem to support the theory. In some scores of instances which might readily be quoted, there have been *three* deaths from the same or similar accidents, at the same time, or immediately succeeding; or three persons whose surnames, or Christian names, or initials were alike, follow each other on the Coroner's Rolls, although their deaths occur in different parts of the district.

THE COUNTY COURT.

THIS Court was established in March, 1847, under an Act passed in the previous year. Up to that time, and from 1839, there was a court for the recovery of small debts, called the "Rochdale Court of Requests." Courts of the like kind were in existence in various towns in the kingdom; but the Act of 1846 abolished all such courts, and established one uniform mode of procedure for the recovery of small debts and demands throughout England and Wales.

The first Judge of the County Court was J. S. T. Greene, Esq., who had held a similar office in the Court of Requests; the Registrar (or Clerk) was James Woods, Esq., and the High Bailiff was Mr. Henry Lord. The two latter had also held similar offices in the abolished Court of Requests. Mr. Greene continued to be Judge until 1859, when he was removed to another district, and C. Temple, Esq., Q.C., was appointed in his place. The latter, on his death, was succeeded by John Osborne, Esq., and this gentleman was followed by the present Judge, Crompton Hutton, Esq. Mr. Woods occupied the office of Registrar until 1867, when he died; and Robert Jackson, Esq., was appointed to succeed him. The High-Bailiffship was filled by Mr. Lord until his death, in September, 1873, when the offices of High-Bailiff and Registrar became united in one officer, the present Registrar, Mr. Robert Jackson.

The original district of the Court was of considerable extent; but in 1858 an outlying part was taken away to form a portion of the Bacup County Court District, at which place no court had previously existed. At present, the district extends over the townships of Blatchinworth and Calderbrook, Butterworth, Castleton, Spotland, Wardleworth, and Wuerdle and Wardle.

The number of cases annually entered in the Court has varied from upwards of 4,000 (before the District was divided) to 2,900, or thereabouts, in 1873. In former years, the Court exercised jurisdiction in Insolvency and Bankruptcy. The latter jurisdiction was taken away under the Act of 1869, when the Oldham County Court was constituted a Bankruptcy Court for Rochdale and other places. With the exception of Bankruptcy and Admiralty, the Court has the same jurisdiction as the other County Courts, namely, Equity and Common Law. The Equity jurisdiction is restricted to matters not exceeding £500 in value, and the Common Law jurisdiction to claims for debts or damages not exceeding £50.

The mode of procedure in the County Court may be briefly mentioned:—A plaint is entered, upon which a summons issues to the defendant to appear on a given day, when the cause is dealt with by the Judge or Registrar. Non-payment of an amount adjudged is followed by execution against goods, or by a judgment summons and commitment. The fees are regulated by the Lords of the Treasury, and have undergone various revisions. The present scale is as follows:—Plaint, 1s. in the pound; Hearing, 2s. in the pound; Admission, 1s. in the pound; Judgment Summons, 3d. in the

pound (with a fee for service of 6d. or 1s.); and
Execution or Commitment, 1s. 6d. in the pound.
Parties may appear by attorney, and there are in the
town several able advocates who practise in the Court.
The sittings are held twice every calendar month at the
Public Hall, Baillie Street. Subjoined is a statement
of plaints entered from 1866 to 1873 : — 1866, 2,942 ;
1867, 2,525 ; 1868, 2,824 ; 1869, 3,036 ; 1870, 3,217 ;
1871, 3,516 ; 1872, 3,435 ; 1873, 2,937.

THE POLICE FORCE.

FEW institutions have undergone more changes during the past fifty years, than the systems adopted for the prevention of crime and the detection of offenders. Up to 1823, Rochdale, as well as other places, including the great Metropolitan District and city of London, was watched by old men known by the cognomen of " Charlies."

The appearance of these guardians of the night as occasionally represented in dramatic entertainments, and as described by Shakespeare, must have been extremely ludicrous.

To assault "Charlie," to overthrow his "box," to take from and spring his terrible rattle, to extinguish the light in his antique lantern was considered capital fun. If assaulted, poor old Charlie was powerless to pursue. He was, as a rule, physically infirm, very often asthmatic, generally under the influence of gin or beer, always wrapped in great coats and capes. Such men did not, indeed could not pay much attention to the apprehension of offenders against the law.

The only duty they discharged with any approach to efficiency was the "calls" relative to the hour of the night and the state of the weather. At times, no doubt, their articulation was very imperfect, if not altogether indistinct.

An additional duty to which they paid particular
attention was the calling up of servant girls, a duty, it
is said, that "Old Charlie" seldom neglected. Many
of the old residents remember several persons who held
the office of watchman as far back as 1820. It is
reported that one of those vigilant officials, called "Old
Stock," was musically gifted, and that he accompanied
the monotonous call of "Two o'clock and a stormy
morning" with an enthusiastic scraping of his fiddle.
This musical watchman was a great favourite with
female servants, for it is asserted that he often neglected
"going his rounds" to give them a little music. It
seems, however, that the musical part of his duty was
chiefly confined to Monday mornings as the clock
struck twelve, at which time the watchman commenced
to fiddle for the purpose of arousing servant girls—that
being the "washing day." The servants of those days
must have commenced work at such an early hour of
the morning as would seriously alarm the domestics
of 1874.

The last watchman employed by the inhabitants was
named Lord. He had no pecuniary allowance for
discharging the duties of his office. His nocturnal
wanderings were confined to the centre of the town.
All the compensation he received was what the inhabitants voluntarily gave him.

In 1825, an application was made for, and a local Act
obtained which, amongst other regulations, contained
provisions for the watching of the town. Immediately
the Act came into operation, the Commissioners
appointed twelve watchmen and a captain of the watch
who, for the first time, were paid out of the rates. No

chief-constable was appointed until after the riots in 1829, commonly known as the "New Bailey Fight." After those disturbances the Commissioners decided to appoint a chief-constable, which appointment took place in August, 1829. Mr. Charles Johnson, of Manchester, was selected to fill that office, which he held for about seven years. He was succeeded by Mr. Samuel Mills, after whom the situation was filled by Mr. J. Butterworth, till the formation of the county constabulary. From that date, up to its incorporation, the town was watched by county police officers. When incorporated, and the council elected, it was resolved to maintain a separate police establishment. Accordingly, a borough constabulary was formed, and Mr. Callender was the first chief-constable appointed.

The borough police commenced duty on the 13th April, 1857. Since Mr. Callender's time the office has been held by Mr. Sylvester, Captain Davies, and the present chief-constable, Mr. Stevens.

The force consists of chief-constable, four inspectors, seven sergeants, and fifty-one constables, total sixty-three. The force was augmented in 1872, in consequence of the extensions of the borough from forty-four to the number given. The constabulary of the borough, according to the report of Her Majesty's Inspector, is maintained in a state of great efficiency.

6

THE POLICE COURT.

THE institution of Justices of the Peace is very ancient. Previous to 1327, there were Conservators of the Peace in every county, chosen by freeholders out of the principal men of the county to perform similar duties; but by a statute of Edward III. a change took place in the practice, and ever since the election of justices has been taken from the people and exercised by the crown. The appointment has always stood high in popular estimation, and is eagerly sought after by men of station. As it is practically in the hands of the Lord Chancellor, it is a frequent charge brought by one political party against another, that the appointments are given as rewards for political services, but owing to the frequent alteration of power among parties of late years, the undue preponderance of one set of politicians is speedily neutralised by the acts of their successors. Up to the year 1839, however, all the magistrates in Rochdale were members of the established church, when for the first time a dissenting magistrate was appointed in the person of Mr. George Ashworth.

Our inquiries enable us to point out the various places in which petty sessions have been held in the town and borough for a long time past. The corner of Cheetham-street was an old place of meeting of the magistrates, in a house which stood near to the shop now occupied by Mr. Taylor, the earthenware dealer. From this there was a migration to the Old Swan Inn, somewhere near where the White Swan now stands. When this was abandoned the next place of meeting was near the present County Police Office, in Yorkshire-street. The Wellington Hotel was next selected, and then, no doubt, for good cause, another change was made, and the petty sessions were held for a great number of years at the Flying Horse, in Packer-street. It is within the recollection of many of our readers that the next place chosen were the Council Rooms, in Smith-street, which were always found not only inconvenient in point of accommodation, but also somewhat undignified in appearance as a suitable place for the administration of justice. Then followed the latest change of all, namely, that to the "Palace of Justice" in our magnificent Town Hall. The sittings of both borough and county magistrates are held here, on the respective days appointed; and thus, for a time, a long time, one would suppose, Justice has found rest for the sole of her foot. A more appropriate spot could scarcely be found, except that it is sometimes said there is rather more atmospheric air stirring thereabouts than is exactly necessary or agreeable.

Mr. John Lee, one of the earliest of the clerks to the magistrates, resided on the premises now occupied by the county constabulary. Mr. Wm. Taylor was the next magistrates' clerk, and Mr. James Woods and Mr. Robert Jackson followed. About the year 1839, when Mr. George Ashworth was made a justice of the peace, a Primitive Methodist minister was given into custody by the Rev. Mr. Steele, a magistrate, and curate of Littleborough Church, for preaching in that village, but

he was released on the order of Mr. G. Ashworth, who
afterwards appointed Mr. William Heaton as his clerk,
and from that date the clerkship to the magistrates was
divided into two departments.   Prior to the incorporation of the borough, in 1856, there appears to have
been no specially recognised chairman of the bench, the
practice being for the senior magistrate on the rota for
the day to take the chair.   For years the local authorities
were of opinion that it was derogatory to the dignity
of the Mayor of Rochdale, as chief magistrate of the
borough, that he should not occupy the chair at the
petty sessions, and no doubt that was one reason why
steps were taken to obtain a separate commission and a
borough bench, which were granted by the Lord
Chancellor in October, 1872.

We understand that in days long past—say forty
or fifty years ago—it was the invariable practice for the
magistrates of the day to give the chair to the Rev. W.
R. Hay, the vicar, even although he might happen to come
into court after its opening.   This may be explained
for the reason that the Rev. Vicar had had a legal
education, and could, therefore, guide the bench to right
decisions in all difficult matters on points of law.   The
position was not assumed as of right; but conceded
from pure courtesy and respect, and for the reason
before mentioned.

As soon as the borough bench was established there
was a change made in the mode of paying the magistrates' clerks.   Mr. Joseph Heap, who was previously
joint clerk with Mr. Robert Jackson, was appointed
sole clerk to the borough bench, at a salary of £500
per annum; and as the police court fees now amount

to about £900 a year, it will be seen that a considerable
profit is realised by the corporation from this source.
The following are the names of the magistrates:

THE BOROUGH.

Robert Taylor Heape, Esq., Highfield; Jonathan Nield,
.Esq., Dunster; James Butterworth, Esq., Rake Bank;
Richard Hurst, Esq., Spring Hill; Robert Leach Twee-
dale, Esq., Healey Hall; Clement M. Royds, Esq.,
Greenhill; James Brierley, Esq., West Hill; James
Petrie Esq., South-street; Edmund Ashworth, Esq.,
Oakenrod; Thomas Booth, Esq., Harelands; John
Leach, Esq., Moss House; Henry Fishwick, Esq., Carr
Hill; John Tatham, Esq., Moss Cottage; Thomas
Healey, Esq., Howarth Cross; Charles Whitaker, Esq.,
Rylands; William T. Shawcross, Esq., Heybrook;
Robert Jewison, Esq., Yorkshire-street.

THE COUNTY.

Rev. F. R. Raines, Milnrow; James Maden Holt, Esq.,
M.P., Stubby Lee, Bacup, near Manchester; James
. Holt, Esq., Yorkshire-street; Geo. Tawke Kemp, Esq.,
Beechwood; John Aitkin, Esq., Lane End, Bacup;
Charles Cheetham, Esq., Ryecroft House, near Hey-
wood; Thomas Bright, Esq., Greenbank; Edward
Greenwood Kay, Esq., Mill House; John Tweedale,
Esq., Beightons; R. H. Hutchinson, Esq., Greenbooth;
James Griffiths Dearden, Esq., Orchard; Joseph
Brierley, Esq., Lauriston House; Joshua Radcliffe,
Esq., Balderstone Hall; John Robinson, Esq., Mount
Falinge; Edward Hoyle, Esq., Bacup; Henry Newall,
Esq., Hare Hill, Littleborough; T. B. Willans, Esq.,
Harefield Hall, Heywood; James Heap, Esq., Cliffe
House, Milnrow; E. A. N. Royds, Esq., Brownhill.

THE POST OFFICE.

"Heaven first taught letters for some wretch's aid,
Save banished lover, or some captive maid:
They live, they speak, they breathe what love inspires,
Warm from the soul, and faithful to its fires.
The virgin's wish, without her fears impart,
Excuse the blush, and pour out all the heart;
Speed the soft intercourse from soul to soul,
And waft a sigh from Indus to the pole."

IT is unnecessary to enlarge upon the benefits of a well-organised and efficiently conducted public postal service in an enlightened and wealthy country such as ours. Without the help which the post office affords to every one in the realm, from the highest to the lowest, it would be difficult, if not impossible, to carry on the ordinary affairs of human life. We have the happiness to live in a country, and at a time, when the daily operations of the postal service are seen in their utmost efficiency; and almost every one can bear witness to the great improvements which have taken place from time to time within recent years, all tending to the convenience and advantage of the public. The rapid and regular means of postal communication which now exist, aided, of course, by the railways and ocean steamers, must strike the mind with wonder; and it is evident that such a method of communication, by letter, with every part of the world could only be provided and carried out by the powerful

state-sustained machinery which we find in connection
with our post office establishment. Not only is this
secured to us, but it is supplied, also, at the smallest
possible cost. A "Queen's head" carries a letter from
one end of the kingdom to the other with safety and
expedition, the outlay being one penny only; and even
for the still smaller expenditure of a halfpenny, the
"Times" newspaper, supplements and all, can be sent
from Land's End to John o' Groats! With Dominie
Samson, we can only exclaim, "Prodigious!" Without the post office, commerce would dwindle and fade;
the stability of kingdoms and peoples would be
jeopardised; and we can easily imagine into what
desperate straits true lovers would be plunged if the
postal authorities were to become bankrupt or "shut up
shop." The sweet and tender nothings with which love
letters are crammed would be written in vain, and the
"soft intercourse" to which Pope alludes in our motto
at the head of this section, would be rendered utterly
impossible, and chaos would, indeed, have come again.
But it is not in the transmission of letters only that the
post office is found so really valuable. Its book and
sample post; the post-card system; and its money order
and saving bank departments, are all most important
boons to the public in almost every part of the kingdom.
That the post office does its work well, not only in these
matters, but also in its telegraphic operations, the public
are well convinced; and, although in its saving bank
department, the rate of interest allowed to the depositors
is small, this is more than counterbalanced by the
absolute security which is obtained for the sums
deposited. That a great undertaking like the post

office should be free from blame at all times is more
than could be expected, but the complaints are few
indeed compared with the vast and extensive duties
which it performs.   Perfection is not to be obtained in
any human institution whatever, but it may be safely
stated that the post office keeps abreast of the times,
and does its utmost to perform its duty faithfully and
honestly to the public at large; and there is no doubt
that the strict supervision which is exercised by the
various heads of departments is productive of much
good.   The year 1840 brought about a great alteration
in the postal system of the country, owing, mainly, to
the exertions of Mr. (afterwards Sir Rowland) Hill.
The immediate effect of the introduction of his plans
was a marvellous increase in the number of inland
letters transmitted through the post; and the system of
a tariff of payment by weight, regardless of distance,
was a marked and salutary improvement upon the old
system which existed of a varying rate, regulated by
distance and weight.   This, coupled with the use of
postage labels for the prepayment of letters, has been the
means of making the post office one of the most valuable
and deservedly popular services of the country.   And,
with regard to postage labels, it may be observed that at
the present day there is scarcely a civilised country under
the sun which has not adopted, and which does not now
use that method of prepaying letters carried by the
general post.   But to England belongs the honour of
inaugurating the system; from which honour, however,
the name of Sir Rowland Hill can never be disconnected.
A grateful country rewarded Sir Rowland for his great
services in the paths of postal reform; and we cannot

think of the post office in this country without cordially recognizing and duly appreciating the good work which he was the means of effecting.

The post office in Rochdale has been as unsettled as the " Wandering Jew " ever since its introduction, and it is to be hoped that it will soon settle down in Packer-street, in the handsome residence which is now being provided, and there prosper and gather moss. The first time we met it was in the building which is at the present time occupied by Messrs. Porritt, at the corner of King-street, on the South Parade; and it has been dodging about that neighbourhood ever since. From thence it was removed to the corner of Drake-street, to the shop now rented by Miss Ashworth; next its sorrowful countenance was seen in the premises now occupied by Mr. Frankell, at the bottom of Drake-street. Then it took shelter at the bottom of the Walk, but returned to its old haunts, and nestled for a time in the building which now serves as the County Court Offices. It next put in an appearance at Messrs. Wrigleys' premises, at the bottom of Yorkshire-street, and found its way into Baillie-street, in Mr. Hurst's buildings. From these it found a temporary abode in the Town Hall Chambers, South Parade, and then it struggled into Drake-street, at the end of Nelson-street, where it is at the present time sojourning. In the year 1835 the charge for postage of a letter, from London to Rochdale, was 11d.; from Liverpool, 7d.; and Manchester, 4d., but if it came round by Bolton, from Manchester; it was 6d. After that came the uniform charge of 4d., and gradually it lowered to the settled price of 1d.

The new post office, which is in course of erection in Packer-street, is three storeys high, 105 feet in length, and 35 feet in width, built of stone, from the Warwick quarries ; and the back part of the building, in Fleece-street and King-street, is faced with Pratt's best pressed bricks. The public offices are spacious and lofty, and very suitable for the various uses for which they are erected. The sorters' room is at the rear of the building, and 'is 50 feet 10 inches long, and 26 feet 6 inches wide. The roof is glass, and there are windows along the side, so that there is ample light for this tedious work. The telegraph instrument room is on the second floor, and it is 96 feet long by 19 feet 5 inches wide. There are also clerks' and letter carriers' retiring rooms.

The postal arrangements in Rochdale and district have been much improved of late years, and now three times a day, in the borough, the inhabitants enjoy the pleasure of hearing the " Postman's knock." About fifty years ago the post office business was carried on in an imperfect and unsatisfactory manner. The post masters in those days were not very amiable, and were " slow coaches," but their movements were only in keeping with the defects of the general system. The remote villages must have suffered great inconvenience in the days we speak of, from want of proper postal facilities; but now thirteen of the adjacent villages have branch offices, where, in addition to ordinary business, money orders are issued and paid, namely, Milnrow, Whitworth, Smithy Bridge, Smallbridge, Pinfold, Bamford, Blackpits, Healey, Shawforth, Wardle, Spotland-road, Townhead, and Oldham-road. The town is now

supplied with the convenience of twenty-four pillar and
wall boxes, a comparatively modern improvement to
which our forefathers were entire strangers. The number of mail bags despatched daily from the central office
amounts to forty-four, and the total number of letters,
&c., delivered weekly, in Rochdale and the district, is
40,000. The officials who accomplish this work are
Mr. John Downes, the post master (who was appointed
to the office on the retirement of Mr. J. Matthews, who
had been postmaster for many years); Mr. Stephen
Platt, first clerk, three sorting clerks, two junior clerks,
ten letter carriers, three "double" auxiliary letter
carriers, and seven rural messengers. The general
despatch leaves at 8-30 in the evening, and the last
despatch, for all parts, at 9-45.

Previously to the transfer of the telegraphs to the
post office, which took place on the 5th of February,
1870, the premises for telegraphic business were in the
occupation of the Electric and International Telegraph
Co., and have since been retained by the Department;
but as the business has, since the transfer, greatly
increased, the accommodation is now very inadequate.
This, however, will be remedied when the new premises
to which we have referred are entered upon. As an
instance of the requirements of the telegraphing public
of Rochdale, the circuits, which were only three in
number at the transfer, have now increased to about
twenty, giving direct communication with London,
Liverpool, Manchester, Leeds, Bradford, Halifax,
Bolton, Oldham, Bury, Todmorden, Bacup, Littleborough, Middleton, Bluepits, and other parts. The
sub-offices having telegraph accommodation are Whit-

worth, Smallbridge, Milnrow, and the receiving office in Oldham Road. Mr. Gregson is the superintending clerk of the telegraph department, and has held the office for some years.

The charge for sending a telegram, to any place in the United Kingdom, is 1s. for the first twenty words, and 3d. for each additional five words or part of five words. No charge is made for the address, or for delivery by foot messenger, within a mile from the terminal telegraph office, or within the limits of the town postal delivery, even when the distance exceeds one mile. American telegrams may be sent from the Rochdale office at from 3s. to 5s. 6d. per word, regulated according to the state with which the communication is made. Continental rates, for telegrams of twenty words, are as follow:—Austria, Hungary, Bavaria, Baden, and North Germany, 7s.; Belgium, 4s. 2d.; Corsica, 5s. 10d.; France and Denmark, 5s.; Greece (according to route), 14s. 4d. to 19s.; Italy and Papal States, 8s. 6d.

FREE PUBLIC LIBRARY.

THE history of this institution in reality should only date from the adoption of "the Public Libraries Act of 1858" by the burgesses of Rochdale. But it must not be left unrecorded that the calling of the public meeting for this purpose was the result of a long-continued agitation in the local press, by which means the public mind was made fully conversant with the scope and meaning of the Act, and the many and great advantages which would accrue to the town by its adoption.

The public meeting called by the Mayor was held in the Public Hall, on the 25th May, 1870, and it is to be regretted that conflicting interests were so strong, that it was only by a narrow majority that Rochdale was spared the everlasting disgrace of having refused to avail itself of the "Libraries Act." This, however, did not arise from a feeling that a library was not wanted—but rather that a free public library would tend to injure certain institutions that already existed. Such fears are now proved to have been groundless. At the next meeting of the Council (2nd July, 1870,) it was reported that the Act had been adopted "by a public meeting of the burgesses," and the "General Purposes Committee with power to call in the assistance of gentlemen outside the Council," was appointed a committee under the Public Libraries Act.

In the following November, the first library committee was formed, and consisted of the following gentlemen, viz.:—The General Purposes Committee, Mr. Councillor James Booth, Major Henry Fishwick, and Messrs. R. Jewison, William Leach, James Ogden, George Webster, and J. J. Curtis (the last six named being non-members of the Council).

This committee at once commenced its duties—books were purchased and taken charge of by the various members of the committee, until a suitable place could be found for their arrangement pending the completion of the town hall.

After some little time a warehouse (now pulled down) at the end of Packer-street was taken for that purpose, and here the volumes were stowed away—arranged in catalogue. From here they were removed to their present shelves in July, 1872.

The public opening ceremony took place on Wednesday, the 18th September, 1872. Previous to the public meeting on that occasion, a preliminary or semi-public assembly was held in the library itself, when short speeches were made by the Lord Bishop of Manchester, the Mayor, Councillor James Booth (the chairman of the committee from its first foundation), the Rev. W. N. Molesworth, M.A., and Edmund Ashworth, Esq., J.P.

The meeting in the large hall immediately after this, was attended by upwards of 1,400 people, and was addressed by the Mayor (W. T. Shawcross, Esq.), Mr. Councillor Booth, Alderman G. L. Ashworth, J.P., W. W. Schofield, Esq., J.P., the Right Rev. the Lord Bishop of Manchester, Mr. J. R. Shepherd, the Rev. H. W. Parkinson, R. M. Pankhurst, Esq., LL.D., Lieutenant-

Colonel Fishwick, F.S.A., Mr. Robert Jewison, and Alderman Willans, J.P.

From the third report of the library committee, dated 31st March, 1874, we learn that the number of borrowers' cards issued up to that date was 2,998, the issue of books from the lending department amounted to 60,760, being a daily average of 204 volumes.

The reference department had issued 24,604 volumes, being an average of 91 daily. The total number of volumes then in the library was 15,707, the total cost of which was £2,515, or an average of 3s. 2½d. per volume. Full and accurate catalogues of both departments have been prepared by Mr. Hanson, the librarian, and published.

Of the lending library it will be sufficient to state that it contains all the current literature of the day, and, considering the short time since its opening, it is as complete as it possibly could be with the funds at the committee's disposal.

Of the reference department we could say much more did our space permit, for (although yet in its infancy) it contains very many works which might with advantage be particularly mentioned; books which it is a great boon for the inhabitants of Rochdale to claim as their own; books which are not to be found in many public or even private libraries in England, and which, in a few years hence, will scarcely be obtainable at any price. We will also draw attention to the collection of specimens of early printing, which consists of about forty volumes, printed between 1472 and 1575. The earliest printed volume in the library is a Latin book in oak binding, entitled "Turrecremata (Cardinalis J. de) Explanatio

in Psalterium," which was printed by the celebrated
J. Schuszler. The Latin bible (oak bound) printed at
Cologne, by Peter Quentel, in 1527, is also noteworthy.
The woodcuts in it are by Anthony Von Worms, a Ger-
man engraver, who flourished about 1530, and have the
two qualities (dear to the collector) of scarcity and
merit. The works of Josephus (in German) from the
Strasburg press, 1575, is splendidly illustrated by
Tobias and J. C. Stimner, and C. Von Sichem. Of the
modern works, we may add that no less than fifteen
pages of the catalogue are included under the general
head of Rochdale. The fifty-three volumes of Public
Records, (including the "Ducatus Lancashire," "Valor
Ecclesiasticus," &c.) presented to the library by the
committee of the Rochdale Circulating Library, (this
library, long known as Hartley's Library, because the
entrance to it was for many years through the shop of
Hartley and Howarth's, now Mr. Henry Howarth, is
a private subscription library, and was established
1772,) are a great acquisition

Upwards of 100 versions of the bible (or a part of it)
in various languages and dialects, including the raised
letters for the blind, are here collected; many of these
were presented to the committee.

To illustrate how far every branch of literature is
here represented, we note amongst the Friends' or
Quakers' books, the large folio edition (1753) of Besse's
collection of "Sufferings of Quakers," Smith's "Catalogue
of Friends' Books," and by the same Author, "Anti-
Quakeriana."

It may be useful to state, with reference to the
lending department, that persons desirous of becoming

borrowers of books, may do so in three days after the presentation of a voucher, signed by a burgess promising to make good any loss or damage which may arise from injury or detention of a book. Small fines are inflicted for keeping books beyond the time allowed for reading. If a book be not returned at the end of the fourth week, proceedings may be taken to recover the value, in case of refusal to return the same. The loan of a book may be renewed, if not finished with by the borrower, upon application at the library, when the renewal will be entered on the borrower's ticket. And the renewal may be repeated again and again unless the book should be wanted by some other person, in which case, it can be renewed only once afterwards. All books must be returned to the library on or before the last Saturday in July in each year. Tickets are not transferable; and no books are issued without production of the ticket. Nor are books exchanged on the day of issue. The library is open daily, from 10 a.m. to 8 p.m., except on the special days mentioned in the rules; and catalogues and all other information can be obtained on application at the library.

But we must pass on to other topics, yet we will complete this short sketch of the Rochdale Library by saying that it is by far the pleasantest retreat in the town, for, as Chaucer has it :.

> "—— Him was lever han at his beddes hed
> A twenty bokes clothed in black or red
> Than robes riche or fidel or saulrie."

7

THE CEMETERY.

"The sculptured urn, the mimic bust,
The grave in pomp array'd;
Serve but to teach us man is dust!
His life a fleeting shade.

Stop, stranger, whosoe'er thou art,
And to thyself be just:
These mouldering tombs address thine heart:
Catch wisdom from the dust."

IT must be obvious to the reflecting mind that a
Cemetery is an undoubted improvement over
crowded burial places in towns, which from their
situation echo the constant din of traffic, and the
war of ribaldry and dissipation. The practice of
sheltering graves in cemeteries with trees, and adorning
them with flowers is attended by valuable sanitary
results by absorbing what is deleterious, and such as
are wholly unattainable when burials are made amidst
streets and houses, while the sight of luxuriant ever-
green shrubs, and of fresh and beautiful flowers in their
season, soothes and consoles the mind, by virtue of
their sadly pleasing associations and emblematic teaching, and, at the same time, the atmosphere is improved
and renovated. It ought also to be remembered that
the place of interment of departed relatives and friends
is the Mecca to which our memory ever turns, be our
pilgrimage in life where it may. Slightly altered how
pleasing and appropriate are Goldsmith's lines :—

"Where'er we roam, whatever realms we view,
Our hearts, untravelled, fondly turn to you;
Still to our loved ones turn with restless pain,
And drag at each remove a lengthening chain."

THE CEMETERY.

The peaceful associations of the grave are beautifully described by Washington Irving, in the following words:—"It buries every error—covers every defect—extinguishes every resentment. From its peaceful bosom spring none but fond regrets and tender recollections. Who can look down upon the grave of an enemy, and not feel a compunctious throb that he should have warred with the poor handful of dust that lies mouldering before him?" "There" saith Job, "the wicked cease from troubling; and there the weary be at rest. There the prisoners rest together; they hear not the voice of the oppressor. The small and the great are there; and the servant is free from his master." There can be nothing more touching to a contemplative mind than to "pace with measured steps and slow," the paths around which lie interred the mouldering remains of those who once lived and moved in our midst. Here lie in peace the loving father, the kind and affectionate mother, the staunch and ever faithful brother, the bright-eyed and beautiful sister, and the firm and never failing friend. How still, how calm, how silent! No tumult now; no angry passions; no resentments; no envy. Proud man! gaze on these mounds which cover the relics of poor mortality, and lay to heart the lesson which they teach. Beautiful maiden! with blooming cheek, fresh with health and vigour, see, within these graves, are those who were once as beautiful and gay as you. Their race is run; their career is over! Pride, be humble; beauty be modest. And to this complexion must we all come at last! And yet we shrink from such contemplations. What these dead are "why fear we to become?"

Surely this pleasant resting place should make us all in love .with " easeful death," and induce us to address that pale phantom by the most endearing names! Oh! when to us the end shall come, as come it must, may it be said of each one, in the words of the greatest master of our language :

> " Nothing in his life
> Became him like the leaving of it ; he died
> As one who had been studied in his death
> To throw away the dearest thing he owed
> As 'twere a careless trifle."

But let us change the theme, and proceed to a description of the Rochdale Cemetery, which contains so many mournful and abiding objects of interest, and which attracts so many visitors for the purpose either of viewing its beauties, or of paying a tribute of affection to the memory of departed friends.

This beautiful resting place for the dead lies about a mile and a-half west of the town on the Bury road. The ground stands at an elevation of 500 feet above the level of the sea, and commands an extensive view of Blackstone Edge and the adjacent hills. In passing under the Gothic archway, the carriage road divides, that leading to the right conducts to the portion set apart for the Church of England ; that to the left leads to the ground appropriated to the different non-conformist bodies. The Catholic portion of the cemetery lies to the north. The aspect of the cemetery is varied by rising and sloping ground, and is made picturesque and beautiful by curved walks and beds planted with trees, evergreens, and flowers. The division between the consecrated and unconsecrated ground is marked by geological specimens placed at the edge of the carriage walk, so that no very obtrusive barrier appears to divide different sections of the Christian Church after death. The Chapel on the consecrated part of the cemetery is in the Norman style of architecture, the design of which was selected by the late Bishop of the diocese, and although not very elegant in the exterior, is very light and commodious within. The services are performed by the Vicar of Spotland and his curate.

The building on the nonconformist portion of the ground is designed to represent an Ionic Temple, and is very classic and elegant. The services are conducted by the Registrar, but ministers of all denominations attend to conduct the funeral service when required by their friends. The Catholic chapel is a neat Gothic building, but not frequently used, as in a majority of cases the service is performed before leaving the residence.

The attention of the visitor is generally arrested by the number and variety of costly and beautiful monuments erected to perpetuate the memory of departed friends: in walking through the grounds he is struck with the names of some who have occupied honourable, influential, and useful positions in the town of Rochdale. Magistrates, mayors, ministers of religion, and members of Christian churches, are called to mind. The first monument visible on entering is that of Alderman Livsey, whose political principles some years ago so largely influenced the working-men of Rochdale. The granite pillar near to this perpetuates the memory of his friend, John Mason, the founder of the Globe Works.

Nearer the nonconformist chapel, we are reminded by a white marble monument of Alderman Thomas Ashworth, J.P., who was for many years an influential and valued member of the town council; near to him lies Mr. Alderman Moore, a warm and generous friend of all good men and good objects. Not very far from him is seen the name of one, precious to many who were influenced through life by his instruction and discipline, William Littlewood. Approaching a more secluded and beautiful part of the cemetery is seen a tall obelisk in memory of George Ashworth, and his most worthy and excellent son, George Leach Ashworth, whose beneficial influence over the town will be felt for many years to come. Near to this spot is the monument of Robert Kelsall, J. P., and also the resting place of Samuel Bright, who died in Geneva, and was buried here. Close by, lies the body of the Reverend H. W. Parkinson, widely known as a worthy and able advocate of civil and religious freedom, and the founder and for more than twenty years pastor of Milton Church, Rochdale. Monuments will be seen of other ministers who had long laboured in the town, and whose memory is still precious to survivors. The Rev. John Kershaw, Rev. James Molineux, and Rev. John Peters; and on the consecrated ground, the Rev. W. J. ffarrington, of St. James's, Rev. J. W. Parker, vicar of St. Alban's, and many others, who were excellent and influential members of society, will be found resting in this quiet and beautiful place.

The cemetery at present contains 13 acres, but an addition of about 12 acres will shortly be enclosed, which is greatly needed, as about 20,000 bodies have been red here within the last twenty years.

The grounds are very tastefully arranged and well kept; and the credit is chiefly due to the Rev. Robert Jones, the respected Registrar, who is a very skilful amateur florist, and who exercises a kind and watchful care over the lovely and sanctified domain of "God's Acre."

"God's Acre! Yes, that blessed name imparts
   Comfort to those who in the grave have sown
The seed that they had garnered in their hearts,
   Their bread of life, alas! no more their own.

"Into its furrows shall we all be cast,
   In the sure faith that we shall rise again
At the great harvest, when the arch-angel's blast
   Shall winnow, like a fan, the chaff and grain."

RELIGIOUS INSTITUTIONS.

THE town of Rochdale and district will compare favourably with any other town of the same size and importance with regard to the number of its religious institutions, although it has not much to boast of on the question of architecture; but there are to be found in our midst several worthy and beautiful specimens of the builders' art. Sabbath morn is ushered in by a total change on the Town Hall chimes from secular to sacred pieces, the first of which is played at midnight, such as the Easter Hymn and the 104th Psalm on alternate Sundays.

> " How still the morning of the hallow'd day !
> Mute is the voice of busy labour.
>
> * * * * * *
>
> With dove-like wings, Peace o'er the borough broods :
> The massive mill wheel rests ; the anvil's din
> Hath ceased ; and all around is quietness and peace.
>
> * * * * * *
>
> The pale mechanic now has leave to breathe
> The morning air pure from the stenching smoke,
> While wandering slowly up the Roach's side,
> He meditates on Him whose power he marks
> In each green tree that proudly spreads the bough,
> As in the tiny dew-bent flowers that bloom
> Around the roots ; and while he thus surveys
> With elevated joy each pleasing charm,
> He hopes (yet fears presumptuous is the hope)
> To reach those realms where Sabbath never ends."

A stranger passing through Rochdale on that day would see the streets thronged with respectably-attired and well-behaved people, and might infer that the respective places of worship were well filled, but this is not exactly so, as there is ample room for more worshippers in many of them. In very many of our churches and chapels the empty benches and pews give abundant evidence of the indifference so often felt by the general public to matters of such vital importance to their personal well-being. Not that Rochdale can be said to be peculiar in this respect; the attending places of worship being to many thousands a "custom more honoured in the breach than the observance," and can be witnessed in every town in the kingdom, as well as in our own populous valley of the Roach.

ST. CHAD'S.

The mother church of the parish is of great antiquity, and stands on a commanding eminence, the ascent to which is by a flight of 124 steps. The church was erected in the 12th century, and has undergone various changes, alterations, and renovations. The local legend is, that the site of the church was, in point of fact, the place chosen by spirits and fairies for the purpose. On several occasions, as the story relates, the materials brought together for the erection of the church, on an entirely different site, were removed from the place originally selected to the hill or eminence on which St. Chad's stands. That this removal was the work of superhuman agency, was the firm belief of our forefathers in those far-distant days; and we should be sorry to do or say anything which could in the remotest manner interfere with this time-hallowed belief, which has been handed down to us, and which, with vast numbers among us, is received with the greatest deference and respect.

The site ultimately adopted, under such supernatural pressure, led, of course, to the formation of the celebrated church steps; to ascend which is always considered a necessary piece of work to be performed by all visitors to our good old town. To come to Rochdale and not mount the steps is considered a breach of good manners, as well as a serious deprivation of a very agreeable exercise. The steps, in fact, are among our most cherished possessions; and they form a most important thoroughfare, with which it would be very unwise to intermeddle to the great prejudice of the inhabitants.

It is to be very much lamented that the graveyard of St. Chad's should have been suffered to fall into the sad state in which it is to be found at the present day. Many years ago, part of the yard was enclosed so as to preserve it to some little extent; but this has been of comparatively little use as to the preservation of the tombs and gravestones. Meditation among the tombs in St. Chad's yard is, consequently, not the easiest possible thing in the world; the deciphering of the inscriptions, with the lessons which they should convey to the contemplative mind, being now attended with many difficulties. Here and there is to be found a racy inscription or epitaph; but, generally speaking, not much is to be gained, from our tombstone literature by the most ardent searcher after that kind of knowledge.

The churchyard has been the scene of strange occurrences, even in the days of the present generation. Often and often the most turbulent, and, sometimes, disgraceful sights have been witnessed here, when the question of church-rates has been agitated and discussed from time to time. Here has been heard oratory of a very emphatic character indeed, mixed, very frequently, with every element which was calculated to arouse the passions of the populace. It is an undoubted fact that, in the early part of his public career, the present Right Hon. John Bright has more than once made his voice heard in the midst of thousands of his fellow-townsmen in St Chad's Churchyard. The deep interest which he took in the once all-absorbing question of church-rates, no doubt, impelled him, as a Dissenter, to take a very prominent part whenever that subject was to be considered by the parishioners at their annual public meetings. Other men of local renown, many of whom have gone to their rest, were also very prominent at these parish meetings, and there are others who are now among us. Happily, these disorders have all passed away; for, with the abolition of church-rates, the annual exhibition, in public meeting, of strong party feeling on the subject does not occur. We live in less troublous times; but the victory was won by men who are, no doubt, entitled to be held in grateful remembrance by those on whose behalf the great battle was so successfully fought. The church has lost the day; but we firmly believe that that loss has been to her a positive gain. Her own people now give her the help, voluntarily, which used to be exacted alike from friend and foe.

We have mentioned that here and there in the church-yard are to be found some quaint or racy epitaphs. We subjoin a few :—

> " Here lies ye bodi of John Whipp, with 10th of his children, who had *eighteen children* by *one woman*; he departed this life," &c.

This person's chief merit seems to have been that he was the means of adding very materially to the population of his native parish. Such a person would have received small favour indeed at the hands of Malthus.

The epitaph most in esteem is that of the celebrated humourist, John Collier, alias " Tim Bobbin." It is supposed to have been written by himself, a short time before his death, and is as follows :—

> "Here lies John, and with him Mary;
> Cheek by jowl, they never vary;
> No wonder they so well agree,
> John wants no punch, and Moll no tea."

Another epitaph, said to have been also written by "Tim Bobbin," on a deceased sexton of the church, runs thus :—

> " Here lies Jo. Green,
> Who arch has been,
>   And drove a gainful trade
> With pow'rful death,
> Till out of breath
>   He threw away his spade.
> When death beheld his comrade yield,
>   He, like a cunning knave,
> Came, soft as wind, poor Jo. behind,
>   And pushed him int' his grave.

> Reader, one tear, if thou hast one in store,
> Since Jo. Green's tongue and chin can wag no more."

The remaining inscription we shall give is on "Samuel Kershaw," a blacksmith, who died in 1810.

> "My anvil and my hammer lie declined;
> My bellows, too, have lost their wind;
> My fire's extinct, and forge decay'd,
> And in the dust my vice is laid;
> My coal is spent, my iron is gone;
> My last nail driven, my work is done."

The last three are by no means bad specimens of gravestone inscriptions, and will bear favourable comparison with such kind of work in other parts of the country.

We may as well in this place lay before our readers some verses on "Tim's" Grave, published upwards of forty years ago, by Samuel Bamford, the well-known Lancashire author and poet. The verses have provoked many a hearty laugh, and they deserve to be kept in remembrance by the lovers of rare "Tim," of whom we are all so proud.

TIM BOBBIN'S GRAVE.

> "I stoode beside Tim Bobbin's grave,
> 'At looks o'er Ratchda' teawn,
> An' th' owd lad 'woke within his yerth,
> An' sed, "Wheer arto' beawn?"
> Om gooin' into th' Packer Street,
> As far as th' Gowden Bell,
> To taste o' Daniel Kesmus ale.
> TIM.—"I cud like a saup mysel.'
> An' by this hont o' my reet arm,
> If fro' that hole theaw'll reawk,
> Theaw'st have a saup o' th' best breawn ale
> 'At ever lips did seawk.
> The greawnd it sturr'd beneath my feet,
> An' then I yerd a groan,
> He shook the dust fro' off his skull,
> An' rowlt away the stone.
> I brought him op a deep breawn jug
> 'At a gallon did contain,
> An' he took it at one blessed draught,
> An' laid him deawn again."

Within the church are to be found monuments of the most interesting kind. We deem it unnecessary to copy out the various inscriptions which appear on the tablets, because the church is always open · to the inspection of visitors. Access for the purpose of inspection can be had on application to the parish clerk, and ample time will be afforded to the curious inquirer to make his notes either concise or full, or as inclination may dictate. There are to be found here records so valuable, that we hope "the world will not willingly let them die." It is to be wished that proper provision should be made under all circumstances, and in all time to come, for the due preservation of these interesting memorials of past ages.

We consider it superfluous to give a list of all the Rectors and Vicars of St. Chad's from the earliest times. We may, however, call attention to the most noteworthy :—

John Hampson, whose name is found to occur in the old records in 1558, was ejected in 1561. Joseph Midgley, M.A., collated 1595, was deprived of his benefice in 1606. Henry Tilson, D.D., collated between the years 1615 and 1635, afterwards became the Bishop of Elphin. Robert Bath, A.M., collated in 1635, was deprived in 1662. The more recent Vicars are the following: Thomas Wray, D.D., collated 1762, died 1778; Richard Hind, D.D., collated 1778, died 1790; Thomas Drake, D.D., collated 1790, died 1819; William Robert Hay, M.A., collated 1819, died 1839; John Edward Nassau Molesworth, D.D., collated 1839.

The curious inquirer need only refer either to Dr. Whitaker's History of Whalley, or to Baines's History of Lancashire, for a full catalogue of the reverend men who have held the benefice of St. Chad's at various times.

The chief incident in the history of the Rev. Dr. Wray, was the obtaining by him of an Act of Parliament by which he and his successors in office were enabled to grant leases for building purposes of the glebe lands of St. Chad's, whereby the revenues of the benefice were greatly increased and the lands themselves rendered of important value to those who thought fit to become lessees. The facilities for building thus afforded, tended to increase the importance of the town itself; and we have daily before our eyes the immense advantages which have arisen to us, as a community, in consequence of the Act to which we refer. Had no such enabling powers been obtained, the glebe lands might have been comparatively valueless at the present day, whereas, as matters now stand, the benefice of St. Chad's may be looked upon as one of the richest in England, as in fact it is. This is entirely owing to the far-seeing sagacity of Dr. Wray; and in this regard, therefore, if he were not otherwise entitled to grateful remembrance, his memory should be held in esteem alike by the clergy and the laity of Rochdale.

The Rev. Dr. Drake held the benefice of St. Chad's for a period of nearly thirty years. He was much beloved by his fellow-townsmen and parishioners, and his death occasioned the greatest regret to all. Moved by a loving regard for his memory, his bereaved parishioners erected for him a tomb in the New Burial Ground, with a suitable inscription thereon. There are some people among us in Rochdale even now who must

have known the Rev. Doctor as he went about in his
parish receiving, on every hand, the kind salutes of old
and young, gentle and simple. Alas! that time, in its
steady progress, should have so greatly thinned the
ranks of the old veterans who were the contemporaries
of the worthy Doctor, but so it is.

> "Time, like an ever-rolling stream,
> Bears all its sons away;
> They fly forgotten, as a dream
> Dies at the opening day."

Passing over the Rev. W. R. Hay, we come now to
his successor, the Rev. Dr. Molesworth, the present
vicar, who has held the benefice of St. Chad's since the
year 1839. It is worthy of remark that the Rev. Dr.
has still further developed the resources and wealth of
the glebe lands; and to his honour it must be related
that within the last seven or eight years he has voluntarily relinquished a considerable part of the income of
his benefice, in order that the stipends of the other
clergymen of the parish should be increased. This he
worthily accomplished by an arrangement with the
Ecclesiastical Commissioners for England. His present
income, under the arrangement alluded to, is no doubt
very large, but it must be remembered that if he had so
chosen he might, at the present moment, have been in
receipt of every penny of income which the revenues of
St. Chad's yielded, without the least shadow of injustice
to the other clergy in Rochdale, who are now reaping
the benefit of his generosity. His conduct in this
respect cannot be too highly eulogised, and instances of
such abnegation are extremely rare. The clergy, no

doubt, duly appreciate his kindness; and among the laity, by whom the matter is understood, there can be but one opinion on the subject, and that is entirely in the venerable Doctor's favour.

In the early part of his career the Doctor had much to contend with.   Conscious, however, of the rectitude of his conduct he bore up nobly against all assaults, and, at the present day, at an advanced age, he has the consolation of knowing that he has lived down the dislike of which he was at one time the object, and the name of the Rev. Doctor is now honoured, as it ought to be, in every part of the parish of which he has so long been the head.

Looking back on the past period to which we have alluded, and contrasting it with the peace which now prevails in the parish, and beholding the venerable vicar as the central object in the picture, one cannot help recalling to memory, as singularly appropriate to the occasion, the beautiful lines of Goldsmith—

> " As some tall cliff that lifts its awful form,
> Swells from the vale, and midway leaves the storm,
> Though round its breast the rolling clouds are spread,
> Eternal sunshine settles on its head."

Dr. Molesworth was always an able writer and controversialist, and now, in the evening of his life, we may add that

> " Age cannot wither him, nor custom stale
> His infinite variety."

ST. MARY'S CHURCH.

This place of worship is situated in Cheetham Street, and was best known in bygone years as " Baum Chapel."

8

It is not now often so called; its more modern name was "St. Mary, the Virgin," but, no doubt, for some good reason the second part of the title has been dropped, and it is at present called "St. Mary's." It was erected about 1744, and the outward appearance of the building, which is of brick, is not handsome. It has recently undergone considerable improvement and decoration internally, and the wonder really is that so much could be done with such unpromising materials as presented themselves. Great credit is due to those by whom the alterations and beautifying have been carried out. The mode of conducting divine service at St. Mary's is decidedly high; and the present Vicar's Ritualism is well known. How far High Church practices conduce to godliness admits of considerable doubt. The Legislature has expressed its mind on the subject by passing the Public Worship Act of 1874; and, probably, when that statute comes into operation people will see less of the "mass in masquerade," and its accompanying clerical millinery, than previously.

While speaking of this church, we must not forget to mention the "Baum Rabbit." Whether any of the present generation have seen that ghostly rodent, we will not undertake to say. In former days, or rather nights, it used to "revisit the glimpses of the moon" in the chapel yard. It was a rabbit of robust and lively habits; and was plump and well nourished, as if the churchyard herbage agreed with it. It was always beautifully clean, and was even said to be "whiter than snow." It used to be seen in various attitudes; sometimes standing on its hind-quarters, after the manner of the rabbit kind, and demurely brushing its whiskers.

Its aspect was usually somewhat serious, although, at times it had a comical twist of countenance. It has, also, been observed delving into the churchyard mould with great determination, as if in search of hidden treasure. But no one, that we have heard, ever came to close quarters with it. The slightest attempt to hold a parley with the mysterious quadruped was utterly useless; for, being exquisitely sensitive to the slightest sound, it invariably disappeared into thin air when intruded upon, and thus eluded the investigations of the earnest enquirer after truth. Strange to say, it was, apparently, much pleased with the love (but not lovely) music of the feline tribe, to which it listened with mute attention. Clearly, the rabbit was invulnerable to the nocturnal sportsman's small shot, and even air-guns, it is alleged, had no effect on it. After a discharge from any deadly weapon, it used to reappear with the greatest equanimity, and frisk about as if to encourage its assailants to further effort in the same direction. Some people said the smell of the gunpowder was as delicious to it as a pinch of snuff is to an old woman. It was " generally admitted " that it was a rabbit of a ghostly or supernatural character. The story runs that hundreds of years before the erection of "Baum Chapel," a "deed of horror" was committed within the precincts haunted by this extraordinary rabbit; but, unfortunately, authentic particulars of that dark transaction have never been obtained, and we are, therefore, unable to gratify the reasonable curiosity of the reader on the subject.

It is agreed on all hands that, as a rabbit, it was remarkably well-behaved, and never, so far as could be ascertained, committed any serious wrong. Its chief

object seemed to be to "scare folks a bit," and it gave
no token of being influenced by any diabolical agency.
"Doomed to walk," or, rather, haunt the churchyard
for a certain term, it would seem, from recent experience,
that it has performed its allotted task, for very little is
heard in our day of the surprising "Baum Rabbit"
which used to perplex the natives, and fright them from
their propriety. It is with reference to this curious
animal that an ancient local poet, in an angry mood,
wrote the verses which we subjoin. He had to pass
through the churchyard every night on his way home,
and was, to say the least, of a very nervous temperament.

> "Confound that rabbit!
> I wish some chap would grab it,
> And stop its nightly habit;
>   Confound that rabbit!
> Confound its head and eyes!
> Confound its legs and thighs!
> Confound it otherwise!
>   Confound that rabbit!
> Dogs, rush out and squeeze him!
> Worry, toss, and teaze him!
> That is, if you can seize him;
>   Confound that rabbit!"

As to its disappearance, we confess ourselves unable
to solve the query which has been submitted to us,
whether the rabbit can have been caught by some wight
more expert than his fellows, and converted into rabbit
pie.

It may be right to add that if our legend of the
"Baum Rabbit" is new to our readers, it is only a
proof that people may live and learn. As we have
said, it is difficult at this great distance of time to obtain
authentic particulars; but we will venture to back our

story against any other that can be produced, and, what
is more, we are quite certain that ours is entitled to be
regarded as being equally truthful.

Reverting to the church itself, it would appear that
one of the later incumbents was the Rev. J. W. Inchbald,
who was held in the greatest esteem as a clergyman and
gentleman. In his days, this church was the most
popular in the entire parish, and crowded congregations
gave evidence of the respect in which he was held. The
service was conducted with a fervour which touched
every heart; and the eloquent pulpit discourses of
Mr. Inchbald must be remembered by many even at the
present day. To see his church crowded, in every part,
on Sunday evenings, was indeed delightful. But those
days are gone.

Another later clergyman at this church was the
Rev. Henry Clere. He afterwards became the Incumbent of Walsden. Mr. Clere was a plain, kind,
and unassuming gentleman, and was, generally, well
liked by the people. Following Mr Clere, came the
Rev. Mr. Morton, who was in turn succeeded by the
present Vicar, the Rev. Robert Napier Sharpe, M.A., of
whom it is enough to say that he is an exceedingly
earnest and able clergyman, with, perhaps, a little too
much of the priestly autocrat in his manner. "High"
in his views, the laity do not usually count for much
with him, unless, indeed, they see things as he does,
which is not always an easy matter to accomplish.
The interior of the church, since the alterations and
ornamentation which we have mentioned, is well worth
inspection, and must excite the greatest admiration on
the part of those who can appreciate "beautiful things
in beautiful order."

ST. JAMES'S CHURCH.

This church is situated in Yorkshire-street, the principal thoroughfare in the town. Built in 1820, it was consecrated in 1821. It is a handsome Gothic building of stone, with a square tower of the same material, in which are placed four dials, illuminated with gas, supplied gratuitously by the Town Council. The clock is of great public utility, and it is for this reason that the illuminating is at the cost of the town. The church is surrounded by iron palisading, within which there is a burial ground, which is not now used. The church contains about 1,000 sittings, of which one-half are free. The living is a vicarage, in the gift of the Vicar of Rochdale, and is nominally worth about £300 a year. St. James's is one of the favoured churches in the parish of Rochdale, which may, after the death of the present Vicar of St. Chad's, be selected for additional endowment, when the funds arising out of the glebe lands, on their becoming vested in the Ecclesiastical Commissioners, will allow of an increased stipend to the holder of the benefice. The present vicar is the Rev. R. S. Rowan, M.A., who, on the death of the Rev. William James ffarington, in 1863, was promoted, by Dr. Molesworth, from a curacy at the Parish Church, where he had been for some years.

There is not much to relate about St. James's. The late incumbent, Mr. ffarington—who was not, however, vicar, as the constitution of the parish as a vicarage took place after his death—had held the living for upwards of forty years. He was a man deservedly respected by "all sorts and conditions of men;" and his death was very generally deplored. His manners were gentle and affable, and he was an honour to the church and the town. He kept his congregation well together, and was regarded as an earnest and eloquent preacher. To an educated person, it was perfectly charming to hear him read the lessons of the day; and his method of conducting divine service in his church tended to place, in a still more admirable light, the very beautiful and inimitable service of the Church of England. On the appointment of Mr. Rowan to the incumbency, he considered it proper, in the undoubted exercise of his discretion, to make, what he conceived to be, necessary changes in the mode of conducting the service; and this circumstance, to say the least, occasioned disappointment and regret to many members of the congregation. In some instances, it is to be feared, that the feeling which the change brought about occasioned something more than mere diappointment. At any rate, it is a fact, that there was a visible thinning of the ordinary congregation. Some of the old pew holders were offended that there should have been any departure from the practices which prevailed in the time of Mr. Rowan's predecessor, who had, for so long a period, maintained the most kindly relations between himself and his people. It is, no doubt, to be deplored that any dissatisfaction should have arisen; but, at the same time, we are perfectly willing to admit that Mr. Rowan did not act from mere caprice, but from entirely conscientious motives. Mr. ffarington was of the school termed "low," and Mr. Rowan, on the other hand, is undoubtedly "high." Between these two schools of thought there are, it is well known, the most important

and distinctly marked lines of divergence, but it is
quite evident that the congregation preferred the old to
the new practices. We are not aware that this had any
weight with the Rev. Vicar; at all events, he pursued
his own course, and the result is that St. James's Church
is not as popular as it used to be among the generality of
churchgoers, or even among the major part of the congregation. Of Mr. Rowan personally, as a clergyman
and gentlemen, we can speak in the highest terms; but
we do very sincerely regret that things are not now as
they used to be. The harmony which existed has been
disturbed, though there has not been any open rupture
of which the public has had any cognizance. In the
interests of the church, the latter circumstance is matter
for sincere congratulation. As a noteworthy event, we
should mention that, Mr. Rowan is one, among many
other clergymen in the kingdom, who signed the
memorial for the introduction, into the Church of
England, of the practice of auricular confession. This
denotes an extremely advanced view of the power and
authority of the clerical character, and has led to a
considerable amount of public comment. The movement
in favour of the confessional has been generally
condemned; and, for our own part, we sincerely hope
that the day may never dawn which shall witness any
such outrageous practice, as in operation in our midst,
in the Church of England. Mr. Rowan, we believe,
has given some explanation of his conduct in connection
with the question, to the effect that he did not desire
confession to exist in the church, so as to be compulsory
on its members, but simply for the benefit of those
persons who voluntarily presented themselves for that

purpose, before those who were properly ordained and set apart for the work. The Rev. gentleman is entitled to the benefit of his explanation, but the broad fact remains that, at any rate, he is inclined, to a limited extent, to view with favour a practice which ought to be regarded with the utmost disfavour by every sincere lover of the freedom of English churchmen.

ST. CLEMENT'S CHURCH.

This church was built in the year 1835, out of a fund provided by parliament for the erection of churches in the manufacturing districts, which was commonly known, on account of its amount, as the million grant. The site was given by James Royds, Esq., of Mount Falinge, who also afterwards gave ground for a school and a parsonage house. There was a party among the promoters of the building who wished that it should be erected at Brotherod, and the matter was referred to the Bishop of the Diocese, who gave his decision in favour of the present site. The incumbent was, at first, dependent on pew rents for his support, but a few years after the consecration of the buiding Mr. Fildes left, by will, the sum of £2,000 as an endowment of the church. This was further augmented by the Ecclesiastical Commissioners in such a manner as to raise the annual income of the incumbent of the church to £300. Under the Rochdale Vicarage Act the endowment was raised so as to yield an annual income of £500, and the chaplaincy of the cemetery was also annexed to the incumbency by that Act, which made it a vicarage. Subsequently the great tithes of a large portion of the township of Spotland were purchased out of the Fildes' endowment, and the benefice then became a rectory. In the year 1870 a new National School was erected in connection with the church, and the old building was converted into an Infant School. The first incumbent of this church was the Rev. G. H. Cotton, M.A., brother of the Provost of Worcester College, Oxford. He was succeeded, in 1844, by the present rector, the Rev. W. Nassau Molesworth, M.A.

ST. ALBAN'S CHURCH.

This sacred edifice, unquestionably one of the most beautiful churches in the provinces, was erected about twenty years ago. It stands on an eminence (like a city set on a hill) which commands a fine view of the surrounding country. The site of the church was the gift of the late Abraham Brierley, Esq., J.P., of West Hill, Rochdale, and the church itself was built by public subscription. The parsonage adjoining is a handsome and substantial building. The first incumbent was the late Rev. J. W. Parker, M.A., who, in 1866, became the Vicar. Mr. Parker held the living until his very sudden and lamented death, in August, 1874. His successor is the Rev. Walter Cooper, B.A., the late Curate. The internal decorations and fittings of the church are of a most costly and elaborate character, and, in point of beauty and correctness of taste, cannot be surpassed.

The munificent gifts and lavish expenditure of our esteemed townsman, Jonathan Nield, Esq., J.P., have made the church a model of artistic beauty of the highest order. The chancel is superb in its ornamentation and adornments, and must be seen to be appreciated. The font and pulpit are exquisite works of art and correct taste; and, with other parts of the church, excite the greatest admiration. The font was the gift of Arthur Brierley, Esq., and the pulpit that of Mr. Nield. The tower contains a fine peal of bells, the gift, also, of the last named gentleman. To admirers of church ornamentation and refined taste, an examination of the interior of the church will afford the greatest satisfaction. St. Alban's is a standing evidence of what can be done when money and gifts are bestowed with ungrudging hand. It would be well if wealthy Churchmen, in other parts, were to emulate the spirit of munificence and piety of which so many examples are to be found in this church. The poet Keats has said that "A thing of beauty is a joy for ever," and we have here a striking proof of the truth of this axiom.

A tribute of regard to the late vicar, the Rev. J. W. Parker, may not inaptly conclude our brief notice of St. Alban's. A perfect gentleman in every respect, he was, at the same time, of a remarkably quiet and unobtrusive disposition. "He wore his wisdom," as Tennyson says, "lightly, like a flower," and he went down to a comparatively early grave amid the unfeigned sorrow of the whole parish of St. Alban's, where he had gone in and out among the people for a period of nearly twenty years. Anyone who had the pleasure of his acquaintance knew how highly he was to be esteemed; and his public ministrations in the beautiful church, where his manly presence was so frequently and regularly seen, must have been a source of consolation

on many and many an occasion to his attentive auditors.
He was a truly good man; and the respect which was
paid to his memory, on the occasion of his funeral, will
not soon be forgotten. The suddenness of his death
was like the shock of a thunderbolt to his parishioners,
and gave one more proof of the uncertainty of human
life. To use the words of our national poet, "He was
a scholar, and a ripe and good one." Adorning the
Gospel of God, his Saviour, in all things, he has now
passed to that bright world of love and joy, "where
God unfolds his presence, and where shines eternal day."

ST. EDMUND'S CHURCH,
FALINGE-ROAD.

This handsome church is seen on the right as we pass
up Spotland-road. It is cruciform in shape, and in the
decorated Gothic style of architecture, the stone mainly
used being Pierrepoint. On entering the church one is
struck with the light, artistic effect, and correct proportions of the sacred edifice. The square tower which
rises from the transept is supported by four beautiful
columns in Aberdeen granite, above the capitals being
elegant designs in stone, representing the fruit and
foliage of the four seasons. The reredos is elaborately
carved in Hollington stone, with emblems of the Lord's
Supper, entwined round the words, "I am the vine,"
a magnificent design by the Rev. E. W. Gilbert, M.A.,
who was the much esteemed vicar in 1873, in which
year the church was opened. The five-light window
over the communion table, is like all the others in the
church, beautifully stained, setting forth Bible history
in glowing figures, a prominent feature being, scenes

from the Life of Christ, and it also depicts the career of
St. Edmund. The window at the south end of the
church has for its subject the Te Deum, and is considered to be a marvel of artistic execution. It was on
view at the Vienna Exhibition. The window at the
north end represents the Stem of Jesse. The light in
the west façade has an emblem of the Trinity, adoring
angels, and prophets. There is a beautiful window to
the left of the west entrance, illustrating God's hand in
the Creation, and further on we gaze at the disobedience
of Adam and Eve, the Fall and its consequence, Cain
and Abel at work; while, on the other hand of the
same transept, are designs of Noah building the Ark,
the Tower of Babel, and the blessing of the sons of
Judah. In the north and south transepts are four kinds
of sacrifices; Melchisedek, the high priest; and the
Last Supper of the Lord. There is in the chancel a
magnificent raised dais or sanctuary, on the floor of
which is an oaken parquetry of a rich pattern. The
roof is panelled in white deal and oak, the timber ends
being carved and supported on corbels of white Hollington stone. Near the chancel is a memorial plate, in
brass, with the following inscription, ornamented with
the founder's insignia and emblems of office in the
various degrees he had attained in Freemasonry, and
surmounted with his family crest and motto, "Semper
Paratus" :—" This church is erected for the worship of
God, for the good of his fellow-man, and in memory of
his father and mother, by Albert Hudson Royds, of
Falinge, 1873 ; Clement Royds, died 6th September,
1854 ; Jane Royds, died 16th February, 1853. ' The
memory of the just is blessed.'—Prov. x. c., 7 v." The

founder's private chapel is separated from the south side
of the chancel by four beautiful columns in Chapfell
granite, and arches cased with Hollington and red
Duncan stone. The window, when viewed from the
inside, conveys an excellent idea of the founder's wisdom
in doing good to his fellow-man in the erection of a
house of God, for no more appropriate scene than that
of Solomon building the temple could have been chosen
as a subject for the stained glass, the details of which
are, so to speak, the pink of perfection. The bowl of
the font at the west entrance is in white statuary
marble, and is at once massive and elegant. It is
supported by marble shafts of various colours, and is
relieved with figures of four angels. This font is the
gift of Mr. Edmund Royds, a son of the founder, an
inscription to that effect running round it. The ornamental work throughout the building is executed
without plaster or paint, the wood used being simply
varnished. The sculpture has a very pleasing effect.
Immediately over the west entrance, on the outside, is a
tablet commemorating the death of St. Edmund, who
appears bound to a tree, while his persecutors are
shooting arrows into his side. It may be well to recall
the legend. St. Edmund, king and martyr, was born
in 841, and at the age of fourteen ascended the throne
of East Anglia. He was a great friend to the poor,
restored the churches and monasteries, but was
compelled, when he had reigned fourteen years,
to withdraw, with some followers, on an invasion
of the Danes, to a church at Heglesduna, or
Hoxne, on the Wavenley. Here "he threw aside his
temporal arms and put on heavenly, humbly imploring

God to grant him constancy in his passion." The Danes surrounded the church, dragged him forth, bound him to a tree, and pierced him with darts and arrows because he refused to abjure his faith. As a token of the honour in which the saint was held, particularly in East Anglia, at least fifty-five churches were dedicated to his name, fifteen being in Norfolk and seven in Suffolk. This church, which was erected at a cost of £20,000, was opened on May 7th, 1873, with masonic ceremonies, about 500 brethren walking in procession to the church, which was formally opened by Mr. A. H. Royds, Past Deputy Grand Master of the East Lancashire Ancient Free and Accepted Masons, and Grand Master of Worcestershire; the Bishop of Manchester, Dr. Fraser, afterwards going through the usual consecration service. The church contains 474 sittings, one-half of which are free and unappropriated, while twenty sittings in the private chapel are retained for the use of the founder and his successors. The service is low church.

ST. PETER'S CHURCH,
NEWBOLD.

St. Peter's Church, Newbold, situated in a thinly populated but growing district, off Milnrow-road, was consecrated for divine worship in May, 1871. The style of the architecture is pointed Gothic, of a bold and vigorous type, treated to suit the rubble stone and red brick of which the edifice is mainly built; stock brick being introduced in the coigns, bands, strings, buttresses, and arches, in the ornamental panels, mouldings, and cornices, and in other places where dressed stone is more usually employed. The ground plan of the church

consists of nave, north aisle ending towards the east
in minister's and choristers' vestries, south aisle ending
in the organ chamber, and a chancel and semi-hexagonal
apse. The chancel arch is broad, and is supported on
carved corbelled shafts. The six nave columns are of red
and white stone, arranged in bands. The two eastern
capitals, and the eastern responds, or half-pillars, are
carved. In the triangular spandrels, above these
columns, are carved medallions, containing busts of the
writers of the Acts and Epistles, bearing rolls—eastern
books—to represent respectively the number of their
writings, and a few words selected from, and epito-
mising the characteristic spirit of each. This part of the
church is effectively lighted by the sixteen vesica-shaped
stone cusped windows of the clere-story, and by the west
windows, which are placed high up above the narthex.
Below the west window are two carved stone medallions
with subjects from the life of St. Peter—his walking
on the sea, and his standing with Paul at the beautiful
Gate of the Temple. The cost of the sacred edifice,
which has seats for 670 adults, was about £4,000.
The vicar, the Rev. James Richards, M.A., is much
esteemed by all classes of the community. Indeed, as
a result of his indefatigable efforts in a church district
that was brought into existence as such by the passing
of the Rochdale Vicarage Act, and containing a population of about 6,000, almost entirely consisting of factory
operatives, he has been able to gather together a
numerous congregation, who meet for worship in an
elegant building, and whose children may receive a
good education in some really excellent schools, which
are spacious, lofty, and well ventilated. They stand at
the back of the church.

ST. MARY'S CHURCH,

BALDERSTONE.

This beautiful church is situated in Lowerplace, Oldham-road, a thriving village, which has been lately brought within the Borough of Rochdale, and was, in addition to the fine spacious schools and vicarage, built by the liberality of Messrs. Radcliffe. The site is triangular in shape, and at the extreme north-west corner stands the steeple, with a tower and spire rising to a height of nearly 150 feet. The principal entrance is by the tower porch, the next important entrance being through a gabled porch. The church, which is built in the Gothic style, cost £8,000, and it is seated to accommodate 600 persons. The eye is struck by the beauty of the interior, the general effect being enhanced by the shining marbles, granite, and alabaster; the coloured mural decoration; the brilliant, glowing colours of the stained glass. The font is a circular bowl of pure white statuary marble, enriched with carved lilies, on each of the eight stems of which one sees a bud, a half-opened flower, and a full blown lily. Around the rim of the bowl are symbolical devices, by Salviati. The floors of the porches and passages generally are laid with red tiles, the borders being of black and coloured encaustic tiles. The steps of the chancel, and its floors and sanctuary, are of marble, in various patterns and colours. Going back to the west end, and looking towards the east, we observe that there are eight stone arches on either side, dividing the nave from the aisles and transepts. They rest on granite shafts of two colours, alternately, the capitals being

9

carved with foliage, &c. In the spandrels of the nave arches there are six medallions, three on each side, containing the following subjects :—The Annunciation; The Birth of Christ; St. Mary finding Christ in the Temple; The Marriage in Cana; Christ commending His Mother to the care of St. John; and the Deposition from the Cross. At the west end are two similar medallions, containing two subjects symbolical of baptism, viz. :—The Passage of the Red Sea, and The Ark. The pulpit, which stands at the north-east corner of the nave, is of polished Mansfield stone, supported on five shining red granite shafts. The upper part is divided by slender shafts of coloured marble and mouldings into ten panels, containing a medallion of alabaster, carved with sacred monograms and floral ornaments. A carved legend from the prophet Jeremiah runs round the base—" He that hath my word, let him speak my word faithfully." The reredos of this church is most beautiful in design, the workmanship and material being of a rich and costly description. There is a gable, with a moulded and cusped arch, and a carved, traceried open cornice, surmounted by the Agnus Dei. In the centre of the recessed place below is a vesica of white alabaster, containing a red marble cross, and marble inlay around it. Below, and in the lower division, on each of the side compartments, which are marked off from the centre by slender clustered marble shafts, supporting figures of kneeling angels, are subjects carved in lily-white marble or alabaster in relief, the central one being The Last Supper; that on the right, The Crucifixion; and on the left, The Agony in the Garden. The spaces on each side of the communion table are filled up with a diaper on carved stone, an alabaster and marble inlay, while the diapering of the chancel itself is of *fleur de lis* pattern. This symbol is frequently introduced elsewhere in the church with reference to its dedication. The woodwork throughout the church is worthy of minute inspection, as are also the stained windows. The great west window, a memorial one, is filled with subjects relating to the Resurrection. The building was consecrated by the Bishop of Manchester, Dr. Fraser, on July 1, 1872. The present vicar is the Rev. J. R. Parr, M.A.

ALL SAINTS' CHURCH,

HAMER.

This handsome church was erected in the year 1866, at a cost of £3,800, upon a picturesque plot of high land given by the late J. S. Entwisle, Esq., on the Foxholes estate, a few hundred yards off the main road leading to Littleborough, at Hamer Bottoms. The foundation stone was laid by the donor of the site, on the 29th April, 1865, and the church was consecrated by the Bishop of Manchester, on the 22nd of November, 1866. The style of the edifice is early English. The plan consists of a nave and north aisle of six bays each, and a south aisle of five bays, the two most eastern being so widened to the south into a sort of double transept, as to give picturesqueness to the interior. At the west end of the south aisle is the steeple, the lowest stage of which serves as a porch, and is the main entrance. The spire is octagonal, and has four very simple square pinnacles at its springing. There is a north porch and a smaller entrance in the western side

of the south transept. The east window is of five lights,
and the head is fitted with tracery of a very complete
design. The "Crucifixion" takes the prominent place,
and nearly fills the three lights ; under it is the "Last
Supper." The other lights contain smaller groups,
representing incidents in the life of our Lord. Altogether it is a very impressive window. The western
window is of four lights, and contains some beautiful
stained glass in figure subjects. This window was
erected by the late Mr. W. W. Schofield, to the memory
of his mother and father. There is a very pretty little
single-light window, intended as a memorial to the late
curate, the Rev. T. C. Kidd. The subject is, "Sick,
and ye visited me." The churchyard is not a general
burial ground, but there are two vaults for the largest
benefactors of the Church, namely, the late Mr. J. S.
Entwisle, who, besides presenting the land, gave £1,000
towards the cost of the structure ; and the late Mr. W.
W. Schofield, of Buckley Hall, who subscribed £1,000.
The extent of the ground consecrated is about three-
quarters of an acre. There are sittings in the church
for 651 persons, of which 354 are free. There is a
remarkable historical coincidence in connection with the
erection of this place of worship on this site. Richard
Entwisle, the first of that family possessing the estate
of Foxholes, at the time of the Reformation, took a
great interest in that movement in the parish of Rochdale; and in his will, made during the early part of
Elizabeth's reign, he directed that when there should
be no sermon or service in the parish church of
"Rachdale," his friend and neighbour, Ellis Hamer, of
Hamer, should call the poor parishioners together, and

read out to them, from "my little Geneva Bible," on
the Lord's-day, in order that God's name may be
known, and his perfections glorified in the town of
"Rachdale." The coincidence is, that the new church
stands in the centre of the two estates of Foxholes and
Hamer, and that the two properties have become united
and now belong to the Entwisle family. The Rev. J. A.
Lobley was the first incumbent, and was highly respected,
and his departure to America was much regretted. The
Rev. Mr. Fox is the present incumbent. Mr. John
Smith Entwisle, whose name is so closely connected
with this church, lived only two years after it was completed, dying on the 20th of June, 1868, and was
interred in the family vault, in the adjacent churchyard,
on the 26th of the same month. Mr. William Whitworth Schofield, of Buckley Hall, who was also a
prominent benefactor, expired on the 7th of December,
1873, and was buried in the family vault, which is
within a few yards of his staunch friend's grave. Mr.
Entwisle, by his sterling uprightness, kind familiarity,
and thoroughly English character, gained for himself the
respect of all classes; and Mr. Schofield, by his urbanity,
amiability, and generosity, endeared himself to his
fellow-townsmen, among whom he was a general
favourite. Their now vacant seats in the church often
recall to the minds of the worshippers the gap which
death has made in their midst, but the two friends
repose in peace within a few yards of the sanctuary in
which, in their lifetime, they took so deep an interest.

> "Such graves as theirs are pilgrim shrines,
> The Delphian vales, the Palestines,
> The Mecca of the mind."

ST. JOHN'S CHURCH,

SMALLBRIDGE.

The church of St. John the Baptist, Smallbridge, was erected by the late Church Building Commissioners out of a fund called the Million Grant. From the consecration deed it is called the Government Chapel of Smallbridge. The site was presented by the late John Entwisle, Esq., M.P., of Foxholes, the cost of the building was £3,071. 10s. 7d. The Rev. Mr. Hay, vicar of Rochdale, had represented to the Church Building Commissioners that Smallbridge was two miles from the Parish Church of Rochdale, and had a population of above 5,000. The church of St. John was erected simply as a chapel of ease to Rochdale, but a district chapelry was assigned to it in 1844. From the consecration in A.D. 1834 to 1842, the value of the benefice was about £65 per annum, arising chiefly from pew rents and fees. In 1842 a legacy of £2,000 was left to the church by the late Mr. Jonathan Fildes, the interest of which, in the funds, at 3 per cent, raised the amount to £125. In 1849 the Ecclesiastical Commissioners made a grant of £20 per annum, in augmentation of the living; and in 1859 they granted a further sum of £3 per annum. In 1866 the Rochdale Vicarage Bill was passed, under which an additional endowment of £215 was obtained. By the same act the incumbency was constituted a vicarage. The present vicar is the Rev. R. K. Cook, M.A., Honorary Canon of Manchester. His predecessors were the Rev. Nathaniel Milne, M.A.; the Rev. W. L. Barnes, M.A.; and the Rev. W. T. Hobson, M.A.

Mr. Cook's exertions as a parish clergyman have been characterised by zeal, ability, and perseverance. Smallbridge, at one time a rather benighted place, has become, through his painstaking and indefatigable exertions, an intelligent and thriving village, and may be pointed to as an illustration of what can be accomplished when the work of reformation is undertaken in a right spirit and with one simple object—the good of the people. Ever active in his Master's service, Mr. Cook has been the means of building the church and school of St. James's, Wardle, and to him must also be attributed the honour of the erection of the church and school of All Saints, Hamer. At Dearnley a school has been built, and is used for divine service, and it may be said that this, again, has been done through Mr. Cook's efforts. All these are monuments of his industry and fidelity to duty, and it is no small praise that he has laboured with such complete success, amid difficulties which might have appalled less energetic and determined workers. Of the personal character of Mr. Cook, we may add that he is held in the highest estimation throughout his own and the adjoining parishes; and we know of no one who is more entitled to the respect of the community among whom he has so long lived and worked. His friends, and the people of his parish, have laboured with him and heartily seconded his untiring efforts. His great popularity has been a "tower of strength" to him, while his amiabilty and personal worth have surrounded him with "troops of friends," who have, on many occasions, proved themselves "friends indeed." Long, very long, may he be spared to continue his labours of love in the

parish which he has for so many years blessed with his
ministry; unless, indeed, the time should come when
promotion to some wider sphere of usefulness may
present itself.   But of him it may be said—

> " Unskilful he to fawn, or seek for power,
> By doctrines fashioned to the varying hour:
> Far other aims his heart has learned to prize,
> More bent to raise the wretched than to rise."

CHRIST CHURCH,

HEALEY.

The tower and spire of Christ Church, Healey, are
visible for miles round, as the church stands on a slight
elevation, and is a prominent feature in the landscape.
Previously to the building of this church, in the year
1850, the Rev. Mr. Stanier conducted worship in a
warehouse at Broadley, and by his labours brought
together a good congregation.   Unfortunately he did
not live to enjoy the fruit of his labours, and his death
was regretted not only by his parishioners, but by members of other denominations, who were witnesses of the
good which he accomplished throughout the district.
He was buried on the north side of the church.   This
edifice was built in the year 1850; it is of stone, in the
Gothic style, and is a fine commodious building, with
1,250 sittings or thereabouts, of which 500 are free.
The living is a vicarage, of the annual value, nominally,
of £300, and is in the gift of the Crown and Bishop
alternately.   The Rev. R. Minnitt is vicar, and has held
the appointment since the consecration in 1850.   Inter-
ments are still allowed to take place in the graveyard.
There is, connected with this church, a national school.

ST. STEPHEN'S CHURCH.

This church, in the connexion of the late Countess of Huntingdon, was erected in 1811. Externally of substantial though unattractive appearance, it is, nevertheless, a very commodious place of worship, and is calculated to seat a thousand persons.

Previously to the opening of this church, services had been held in the old Theatre, conducted by the Rev. J. Nelson, who died in Rochdale before the building was completed.

The Rev. J. K. Foster was the first minister, and continued so for several years, when he became President of Lady Huntingdon's College, at Cheshunt. After his removal the congregation rapidly declined. He was followed by the Rev. S. T. Gibbs, who laboured here about three years. The Rev. E. C. Lewis became the minister in 1839, and has continued to the present time. Under his ministry the attendance gradually increased, and has maintained its efficiency for many years. In 1865 Mr. Lewis was unanimously elected the President of the Conference of the Countess's Connexion, and at the close of its sittings received high commendation for the ability displayed in conducting its business.

The prayers of the Church of England are required to be read, according to the discretion of the minister, as is the case in all the late Countess's chapels, necessity, not choice, having compelled her Ladyship to secede from the Establishment, while she continued attached to its services, its articles of faith, and its evangelical ministrations.

The organ of St. Stephen's is one of the finest in the town, and was erected upwards of twenty years ago, at a cost of about £500.

Mr. Lewis, now that the Rev. John Kershaw, late of Hope-street Chapel is dead, is the oldest Dissenting minister in the town. In disposition he is kind, affable, and genial, and has friends amongst every religious denomination in the parish. As a preacher he is extremely popular, and his sermons, which are preached extempore, are models of excellence, and are clear, forcible, and convincing. He illustrates his texts in the most vivid manner, and his style is captivating and impressive. The entire service at St. Stephen's is beautifully rendered; and the congregations are frequently full and sometimes overflowing. On special occasions numbers of persons from other places come to hear Mr. Lewis preach. The ordinary congregation is highly respectable and intelligent.

ST. JOHN'S CATHOLIC CHURCH,

ANN-STREET.

This is the first Roman Catholic place of worship erected in this town. It is not very ornate in its external appearance, having in front a building used as an institute and school, and at the back the priest's residence. Still, when we enter, we find its interior bears an artistic resemblance to churches of greater pretensions, and the decorations of the altars are very effective. The church is 100 feet in length, from the main entrance to the high altar, and affords comfortable sitting-room for 500 persons. It was built by sub-

scription, in 1829, by the late Dr. Turner, Bishop of
Salford, who was then a humble but very zealous and
devoted priest, and had charge of a little flock who had
previously met for worship in a room behind Alderman
Willans's woollen warehouse, in Clegg-street, behind
John-street. Father Turner had to contend with many
difficulties, especially pecuniary ones, in carrying out
his object. Subscriptions came in from Bury, Haslingden, and other places in the neighbourhood of Rochdale,
but these funds were soon exhausted in building operations, almost as soon as they came in from time to time,
and it is related that the hard-working Father, one
Saturday, sold his own watch to make up the deficiency
in the men's wages. The church, however, was opened
with great rejoicings in 1829. Father Dowling, who
was much esteemed by all classes for his warm-hearted
charity, and who was regarded as the very model of a
faithful and loving pastor, took charge of the congregation in 1835, and remained at St. John's till his death,
which occurred in 1871. Father E. O'Neill, who is also
very much respected, succeeded him, and in 1873 opened
the front entrance, under the school, already mentioned.
The education, conducted under the superintendence of
the Franciscan Order of Nuns, is excellent. They have
a convent close by, which was purchased by Father
O'Neill, who has also recently established a girls' school,
and another for infants. Attached to the convent is a
handsome plot of land, known as Bellegreen, and
measuring two acres in extent. The boys' school is in
a very efficient condition, and the young men's association, in connection with the newsroom adjoining the
church, is also in a flourishing state.

ST. PATRICK'S CATHOLIC CHAPEL.

In the year 1861 the Rev. M. Moriarty commenced a mission in Rochdale, in an Assembly-room, in Yorkshire-street, opposite St. James's Church, and gradually he increased his congregation. The same year, the room not being sufficiently large for the congregation, a building was erected in Watts-street, which was made to answer the purpose of a chapel as well as schools. In 1867 a chapel was erected in close proximity to the schools, and the internal dimensions are :—Length, 95 feet by 40 feet; the height, to ridges, 50 feet. There is a gallery extending the full width of the building, about 30 feet from the entrance or front wall, which will seat about 200 persons. The body of the chapel will accommodate about 500, the floor of which is on an incline from the entrance to within six feet of the chancel, so that those seated at the back can comfortably see the minister at the altar. The edifice is not built in any special style, but is an attempt at Gothic. It is composed of brick obtained in the neighbourhood, and blue Staffordshire bricks are introduced round the windows and doors. The whole is surmounted with a stone belfry and an ornamental stone cross. Between the chapel and the schools a comfortable looking parsonage has been erected. On the 6th of October, 1867, the chapel was consecrated by Dr. Turner, the late Bishop of Salford. The Rev. M. Moriarty still presides over the flock that he has gathered together by his own exertions, but their ranks are continually thinned by emigration.

BAPTIST CHAPEL,

It is now upwards of a hundred years since the
Baptist Church originated in Rochdale. Prior to the
year 1773 there were a few godly folk, members of the
Baptist churches at Bacup and Wainsgate, who resided
in Rochdale, and who, Sunday after Sunday, used to
cross the hills, to their own place of worship, to attend
the ministry of Mr. Hirst or Dr. Fawcett; after a while,
however, they succeeded in obtaining the services of
these and other ministers in their own houses, and as
the result of their preaching, nine persons were baptized,
in the river Roach, on the 12th October, 1773, in the
presence of a great crowd of people: this baptism took
place nearly opposite where the New Town Hall stands.

The first meeting house that the Baptists occupied,
was a room attached to the Bull Inn, then situate nearly
at the bottom of Yorkshire-street, almost opposite the
present Market Place, and was known as the "Bull
Chamber." In this room they continued to meet till
the year 1775, when, encouraged by the ministers who
visited them, they procured a plot of ground in Town
Meadows, and began the erection of a place of worship
14 yards by 12 outside. The whole expense exceeded
£400, a sum far beyond their ability to furnish, but a
great part of which, through the exertions of the
ministers who visited them, and the kindness of
neighbouring churches, they were soon enabled to raise.

For many years after the erection of this building it
remained without pews, but after Mr. Littlewood's
settlement as pastor of the church, which was in 1786

(he being the third pastor), they were enabled to fill the bottom with proper seats, and as the congregation gradually improved, it was thought advisable, in the year 1798, to erect a gallery. This was done at a cost of £300, which was principally raised among the members themselves. The chapel in Town Meadows was occupied till the year 1833, when the present building in West-street was opened, the total cost of the chapel and lands being £3,332. 15s. Towards this amount the late Rev. W. Stephens, who was then pastor, voluntarily resigned an endowment of nearly £70 per annum, left by Miss Betty Stott, of Smallbridge, for the benefit of the minister; the estate being sold for upwards of £1,400, which was devoted to the building fund for the new chapel. West-street chapel was described by Mr. Stephens, at the time of opening, "as a plain, but elegant and commodious building, and in a very good situation." "The school-room," he said, "though beneath the chapel, is both lofty and spacious, and is provided with every convenience." Some who are now living, and who recollect the transit from Town Meadows to West-street, will endorse the description given by Mr. Stephens. The school-room, however, under the present chapel has been superseded by a new and elegant school, erected behind the chapel, and fronting Buckley-street, the memorial stone of which was laid on the 12th June, 1873, by Mrs. Kelsall, and has been erected at a cost of nearly £3,000, including land and fencing, together with a neat lecture room at the front of the building.

The church, since its formation, has been favoured with a settled ministry for about ninety-two years and nine months, leaving rather more than seven years for vacancies, and of the nine pastors who have been the choice of the people, three have laboured for seventy-two years, leaving the remaining twenty years for six pastors.

The three who só honourably and so long sustained the office of minister, were the Rev. Thomas Littlewood, the Rev. William Stephens, and the Rev. W. F Burchell, the last of whom still survives, and is residing at Lee, in Kent.

The following is a list of the ministers who have served the church from its commencement down to the present time, viz.:—Rev. A. Greenwood, 1775 to 1781; Rev. John Dracup, 1781 to 1785; Rev. Thomas Littlewood, 1786 to 1817; Rev. William Stephens, 1818 to 1837; Rev. Benaiah Hoe, 1837 to 1838; Rev. W. F. Burchell, 1839 to 1860; Rev. E. C. Pike, B.A., 1861 to 1866; Rev. Samuel Chapman, 1867 to 1870; Rev. T. Harwood Pattison, 1871, present pastor, who has, however, accepted the pastoral invitation of the first Baptist Church, Newhaven, Connecticut. Mr. Pattison's departure will be much regretted by his own church and his friends generally.

A marble tablet, provided by the pupils of the late Rev. T. Littlewood, who, in addition to his pastoral work, had a seminary at Townhead, was erected to his memory behind the pulpit, in the chapel, at Town Meadows, and is now fixed under the front gallery in West-street chapel.

There is a fine Oil Painting of the late Rev. William Stephens, the work of his own hands, kept in the vestry, behind the chapel, in West-street.

PARTICULAR BAPTISTS,

HOPE CHAPEL, HOPE STREET.

This cause was commenced by a few persons who left Town Meadows Chapel, of which place Mr. Thomas Littlewood was the settled minister, about 1807. At first they met in Greenwood's School-room, Drake-street, and invited Mr. John Warburton to become their minister.

Their numbers increasing, they commenced building a chapel in 1810, and called it "Hope Chapel." At the time it was built it was surrounded by fields and gardens, but after some time houses were built and a street laid out which took its name from the chapel. After a few years Mr. Warburton left Rochdale and went to Trowbridge, in Wilts, and Mr. John Kershaw, who had been raised up amongst them, was invited to take the charge of them as the settled minister, which, after due consideration, he accepted in March, 1817, and continued with them until the time of his death, which took place January 11th, 1870, in the 78th year of his age, and the 53rd of his pastorate over the church. In 1848 the chapel was enlarged at a cost of £900, and in 1855 a large school-room was built which cost upwards of £800. In the year 1867 the Minister's Jubilee was celebrated, and Mr. and Mrs. Kershaw were each presented with a gold watch, and Mr. Kershaw with a purse of gold containing £250. The church has recently elected Mr. Richard Lovesey, of Cheltenham, as resident minister.

Mr. John Kershaw was a kind, loving, and faithful pastor; and his long connection with this church had

endeared him to friends and members. Among his
dissenting brethren in the town and neighbourhood he
was regarded with the kindliest feelings; and his
presence at public religious meetings, when other
ministers were present, always gave pleasure, while his
sound and practical utterances carried conviction to
every hearer. At the time of his death he might be
looked upon as being the father of the Dissenting
ministry in Rochdale. He was an especial favourite
with young people and children, for

> " His ready smile a parent's warmth expressed;
> Their welfare pleased him, and their cares distressed;
> 'To them his heart, his love, his griefs were given,
> But all his serious thoughts had rest in heaven."

BAPTIST CHAPEL,
DRAKE-STREET.

This chapel was opened in January, 1854, having
been built by subscription, towards which the late
Henry Kelsall, Esq., of the Butts, was the largest contributor, to accommodate a small congregation which
had been gathered by the labours of Mr. Todd, who
came from Bacup, in March, 1847, at the invitation of
H. Kelsall, Esq., and from that time till the opening of
the chapel worked zealously, gathering children for
Sunday School instruction, and their parents for public
worship and preaching, in a Mission Room, first in
School Lane and afterwards in Church Stile. After the
opening of the chapel he continued to minister to the
people until November, 1862, when he removed to
Lancaster. Mr. Alexr. Pitt, of Burton-upon-Trent, was
selected to succeed Mr. Todd, and took the pastorate of
the people in September, 1863; until this the Drake-

10

street cause held the position of a branch of the older
church at West-street, but now became a separate
church by the dismissal of a number of members from
that church and the union with them of a number of
newly baptized converts. Under the energetic ministry
of Mr. Pitt the church and congregation rapidly
increased, and the chapel was improved and enlarged
by being fitted up with pews, of which, till now, it had
been nearly destitute, and the addition of a good
capacious gallery. The teaching of the Sunday School
and the holding of public worship in the same building
were now found very inconvenient, and H. Kelsall, Esq.,
the original promoter of the cause, now built, at a cost
of £1,200, the excellent school buildings and chapel-
keeper's house in the rear of the chapel, and presented
the same to the church and people at Drake-street, one
large room in the building being appropriated to the
use of a Ragged School, which is still carried on therein
and is supported by his daughter, Mrs. Kemp. The
new schools were opened in January, 1865, and the
opening celebrated by the holding of a very full
and joyous tea meeting. Some time after this
the chapel was still further improved by the putting
in of skylights, it having been previously rather
dark, and the painting thereof throughout, and
also the planting of the ground surrounding the chapel
and the asphalting of the paths and the yard between
chapel and school. All these improvements, the pews,
galleries, painting, &c., were paid for by subscription,
within a short time of their completion, without the aid
of that now popular institution, the Bazaar. In
September, 1871, Mr. Pitt resigned his pastorate and

removed to Liverpool to take charge of the South Bethel Mission there, and since that time the church has been without a settled pastor, but nevertheless it is prosperous and increasing, and the school also is in a flourishing condition. It possesses a small library, and there is held within it a Young Men's Mutual Improvement Class, a Sick and Burial Society, and a Band of Hope. The land on which the premises stand is a rectangular plot extending from Drake-street in front to Henry-street at back, into which latter street the school opens, but is connected in its upper room with the chapel by a bridge over which the children pass from the school to their seats in the chapel. The whole is freehold and free from chief rent, is held in trust for the use of the Particular Baptists; its estimated value is about £5,000, and it is free from debt. It contains sittings for 412 persons, beside school and choir.

EBENEZER BAPTIST CHAPEL,

WATER STREET.

This church was formed of members formerly in connection with the West-street Church, and met at first for divine worship in Baillie-street, on the 8th of January, 1867; it continued there up to the time of its removal to the chapel in Water-street. The last mentioned place was built in 1834, by the New Connexion Methodists, and was purchased from them by the Baptists, and re-opened for divine service on the 1st of May, 1870. The alterations and improvements made in the chapel at that time, were still further supplemented by the erection of an organ, opened in October, 1873. The Rev. Alfred Pickles, who was settled as the first pastor of this church, on the 17th of August, 1869, still continues his labours. In addition to the Sunday-school, there are Tract and Sick and Burial Societies in connection with this chapel.

PROVIDENCE CHAPEL,
HIGH STREET.

This building was erected in 1806, for the ministry of the Rev. Joseph Cooke, who had been expelled from the Methodist connection on doctrinal grounds. After his death it was offered for sale, and purchased by a mere handful of people for the, at that time, large sum of £1,600—an act of courage for which lovers of Christian liberty ought to be ever grateful. Vested in trust, it still remains one among a number of congregational chapels, a testimony to the growth of principles which, in those days, had few adherents in Rochdale.

These few were probably influenced by the advice of ministers in the neighbouring towns, who had given themselves in part to evangelistic labours in Rochdale and its neighbourhood. The most distinguished of these labourers was the Rev. William Roby, who, in addition to his pastoral and itinerant duties, added that of instructing young men intended for the ministry, who also shared in the labours of their tutor, wherever an opportunity presented. Thus Rochdale and the adjacent villages of Wardle and Ridings were favoured with religious teaching at intervals of more or less regularity.

The first congregational minister who made Rochdale his home, was the Rev. John Ely. He commenced his labours in Providence Chapel a few months after its purchase in 1814. The debt on the chapel was a source of constant anxiety, during the first half-dozen years of his ministry; but, during that time, the young minister had so won the esteem of the church and congregation that, rather than lose him, they were willing to make an effort to accomplish what had previously been deemed an impossibility, and they removed their debt. After this, prosperity was uninterrupted, until the removal of the pastor to Leeds. Amongst the external evidences of this prosperity may be mentioned the several circumstances of the establishment of branches at Smallbridge and Calderbrook, 1824, and the erection of an organ in the chapel, 1822. The late distinguished John Roby, Esq., banker, and subsequently the accomplished author of "Traditions of Lancashire," was the first organist. The termination of the ministry of the Rev. John Ely, in Rochdale (1834), was accompanied by the profoundest and most wide-spread regret, not only amongst the congregation, but in the town generally. We are told that during the latter part of his ministry, "the congregations became overflowing on the Sabbath, and at the week evening services few seats were unoccupied." During Mr. Ely's ministry other work was done, viz.: The establishment of Sunday Schools, at first without any separate building for the purpose, but afterwards a school was erected in High-street, which ultimately became over-crowded, and is now let as a warehouse. After this another school was erected, as a local branch, at Moore-street.

The Rev. T. C. Carlisle, became the successor of the Rev. John Ely, at Midsummer, 1835. During his ministry, a large secession of the members of the church took place, which, together with other circumstances, led to his resignation in September, 1837, a little more than two years after he had become the minister. After this those who had seceded were restored to church fellowship. It may naturally be supposed that a church and congregation that had known separation and re-union so recently, would require a pastor of no common order to heal wounds in which the process of healing had only just commenced.

In the Rev. David Hewitt was found a man who possessed energy, ability, and discretion, which, with his geniality of disposition, were sufficient for the occasion. Having spent twelve years in successful labours, he resigned his charge in July, 1850. During his ministry, in the year 1847, the present Sunday and Infant Schools were erected at a cost of £1,300.

In the interval (two years) of the vacant pastorate two important events took place—one, the removal of debt (£1,357) from the school and chapel; the other, the separation of a large part of the congregation, who afterwards erected Milton Congregational Church.

The Rev. William Spencer was the next minister, and commenced his labours in August, 1852. His ministry began auspiciously; a variety of circumstances arose, however, which taken singly were trifling, but in combination, led an amiable man to relinquish a charge, in which he was universally esteemed.

The Rev. G. Snashall commenced his labours in July, 1859. His ministry seemed to be successful until shortly before his resignation, when, unhappily, a dispute arose which ended by the termination of his ministry, and the secession of a number of the congregation, who afterwards became the United Presbyterians.

The Rev. J. C. Mc.Cappin entered upon his labours in April, 1867, and relinquished the pastorate in March, 1871. Nothing remarkable occurred during his ministry, beyond the death of Mrs. Mc.Cappin, which cast a gloom over the remainder of his ministry, and finally led to his resignation.

The Rev. R. G. Williams, who is the present pastor, possesses the esteem and affection of the entire church and congregation. His preaching is considerably above the average as regards ability, and is thoroughly evangelical in tone.

Since 1814 various alterations have been made in the building. One of the earliest of these was the addition of an ornamental portico, which added considerably to its exterior effect, and a little to its interior accommodation. The last of these alterations was made in 1864—the jubilee of Independency in Rochdale. Then the whole of the bottom was renewed, a new rostrum erected, and considerable alterations were made in the orchestra; besides which a tablet was erected in memory of the Rev. John Ely, and another in memory of the late John Roby, Esq., at the expense of his widow. In 1853, the organ, which had done duty for thirty-one years, was removed, and the present one, which is said to have no superior in Rochdale, took its place.

The chapel will seat 750, is well lighted and comfortable. The interior decorations have been very tastefully done.

MILTON CONGREGATIONAL CHURCH,

SMITH STREET.

This church owes its origin to a secession from Providence Chapel, High-street, in March, 1852, the cause of which was a difference of opinion upon the choice of a minister. Among the numerous seceders may be named Messrs. R. Pagan, J. T. Pagan, A. Stewart, R. Kelsall, J. J. Curtis, T. Fisher, R. Clegg, Challinor, Tinsdale, and J. Ashworth.

Their first place of meeting was in the Public Hall; the upper room being used for service, and the lower one as a Sunday School, the first officers of which were Messrs. J. T. Pagan and J. J. Curtis, superintendents, and Robt. Craig, secretary. The week-night services were held in the Commissioners' Room, Smith-street. It was at once decided to form a church upon Congregational principles, and the Rev. Robert Vaughan, D.D., of Manchester Independent College, was requested to officiate at the formation of the church, and to administer the ordinance of the Lord's Supper for the first time. The first deacons of the church were Messrs. Southworth, Dawson, Hoyle, and I. Grindrod. The next step was the choice of a pastor, which fell upon the Rev H. W. Parkinson, who had formerly been a student at Coward College. After the settlement of a pastor, the next question was the building of a place for worship, and on Good Friday, 1853, a tea meeting was held in the Commissioners' Room, after which the question of ways and means was discussed, and a magnificent sum was raised. Among donations were the following :—Messrs. A. Stewart, £500; R. Pagan, £500; R. Kelsall, £500; T. Southworth, £500; and smaller sums raising it to nearly £3,000. It was then decided to build a handsome stone church on land occupied as a garden by H. Kelsall, Esq., J.P., which was planted with fruit trees. The first estimate was £3,500, but the ultimate cost was above £5,000. In the early part of next year the corner stone of the building was laid by Andrew Stewart, Esq., and the building was completed and opened, without any accident, in 1855, on which occasion the Rev. R. Raffles, D.D., of Liverpool, preached in the morning, and Rev. T. Binney, of London, in the evening; from which source the handsome sum of £1,700 was realised; which, with previous subscriptions, removed the entire debt and left a balance which was spent in painting and renovating the church and schoolroom.

Of the late minister, the Rev. H. W. Parkinson, who died suddenly in August, 1874, we may be permitted to remark that in point of ability he was undoubtedly above the average, and held a high position in the esteem and affection of his congregation and friends. He was also much respected by the general public, and was a writer of no mean eminence. He was kind-hearted and amiable, and his death was a very great blow to his church and friends. His funeral, which was public, was attended by a great number of the influential and wealthy inhabitants of the town, and gave ample proof of the high esteem in which his memory was held, and of the "golden opinions" which he had won and worn in their fullest gloss. We are pleased to add that since his death a very large sum of money has been raised on behalf of his widow and children, the principal contributors being gentlemen occupying high social position in the town and elsewhere. The amount raised exceeds £3,500.

METHODIST NEW CONNEXION.

In the year 1814 Mr. William Whittle Barton, a native of Liverpool, settled down in Rochdale, and finding no church of the Methodist New Connexion in this town, he commenced a class in his own house, in the year 1815, and preached in cottages in various parts of the town. In 1820, a garret was rented in St. Mary's Gate, and here for a time, the Rev. W. Driver, and other early ministers of the connexion preached. The cause flourished, and the room being found too small to accommodate the increasing numbers, it was determined to build a chapel, and accordingly a chapel was erected in Zachary, and opened for public worship on the 2nd June, 1822, by the Revs. A. Jackson, S. Woodhouse, and T. Allin. This chapel seated about 270 persons, and cost £400. The place afterwards proving inadequate to meet the growing demands of both church and school, it became necessary to obtain further accommodation. A garret was therefore rented in Holland-street, and devoted to school purposes. In process of time, the Zachary Chapel gave place to a much larger one, which was built in Water-street, at a cost of £1,000, and was provided with a commodious school on the basement story. On the 3rd of October, 1868, a still larger chapel was commenced in Molesworth-street, the late G. L. Ashworth, Esq., J.P., laying

the foundation stone in the midst of a large assembly.
The Rev. Thomas Masterman, the pastor, was the prime
mover in this undertaking which he thought was
necessary to meet the requirements of the age. The
chapel cost over £3,000, and is built in the Italian style;
it is well proportioned and convenient. The lower
storey comprises the school-room, 57 feet by 42 feet;
it is lofty and well lighted. The chapel is 63 feet by
42 feet inside, with galleries, orchestra, ministers'
vestry, large band-room for general purposes, and a
small vestry for the use of the choir. On the 10th of
October, 1869, it was opened by the Revs. S. Hulme,
and C. Donald, and its compactness and completeness
gave much satisfaction. The Rev. Wm. Woodward is
the present pastor. Mr. Barton, to whom the connexion
is indebted for its position in the town, was a prominent
public character for a great number of years. He is
mentioned in a previous part of this work; and was
Town Surveyor from 1818 to 1858. He was a vigorous
opponent of church rates and of public abuses; and
was held in much and deserved esteem by his party.
On his death, in 1859, he was honoured with a public
funeral, in recognition of the services which he had
rendered to the town and people.

PRIMITIVE METHODISTS,

SMITH-STREET.

It has been the pride of the Primitive Methodists to
carry out the words of the parable, "Go out quickly
into the streets and lanes of the city, and bring in
hither the poor, and the maimed, and the halt, and the

blind;" and to their praise it must be stated that no place can be too humble, nor back slums or alleys too wretched wherein to proclaim the grand truths of the gospel. About fifty years ago missionaries from Manchester visited Rochdale and preached in the open air, and services were also carried on in a cellar in Cheetham-street, near where the "Three Crowns" public-house now stands. An amusing incident occurred at one of their open air services. The Rev. John Verity while "holding forth" in Cheetham-street, perched on a chair, received from an officer the dictatorial command to "move on." Verity politely said to the constable, "I hope you will permit me to dismiss the people first?" The officer consented, and then Verity went into a lengthy explanation as to what he had intended to have stated if he had not been interrupted by the official; that it had been his "intention to have told them that Christ had died for sinners, and that they might be saved;" and in this strain, for half an hour, he informed the people of his intentions if he had been allowed to have done so, during which time the "guardian of the law" was on the tiptoe of expectation at the conclusion of every sentence to hear the "dismissal" given to the flock, but finding that the explanation had not a full stop and continued to roll on, he retired from the scene in hopeless disgust. The Primitives next rented a large room in Packer Meadow, at the top of King-street, where they sojourned for seven or eight years. The congregation increasing, it was decided to build a chapel, one storey high, in Drake-street, opposite Water-street, which cost about £400. In the course of time this place was not large enough for the ever-increasing worshippers, and the old chapel was pulled down and a larger one built upon the site, the cost being about £1,200. In 1863 it was determined to have a still larger chapel, more convenient and better lighted, and one was built in Smith-street, at a cost of £2,500. The stone was laid by the late Mr. G. L. Ashworth on the 1st of August, 1863. The front of the chapel is faced with Yorkshire pierpoints. There is a pilaster at each corner, having mounted bases and caps, with Yorkshire stone dressings. The front is a gable one, surmounted with a bold block cornice. The entrance doorway consists of moulded pilasters, together with moulded caps and bases, and finished on the top with a moulded circular block cornice, with a keystone in the centre. There is a double flight of steps to the front door. The size of the building is 58 feet by 45, and 30 feet from the floor to the ceiling. The schoolroom beneath the chapel is 12 feet high, and well lighted on all sides, and but 4 feet below the level of the main street. It seems necessary to explain that the late chapel in Drake-street was sold by the trustees for a Burgess Hall, under the idea that it would be only so used, but this purpose has been departed from, and the building is now used as a Music Hall, much to the disappointment and regret of those by whom it had been used as a place of worship, and who have had no hand in such obvious desecration to such apparently "base uses." No doubt the change of intention arose from the fact that as a Burgess Hall the building would not pay, and the proprietors were therefore obliged to dispose of it in the manner which would prove most beneficial to those who were pecuniarily interested in the transaction.

SOCIETY OF FRIENDS.

The Society of Friends, commonly called "Quakers," have a Meeting House in George-street, Rochdale, which was erected in the year 1808. It is an extremely plain, unpretentious structure, which only reminds us "that man looketh on the outward appearance, but the Lord looketh upon the heart;" and no one would expect to find in such a place of worship, either gaudy decorations, surpliced choirs, wafted incense, "or gorgeous priest in pomp arrayed." Neither does the peal of an organ resound through the building, but the plain unaffected voice is heard in supplication, and in directing the way to salvation, when the Holy Spirit prompts to those sacred acts. "Their prayers and praises are, for the most part, silent and inward. They prefer to make melody in their hearts unto God, considering such to be more spiritual than the outward services of the voice."

Previously to the year 1808 the members of this society, from Oldham and Rochdale, were in the habit of assembling at Turf Lane End Meeting House, which is four miles from Rochdale and two from Oldham, but they ultimately erected a place of worship in each town, the one in Rochdale being situated in George-street, as before mentioned. It contains seats for 300 persons, but the congregation numbers at present about 80. It is here the Right Hon. John Bright regularly attends for worship when at home; but we believe he does not ever address his fellow-worshippers on such occasions. He takes part in the affairs of the society at their business meetings, which are held from time to time, and evinces a great interest in the welfare of the society. Of course, as might be expected, the Friends are really proud of their distinguished brother, who is, notwithstanding his great eminence, as quiet and unobtrusive as the humblest among them.

WESLEYAN METHODIST CHAPEL,

UNION-STREET.

The history of Methodism, in Rochdale, dates from the middle of the last century. The first mention made of Rochdale in Mr. Wesley's Journal, is under date 18th October, 1749. Mr. Wesley was on his way from Leeds, and says:—" I rode, at the desire of J. Bennet, to Rochdale, in Lancashire, as soon as ever we entered the town we found the streets lined, on both sides, with multitudes of people, shouting, cursing, blaspheming, and gnashing upon us with their teeth. Perceiving it would not be practicable to preach abroad, I went into a large room open to the street, and called aloud, 'Let the wicked forsake his way, and the unrighteous man his thoughts.' The word of God prevailed over the fierceness of man, none opposed or interrupted, and there was a very remarkable change in the behaviour of the people as we afterwards went through the town. We came to Bolton in the evening. We had no sooner entered the main street than we perceived the lions of Rochdale were lambs in comparison of those at Bolton. Such rage and bitterness I scarcely ever saw before in any creatures that have the form of men," &c., &c.

Mr. Wesley does not mention any more visits to Rochdale for a long period. But we find him paying a visit to Bankhouse, near Rochdale, on the 3rd April, 1752;

and these visits were often repeated long before
any society was formed in Rochdale. The society
at Bankhouse, near Bagslate, was visited by the
preachers from Bury, though Bagslate is only two miles
from Rochdale. And about this period too, Smallbridge
was regularly visited by preachers from Colne, thus
shewing that Methodism was not established in Rochdale as early as other neighbouring towns.

About 1760 a society was formed, and a preaching
room was secured at Waterside, near the river, on a
part of the site now occupied by the Town Hall and its
approaches. The room would be about the centre
of the eastern esplanade. The Methodists afterwards
occupied a building in Temple Court, Blackwater-
street, now Temple-street, and subsequently removed
to a new chapel in Toad Lane, about the year 1770.
In that year Mr. Wesley writes in his Journal, 29th
April, 1770, "I preached in the new preaching house at
Rochdale." His visits to Rochdale appear to have
become more frequent, as we find him preaching here
on the 16th April, 1774; 17th April, 1776; 24th August,
1778; 12th April, 1779; and 6th April, 1780. This
new preaching house must have been the one in Toad
Lane. The lease for the land is dated 18th May, 1778,
and is from James Taylor to Messrs. Cockroft and
Clegg, for 669 yards, at a rent of £5; and as the plan
shews the form of the chapel, with its entrances, &c.,
the deed must have been completed after the erection
of the chapel.

John Valton and George Snowden were stationed
at Manchester in 1781. Their ministry was eminently owned of God; there was a general revival

of religion throughout the circuit, and a great ingathering of souls was the happy result. The chapel at Stockport was enlarged, and a new one erected at Ashton. But the assistant preacher declared that "this work would have been more extensive had it not been for two or three of the leading members of the Rochdale society, who demanded an unjust share of our labours. Their opposition was so strong that it quite broke my spirit and cramped my future usefulness. It obstructed all my intended visits to the populous villages. Alas! how often have godly ministers had to make the same complaint."

Of his visit to Rochdale, on 26th and 27th August, 1787, Wesley says:—"The house at Rochdale was well filled at five a.m. I have not seen so large a morning congregation, in proportion to the town, since I returned to England. I was invited to breakfast at Bury, by Mr. Peel, a calico printer, who, a few years ago, began with £500, and is now supposed to have gained £50,000. Oh, what a miracle, if he lose not his soul!"

"23rd April, 1788. In the evening I preached to a lively congregation at Rochdale. Formerly we had much trouble here, but it is past, and they now hold the unity of the spirit in the bond of peace."

In 1790, Wesley went from Bolton into Yorkshire. The manuscript of his journal is lost from April 10th to May 24th. He must, however, have passed through Rochdale, for it was within remembrance of old people, and amongst them Miss Stott, who said, "that she saw Mr. Wesley walk up Packer-street and up the Church Steps, which he counted as he went up."

11

The chapel in Toad Lane appears to have been occupied by the Methodists more than twenty years. The society established by the late Countess of Huntingdon afterwards occupied the building. Subsequently it was used as a theatre and assembly room; and there is now erected on the site the central store of the Rochdale Equitable Pioneers Society. The Methodist chapel was built in Union-street, and opened on Sunday, the 22nd May, 1793, by the Rev. Joseph Benson, M.A., and the Revs. J. Roberts and Thomas Hanby. In this chapel, on the 25th November, 1821, the Rev. Adam Clarke preached a sermon in behalf of funds of the Sunday School (xvii. c. John, 3 v.). A very large congregation was assembled, and while they listened with rapt attention, suddenly a cry was raised that the gallery of the chapel was falling. A scene of intense consternation and confusion ensued. From the pressure many persons found themselves in very different parts of the chapel to those they had first occupied, and knew not how they had got there. One person who sat in the front of the gallery managed to jump into the pulpit as a place of safety, though what course she took in her fright could not be recalled by her. One well-known individual would not allow any person to leave the pew in which he sat, comforting them by saying, "Sit still, friend, we are going gradually," evidently thinking little respecting those underneath. Another, the late John Howard, declared that he saw the ceiling open. The rush of those who fled from the chapel was so terrific that it forced the large doors outwards. Some few were hurt, but no life was lost. The alarm was caused by the breaking of a slender form on which some

persons stood to see the preacher more easily. Dr.
Clarke exhorted the alarmed congregation to be quiet,
but Mr. Robert Heape, senior, of the Hartley, by
gesture and voice, urged the leader of the choir (Robert
Nuttall) to sing, and he struck up " Praise God from
whom all blessings flow," to the tune of the old hun-
dredth psalm. In a moment the instruments took up
the solemn sound, quiet was immediately restored, and,
with a sense of relief, safety, and gratitude, the whole
congregation joined heartily in the song of praise. Dr.
Clarke finished his sermon. The collection in no wise
suffered, the amount being about £80. This chapel
was used for worship exactly thirty-two years; the last
services being held on Sunday, 22nd May, 1825. From
a record of that period we learn that " by some defect
in the original construction of the roof, the whole edifice
had become unsafe." Competent judges declared that
the large congregations which on particular occasions
attended were in imminent danger of being suddenly
buried beneath its ruins. The present chapel was
erected in the year 1825-6, and was opened Thursday,
March 16th, 1826, when sermons were preached by the
Revs. Robert Newton, David Stoner, and Theophilus
Lessey. On Sunday, the 19th March, Mr. Wm. Dawson
preached; and in the afternoon and evening, the Revs.
Philip Garrett and Jabez Bunting, M.A. Although
Rochdale was then suffering much distress from the
effects of the American tariff, which practically excluded
the exportation of the flannel manufacture of this
neighbourhood to the American states, and throughout the empire there was much commercial depression,
which was severely felt in Rochdale, the collections

amounted to £302. 7s. 7d., in addition to the sum of £1,840 previously subscribed.

This commodious chapel, which, at the time of its erection was one of the largest in the connexion, is 87 feet long and 69 feet in width (outside), and is capable of seating 1,650 persons. The cost of erection of the chapel and alteration of the ministers' houses, was about £5,000. The Sunday Schools, which were erected in 1819, were found unsuitable in their arrangements for the educational requirements of the time, and were taken down in the year 1858. A more convenient and excellent building, well adapted for all educational purposes, was erected on a larger scale, at a cost of £1,600. It is only just to record the praiseworthy labours of the Rev. Charles Garrett, to whose deep interest in this movement the success of the scheme is to be ascribed. The chapel contains a very excellent organ, built by the late Mr. Richard Nicholson, about the year 1840, at a cost of 400 guineas. In the year 1835-6 a large secession from this congregation and society took place, and eventually formed the congregation now assembling in the Methodist Free Church, Baillie-street.

In reviewing this brief sketch of the past history of Methodism connected with Union-street Chapel, it is pleasing to recall the particulars of its present outgrowth, and, as far as we have the information, we have here endeavoured to enumerate the particulars. Up to the year 1795, Rochdale was supplied by the Methodist preachers of Manchester, as it was then included in the circuit under their pastorate. In the year 1795 Rochdale became the head of a circuit. Bacup, Newchurch, and Heywood were then included within its limits. Bacup and Newchurch were constituted a circuit in 1811, and Heywood in 1853. The Rochdale circuit, for greater convenience of managing its pastorate, was divided, in 1868, into the Union-street and Wesley circuits. Wesley chapel was built 1867, in Castlemere-street. The Union-street circuit contains seven Chapels, nine Sunday Schools, three Day and Infant Schools. The Wesley circuit contains seven Chapels, eight Sunday Schools, four Day and Infant Schools, and the two circuits contain 1,850 members. After this recapitulation we may be permitted to look back to the period when, 125 years ago, the Rev. John Wesley entered Rochdale, and recall his testimony as to the manners and habits of the people in 1749; and then remembering the opposition which he met with during the mission he pursued for forty years after. We notice with pleasure such untiring energy—an attentive congregation waiting to hear him at five o'clock in the morning, hanging on his lips and treasuring his words. Mr. Wesley died 2nd March, 1791. And now the work which he begun has, by the blessing of God, extended to thousands in this town and neighbourhood, and every Christian church has benefited, and the general population raised to a higher standard.

UNITED METHODIST FREE CHURCH,

BAILLIE-STREET.

Baillie-street Chapel, belonging to the United Methodist Free Churches, was opened for Divine worship on January the 8th, 1837. The original cost was about

£4,000. In 1840 it was enlarged by the addition of a spacious gallery at an expenditure of upwards of £1,763 ; and, in 1856-7, nearly £1,000 was expended on new vestries, &c. In 1867 other important alterations and improvements were made, involving an outlay of some £1,400. The total cost, therefore, has been upwards of £8,000. It is the largest place of religious worship in the town, having accommodation for 1,800 hearers. In the basement story is a school-room, library, ministers' vestry, class-rooms, and every convenience for tea meetings, &c. The chapel is light, well ventilated, and warmed, and all can see and hear the preacher. The lower part of the chapel being arranged on the amphitheatre plan, the acoustic properties of the building are all that could be desired. There is a splendid organ which was erected in 1845, and which has since then been enlarged and improved. The societies in the circuit of which Baillie-street is the head have a membership of 2,031. The Sabbath-day scholars number 6,386, taught by 929 teachers. There are four itinerant ministers, forty-five local preachers, and ninety-four class leaders in the circuit, with nineteen other chapels within a radius of three miles from Baillie-street. Liberal Methodism is thus well sustained in Rochdale and the neighbourhood.

In the year 1864 Mr. Oliver Ormerod laid the foundation stone of Castlemere Chapel, a fine spacious edifice, off Drake-street, which has 1,250 sittings, and it cost about £8,500. It was opened for Divine worship on September 6th, 1865.

UNITED PRESBYTERIAN CHURCH.

This handsome church is situated in Manchester-road, opposite the pleasure grounds, and was built in the year 1868, at a cost of about £6,000. In the basement storey there are class rooms and a vestry room. The building will accommodate about 800 persons; 660 on the ground floor, and 140 in the gallery. The total length inside is 85 feet 6 inches, and the width 43 feet, with transepts 24 feet by 14 feet. There are three entrances : one in the centre of the front elevation, one through the tower, which is at the north-east corner, and one on the south side near the front of the building. There are two entrances to the schools. The church is neatly pewed with pitch-pine, and the wainscoting and doors are made of the same wood. The pulpit is very handsome. In shape it is octagonal, and made of stone, with black marble columns, having moulded bases and carved capitals. The principal walls are composed wholly of stone, the outside being faced with Yorkshire pierpoints. The style of the edifice is Gothic, of a period known as the early decorated. At the north-east corner there is a tower, and it is intended to surmount it with a spire, 130 feet high from the ground, as soon as the funds will permit this extra outlay. In 1866 this religious body was formed by gentlemen who had left Providence Chapel and other denominations, and for two years their services and Sunday School were held in the British School, Baillie-street, where the congregation increased rapidly.

The Rev. A. H. Drysdale, the present pastor, was inducted in August, 1867, and he is very much respected.

His abilities are of a high order, and his pulpit
discourses are the subject of much eulogium; and, apart
from his ministerial office, we believe that his literary
tastes are of the most elevated kind. Mr. Drysdale has
made a great number of friends in Rochdale outside his
own congregation; and the kindly feeling which exists
between himself and the other ministers of religion in
the town proves the amiability of his disposition, and
his desire to sink minor differences on theological
questions on which all men do not think alike.

UNITARIAN CHAPEL,
BLACKWATER-STREET.

This is not only the oldest dissenting chapel in
Rochdale, but the oldest place of worship of any kind,
except St. Chad's Parish Church. During the Com-
monwealth the Revs. Robert Bath and Zachariah Taylor
were vicar and curate, respectively, of the Parish
Church; but in the year 1688, in King Charles the
Second's reign, the Act of Uniformity was passed, and
the above-mentioned clergymen were required to subscribe to the Thirty-nine Articles of the Church of
England, or else be evicted from their livings. They
both preferred liberty of conscience and freedom, to
holding their livings on such terms, and were accordingly evicted. But the Rev. Robert Bath, being a
popular preacher, continued to gather large numbers of
his parishioners around him, thus forming the first dissenting congregation in Rochdale. But it was not till the
year 1689, when William the Third passed the "Tolera-
tion Act," that the Rochdale Presbyterian dissenters
dared to meet together in a meeting-house of their own,

without fear of molestation from the authorities: The
first meeting-house or chapel seems to have been in
existence from the year 1690 till 1716, when a new one
was erected and duly licensed as "a meeting-house of
dissenting Protestants," at the Quarter Sessions, held
at Manchester, October 17th, 1717. This chapel, like
many others erected by the Presbyterian Nonconformists
of those days, was dedicated to the worship of Almighty
God, with an open trust deed. The Puritan Presbyterians had suffered so much persecution upon matters
of creeds and doctrines, that they refused to specify in
the trust deeds of their own chapels, the particular
doctrines to be taught therein ; and, as a consequence,
very many of them, Blackwater-street Chapel being one,
gradually drifted away, upon the current of free inquiry
from the old orthodox dogmas and creeds held by their
founders, to the full realization of individual freedom
and right of free enquiry, held by modern Unitarians.
The old chapel existed from 1717 till 1856, when it was
pulled down, and the present neat, though rather small
chapel was erected. It is built in the Gothic style, with a
central nave and south aisle. It is 66 feet in length and
34 feet in width, and will seat about 200 persons. There
is a small endowment attached to the chapel. The Rev.
Thomas Carter is the present minister, being the twenty-
second in order of succession from its foundation.

UNITARIAN CHAPEL,
CLOVER-STREET.

This chapel was built in the year 1818, but has since
been considerably altered and improved. In 1868 new
Day and Sunday Schools were erected immediately

behind and adjoining the chapel, which have added very
materially to the convenience and usefulness of the
institution, as previously to the erection of the new
schools the teaching was done in the bottom part of the
chapel.

The chapel and congregation had their origin as
follows :—In the year 1803 a Mr. Joseph Cooke was
appointed as one of the itinerant ministers at the Wesleyan Methodist Chapel, Union-street, Rochdale. His
abilities as a preacher were not of the common kind,
and he soon became very popular. In the course of his
experience amongst the Methodists he had often noticed
persons of that persuasion who talked as though they
thought religion consisted principally in raptures and
impressions, and who made their own imaginations and
feelings, rather than scripture, the criteria of religious
truth. This he considered a serious error, and he was
desirous of putting a stop to it. He therefore preached
two sermons—one on " Justification by Faith," and the
other on " The witness of the Spirit." In these sermons
the doctrine expounded was considered by the Methodist
Conference which met at Leeds in August, 1806, to be
contrary to the teachings of Wesley. Mr. Cooke was,
therefore, called before a committee of the Conference
and given an opportunity of retracting. But as he
could not do so, and considered himself that the
sermons were quite in accordance with Wesley's own
teachings, he was forthwith expelled from the Methodist
body. But a considerable number of the Methodists in
Rochdale having embraced Mr. Cooke's views, they
invited him to settle amongst them and become their
minister. He accepted the invitation, left Leeds, and

was received by these friends with great cordiality. They accordingly then left the Methodist Connexion, commenced a subscription, and a large and commodious chapel was built in High-street, Rochdale, to which the name of "Providence" was given. While this was doing Mr. Cooke had the pleasure of addressing large and crowded congregations. Hundreds flocked to see and hear the man of whom report said that he preached such strange things that the Methodists would have him no longer, and since they had turned him out he had laid aside the Bible and put common sense in its place.

The new chapel was opened in 1807, and Mr. Cooke continued to preach there till his death, which took place, after a severe and protracted illness, on March 13th, 1811. He was interred inside the chapel, in the aisle just in front of the pulpit.

During Mr. Cooke's life the congregation at Providence Chapel consisted of from five to seven hundred people. After his death they were for a time indebted to three young men, whose names were John Ashworth, James Wilkinson, and James Taylor, for the principal supply of the pulpit; but, very shortly, additional assistance was invited from the Independent Calvinists. This, however, by a large majority of the congregation, was deemed a very inconsistent step, as Mr. Cooke was a most decided Anti-Calvinist, and by far the greater number of the congregation could not bear to hear Calvinism. Some, therefore, when these men came, stayed away from the chapel; others said nothing for some time, preserving silence for the sake of peace, and being wishful that the congregation should remain as

Mr. Cooke left it.   Measures were afterwards taken for
securing the services of a regular minister, and
ultimately a Mr. Bowman, of Ipswich, who had been
a local preacher amongst the Methodists, was appointed.
For a short time he gave satisfaction, but ere long the
strain of his preaching began to alter, and some parts
of his discourses were not only opposed to Mr. Cooke's
later sentiments, but to the very doctrines for which he
was expelled from the Methodists.   The great majority
of the congregation were astonished that the man should
act so directly contrary to his previous professions,
whilst the rest approved of his conduct.   This, and
other differences that arose at the time, which was
about nineteen months after Mr. Cooke's death, caused
about three-fourths of the congregation to leave the
chapel, some going to one place and some to another;
but the · greatest part resolved neither to be separated
from one another, nor join any sect or party.   They
therefore requested the three young men to continue
their labours amongst them, and they consented.   But
having no place in which to assemble for public worship
a large room was sought for, and till this was found
they were kindly accommodated at Blackwater-street
Chapel.   Very soon, however, a pretty commodious
room was found in Drake-street, Rochdale, then known
as Greenwood's School, and this room continued to be
occupied by them as a preaching room and school
until the completion of the chapel in Clover-street, in
the year 1818.

For some time after Mr. Cooke's death the congregation were known as " Cookites," and their views on
religious doctrine were but little removed from the

doctrines generally entertained by the Methodist body. But, being anxious enquirers after truth, they began to examine and judge of the Scriptures for themselves, and gradually became what are generally known as Unitarians, or believers in the simple unity or oneness of God, though at the time they embraced this doctrine and rejected the doctrines of orthodoxy, they thought themselves the only people in the world who believed as they did, but they were happy to find afterwards that in this notion they were greatly mistaken.

For about twenty years after the opening of Clover-street Chapel the services were conducted gratuitously, or nearly so, by the three ministers above-mentioned. For a few years more, by Messrs. Taylor and Wilkinson alone, and then solely by Mr. Wilkinson till his death in May, 1858.   Then, for a period of about four years, the pulpit was supplied from the Manchester Home Missionary Board and other sources.   In February, 1862, the first settled minister was appointed in the person of the Rev. James Briggs, previously student of the Home Missionary Board, Manchester, who resigned from failing health in 1864; and, in 1865, the Rev. Joseph Freeston, of Manchester, succeeded him, and remained till July, 1869, when he resigned; and was followed in February, 1871, by the Rev. J. C. Hirst, who had also been a student of the Home Missionary Board.   He continued as minister till June, 1874, when he left Rochdale for Scarborough.   The pulpit is now (December, 1874) vacant.

HOLLAND STREET CHURCH AND SCHOOL.

This school and place of worship are not connected
with any of the general denominations, and, have no
special name. The origin was the secession of
twenty-seven teachers, in 1851, from the Wesleyan
Methodist Association Sunday School, Baillie-street,
which occasioned a considerable number of scholars to
leave also, who naturally urged the teachers to commence a school, to which the teachers yielded, and they
first met in Sunny Bank House. There was immediately a large accession of scholars, who were instructed
by twenty teachers. Every room in the house was soon
filled, and the late George Ashworth, Esq., of Roche
House and Sunny Bank Mills, allowed them the use of
a room in his warehouse adjoining, where a congregation, in addition to the scholars, assembled, and a regular
service and preaching were commenced. After eighteen
months' trial, and finding that the work and effort were
likely to be permanent, Mr. Ashworth, seeing and
sympathising with the good work that was evidently
going on, erected a fine brick building for the congregation and scholars. The main building is 72 feet in
length and 36 feet in breadth, and there is a wing
attached of 30 feet by 16 feet. The ground floor is
occupied by ten separate class-rooms, an infant class-
room, and a library. The upper room is used for
religious service, and there are also three separate
class-rooms, a vestry, a band-room, and a night school
room. At the present time the teachers number 44, and
the scholars 462. The services are conducted by

preachers from every denomination, who have willingly and effectively supplied them. On week evenings the Sabbath school class-rooms are used for the Methodist class and prayer meetings. The night school is taught on four nights of the week. The sittings in the preaching room are all free, and there is no collection ever made from the congregation, the necessary expenses being raised by weekly voluntary contributions. The cost of the night school is, however, entirely defrayed by the firm of Messrs. G. Ashworth & Sons, as it has been for some thirty-five years, and is under the able supervision of Mr. J. J. Curtis, who was engaged at its commencement as the teacher.

CHAPEL FOR THE DESTITUTE.

"The poor ye have always with you."

On the 4th of October, 1858, Mr. John Ashworth, who at that time was a master painter in Rochdale, opened this chapel in the Lyceum, and it has been the means of doing great good amongst the poor and itinerant class of the population. The origin of this place of worship will be best explained by the following quotation from Mr. Ashworth's first report:—" It was during a visit to London, in 1851, that the thought was suggested. I had seen its palaces of glass, brick, and stone, visited its museums, galleries, and other splendid places of attraction; also, its prisons, penitentiaries, hospitals, houses of refuge, &c.; but the House for the Destitute interested me more than all besides. What I saw and felt on visiting this place produced a degree of anguish from which I have never wholly recovered. Hardened villany, misery, wretchedness, and hopeless

despair were evident on every side; all the woes of the
Apocalypse seemed to have overtaken the miserable
inmates. I felt they were all my brothers and sisters,
and I felt that sin had done it all; and I also felt a
degree of veneration for the men whose Christian
philanthropy had reared this shelter for the lonely
destitute. Infidelity, I knew, had not done it; for
infidelity never did much to mitigate human sorrow, or
lessen human woe, in any age or in any part of the
world. That the Gospel of Christ, applied by the Spirit,
could reclaim these miserable beings, I had not the
slightest doubt; that in all towns hundreds of such are
to be found that never attend any place of worship—
the outcast and feared of society. And yet, is it not
the duty of the man whose heart God has touched to
do all he can for the redemption of such? and if they
will not come to our chapels and churches, go in amongst
them, meet them on their own terms, and provide them
places of worship adapted to their own condition.
Thence arose the determination that, on my return to
Rochdale, such a place should be commenced. But I
am ashamed to say that in consulting cautious friends
and human probabilities everything seemed unfavour-
able to the undertaking, and in spite of all my reasoning
against the work, I was for several years reproaching
myself for neglecting to perform the vow I had made
in London. During an affliction laid upon me in 1858,
I pleaded for deliverance, re-resolved, and prayed that
the Lord would help me to endure labour, misrepre-
sentation, ridicule, or imposition. With these feelings
I determined not to consult any human being, but to go
at once to work, dependent upon God's help and

blessing. I took a small room, got 2,000 small bills printed, worded :—' Ye houseless, homeless, friendless, pennyless outcasts, come! In rags and tatters, come! Ye poor, and maimed, and halt, and blind, come! Of whatever colour or nation, creed or no creed, come! * * * All we seek is your welfare, both body and soul.' These I distributed in lodging-houses, and in various places throughout the town, likely and unlikely, for several days, and with painful nervousness opened the room for the first service on the 4th of October, 1858, with twenty-seven persons present. During the year the congregation steadily increased; now (at the end of the first year) there is an average attendance of 100, and all of these persons who, I believe, never thought of going to any place of worship, and many of them really destitute. I am very glad to be able to testify that there is much improvement in their outward appearance, and their conduct has been respectful and orderly." Mr. Ashworth, in his fifteenth report, states :—"The low lodging-houses are terrible schools for juveniles; but what are known in tramp language as *Fencing-Cribs*, or lodging houses where thieves are harboured and trained, are still worse, and of the many thousands of mendicants that swarm in our cities, towns, streets, and lanes, and well-known by the police, and in our unions and prisons, a very large percentage would be found to sojourn in these bad, polluting houses. They have a vocabulary generally understood amongst themselves, by which they distinguish the true genuine tramp. *Red-Cove* is one who acts the blind old soldier. *Shallow-Cove*, a dry land sailor. *High flyer*, a begging letter writer. *Moon-*

12

face, a professor of religion, and sells tracts. *Lurker*, many trades, and always the one that is slack. *Cads*, settled beggars. *Scrieving-Cads*, writers on smooth stones or footpaths. *Fly-Cads*, occasional beggars, and pedlars. *Shallow Motts*, destitute females. *Star the Glaze*, housebreakers. *Blinker*, sore eyes. *Peter Pindars*, sellers of spectacles, pins, laces, &c. *Calico Face*, pretender to consumption. *Weezer*, the asthmatical. *Flops*, those that pretend to fits, or taken suddenly ill. *Joints*, afflicted with rheumatism. *Doctor*, the union. *Limbo, Trap, or Jug*, prison. These are only a small part of their mystic terms, and others are being daily coined. They have also signs and signals in the lodging houses, chalk marks for the highways, are all constantly pursuing their peculiar craft, and preying upon the generous, and industrious part of mankind. The greater the cheat the more plausible his tale. Few that are willing to work are ever found amongst them. George Brine, one of the oldest mendicants, and one that has cost the country much expense declares that nine out of ten beggars and tramps make it a profession : few individuals escape being fleeced by one or other of this fraternity, and on some of us they have imposed a considerable tax.

"The visitors of one of our Rochdale benevolent societies had great anxiety and trouble with one of the *Flops* who had become suddenly and painfully afflicted in a low lodging house. He was daily attended, and provided with his expenses, a doctor, wine, and many comforts. The doctor could not define his malady, or give him any relief; week after week still found him in great pain. A wag, who understood a little of the

mendicant's profession, hearing of the case, undertook
to cure him for nothing, and went with two of the
visitors in the capacity of a medical man; he felt his
pulse, examined his tongue, shook his head very solemnly,
declared it a bad and dangerous case, but thought he
could give him relief; addressing the sufferer he said,
'Well, my poor man, you seem to be in great pain, but
I think we can soon make you better.   You must have
your head shaved, covered with a large mustard plaister,
and ten leeches on your temple; also mustard plaisters
must be laid on your back, chest, and bottom of your
feet; and we will have all ready for you about ten in
the morning. Good bye, for the present.' The only
answer from the sick man was a pitiable groan; but he
disappeared that evening, and has not been seen in
Rochdale since.''

Mr. Ashworth, in a pamphlet entitled ''My New
Friends,'' gives a very interesting picture of the
inhabitants of low lodging houses, and the following
amusing extract is worthy of notice :—''Wishing to
get some one to volunteer, I laid my hand on the
shoulder of the thin man, who was trying to divide
his hair, and requested him to give a challenge
to the whole house.   There was a general shout from
all, that if I got him I should have the worst in the
lot; they should like to see Bill Guest in a chapel.
'Yes,' said the wooden-leg man, 'if Bill goes, I go.'
'And me,' said the flat-nosed man ; 'And me,' said the
red-slop ; 'And me,' said Jenny Lind ; 'And me,' said
the old man with the large spectacles.   Bill very coolly
observed that they had better mind what they were
doing, or he would surprise some of them.   But the

whole fifteen declared they would go if he went. 'Then
I go,' said Guest; 'and now let me see which of you
dare show the white feather.' We bargained that I
was to call for them at six o'clock, to show them the
way. Exactly at six, I called on my sixteen friends at
the lodging-house. My entrance was the signal for a
general move. Bill Guest had finished dividing his
hair, and had done his best to look smart. Boz, or
Boswell, had fitted on his leg, and all were instantly
ready. Not one had shown 'the white feather.' They
laughed at each other, and were all greatly excited.
'Who will lead up?' was bawled out by the red-slop
man, and it was agreed we should go two abreast, I
and Boz (the wooden-legged man) being the first. In
this order we marched down King-street, over the iron
bridge, through the Butts, to the preaching-room. All
the way we attracted much attention, some remarking
that we were the awkward squad, others that we were
going to the rag-shop, whilst others exclaimed, 'That
bangs all!' But what was to them a cause of
merriment was to me a source of great anxiety.

"I had provided the Religious Tract Society's penny
hymn-book, and handed one to each; then, taking my
place behind a table, I gave out the page. Few could
find the hymn, but all pretended to do so; and when I
set out the tune, the Old Hundred, I found that not one
of the men, and only one of the women, could join in
singing, and that one was the so-called Jenny Lind. I
could have well dispensed with *her* help, for she began
singing before she knew what the tune was, and she
had a screeching voice, the effect of which on my nerves
was something like that produced by the sharpening of

a saw with a file; this caused a general titter through the congregation. I had intended to sing five verses, but was glad to give up with three. What Jenny's success was in singing in the streets and public-houses I know not, but I know I was afraid to join her a second time, though my friends gave me credit for being a tolerably good singer. So ludicrous had been the whole performance, that many of the congregation were almost convulsed with suppressed laughter, and I did not think it prudent to engage in prayer until they were in a more serious state of mind, so I requested them to sit down. ' I then began to tell them all about my reasons for beginning a place of worship for the destitute. I have spoken to many congregations, but to none more attentive than these twenty-seven. O, how my soul did yearn in love to those miserable beings! I then proposed prayer, and told them that they might stand, sit, or kneel, just as they liked; but they all knelt down, and ere we rose the Spirit of God worked with power. Lis Dick, and the old man with the large spectacles, remained on their knees after the others had risen; they both afterwards confessed that they had not prayed for years before."

The agencies at the present time employed consist of one missionary (Mr. Calman) and two bible women, who visit the sick and the poor, and a blind female who teaches the blind to read embossed type. The Sunday services are usually attended by about 200 persons, and the week nights' by about 100.

There cannot be any question that the work in which Mr. Ashworth has been engaged for the past sixteen years, has been of the most praiseworthy character;

and that the class of persons for whose especial benefit his chapel has been instituted were, indeed, "like sheep going astray," having no one, apparently, to give them either help or sympathy. Mr. Ashworth not only provides spiritual instruction for these persons, but their bodily wants are also cared for. His experience will have made him acquainted with strange persons and strange circumstances; and he has, on many occasions, made the public conversant with some of these by means of the stories which are appended to his annual reports. The work in which Mr. Ashworth has been so zealous and unwearied has received important and ready help from the philanthropic and charitable in various parts of the country; and, perhaps, there is hardly a town in the kingdom in which himself and his work are not well known and appreciated. We regret that at the time of our writing, the state of Mr. Ashworth's health is such as to give much apprehension to his friends, but we hope that a change for the better may shortly take place, for it would be a great calamity if he were removed from the sphere in which he has so faithfully laboured, and the poor and destitute be deprived of one who has been to them a true and sincere friend and comforter.

SUNDAY SCHOOLS.

"Oh, day most calm, most bright!
The world were dark but for thy light:
Thy torch doth show the way."

IN the year 1781 Robert Raikes, a printer in Gloucester, founded Sunday Schools. Inclination leading him into a part of his native town inhabited by the lowest class of the people, he was struck with concern at seeing a group of children, miserably ragged, at play, cursing and swearing. To check this deplorable profanation of the Sabbath, he engaged four women, who kept dame schools, to instruct as many children as he should send them on the Sunday. In a short time a visible improvement was effected, both in the manners and morals of the children, who came in considerable numbers.

"'Tis education forms the common mind,
Just as the twig is bent, the tree's inclined."

As to who first introduced the Sunday school system into Rochdale, is a disputed point. It is stated that Colonel Townley, a churchman, of Belfield, in the year 1782, employed a teacher to instruct children on the Sunday in Moss School, Milnrow-road, and that he had consulted Raikes as to the plan that was adopted in Gloucester. However, it is admitted that this attempt resulted in failure.

In the year 1782 Mr. James Hamilton, a Dissenter,
a tin-plate worker, who had his workshop at the corner
of Newgate, Rochdale, was impressed with the utility
of Sunday schools, and he wrote to Mr. Robert Raikes,
asking for information as to how he should proceed in
establishing a Sunday school in Rochdale. Mr. Raikes
courteously gave the information, and Mr. Hamilton
opened a school over his works in White Beaver Yard.
The first Sunday about twenty children attended, and
he was assisted by a young man named John Croft, a
butcher, who resided in Blackwater-street, with whom
John Wesley used to lodge when he visited Rochdale.
The number of scholars rapidly increased, and a few
Sundays after the establishment, Mr. Hamilton enquired
from Mr. Raikes as to what place of worship the
children were to be taken to. Mr. Raikes replied,
"by all means, to the Parish Church." Mr. Hamilton
escorted his little flock into the Parish Church yard,
and enquired from the churchwardens where they were
to be placed. The Rev. Dr. Wray, the vicar, directed
them to be put in an obscure corner of the church, and
told Mr. Hamilton that he was not to bring the "dirty
ragamuffins" there again. Notwithstanding this clerical
injunction, he re-appeared with his ragged flock on the
following Sunday, and the churchwardens and a parish
constable threatened to handcuff the worthy pedagogue.
Hamilton showed a bold front, and succeeded in taking
the children again into the church. He was once more
warned not to bring them there again. Mr. Hamilton's
workshop was found to be inconvenient for the increasing
number of scholars, and he took a large room in Temple-
court, Blackwater-street, and then the youngsters were

called "Templars." A short time after a number of Wesleyans assisted in the work, and the school was removed to the Wesleyan Schools in Union-street. There was an organised canvass throughout the town for pupils, and the result was that Union-street Schools were crowded, and other Dissenting denominations took up the scheme, and the church authorities were stimulated to join in the work. The children of the poor. in those days were miserably clad, which led to the establishment of a "Dorcas" society, and through the exertions of the members of this society, and the Sunday school teachers, the naked were clothed, their minds and morals improved, and the elements of a religious education imparted to them, and Hamilton's "grain of mustard seed" has now grown into a very large tree. It is delightful in our day to witness the annual Whit-Friday procession of Sunday school children, and to see thousands upon thousands of them walking together on that always welcome anniversary, to the strains of lively music, all comfortably and neatly attired, and with joyful faces, and it must be very gratifying to all who labour in the cause, as well as to those who sympathise therein, and aid, in other ways, the great work which Sunday schools are employed in doing. The labour of the teachers is indeed a labour of love, and it is hardly possible to over estimate the large amount of good which these valuable institutions are the means of accomplishing.

About the year 1834 the Rochdale "Sunday School Union" was formed by Mr. James Littlewood, the Rev. John Ely, Mr. Joseph Heap, Mr. Benjamin Hamilton, and Mr. Henry Staley. The work went on slowly at first, but the Union has now become most powerful, the schools of the Dissenting denominations connected with it numbering fifty-four. Mr. John Pollitt has been the secretary for nearly a quarter of a century, and Mr. I. E. Gibbs is the president. During its career it has been instrumental in bringing about several changes in the bye-laws of the town and in local customs of disreputable tendency. The discontinuance of the Bagslate races is one of its laurels, and the bye-law against "pitch and toss" was adopted under its influence, as well as other improvements in the right direction, all which greatly redound to the credit of this praiseworthy association.

EDUCATION.

----"None now,
However destitute, are left to droop,
By timely culture unsustained; or run
Into a wild disorder; or forced
To drudge through a weary life without the help
Of intellectual implements and tools:
A savage horde among the civilized,
A servile band among the lordly free."

THE present system of Public Elementary Education in England has been gradually developed within the last half-century. Although it is often urged that it is not worthy the name of a *national system* at all, yet it must be allowed by persons conversant with the subject that the plans now in operation have done, and are still doing, a vast amount of good to the rising generation; and if every child in the kingdom cannot secure a sufficiently good education the cause lies less with defects of the law than with the parsimony and indifference of individuals or communities, mixed in some cases, it may be, with a trifle of the *odium theologicum*, for the Act of 1870 places it within the power of any constituted district to have a School Board elected, one of the powers of which is to enforce the regular attendance of every child at school for a number of years, and thus do away with the greatest existing hindrance to educational progress.

It may be useful to give here a short sketch of the Governmental Educational Agencies now at work, the

whole action of which is based on the principle of aiding
local efforts. The Education Department rules over the
Public Elementary Schools of the country, and besides
bearing the cost of inspection and examinations, dis-
tributes from the Parliamentary Grant of about a
million annually, grants towards the support of
Training Colleges for Teachers, and the maintenance
of Day and Evening Schools. This money is paid on
fulfilment of certain conditions specified in the Education
Code. The Department of Science and Art encourages
the teaching of drawing in day schools, and also
science and art in special schools, or classes formed for
the purpose by the award of payments and prizes to
schools, teachers, and pupils. For incorrigible and
criminal children there is provided the stern and whole-
some discipline of the Industrial or Reformatory School,
and by magistrates' order children may be committed
to those semi-prisons for a number of years, where they
are trained to industry and supported at the expense of
the Government, of the subscribers to the school, of the
ratepayers, and to some extent of the parent.

If the ladder *from the gutter to the university* is not yet
as complete as could be desired, yet there exist, in the
present system, means by which a child of ordinary
capacity may acquire a reasonably good education at a
very small cost. It is not generally known that the
Education Code provides for the teaching of one or
more of the following subjects (beyond the three R's
and music and drawing, which are specially cared for),
viz.:—Geography, history, grammar, algebra, geometry,
natural philosophy, physical geography, natural sciences,
and the Latin, French, and German languages.

The Department of Science and Art gives scholarships of £5, £10, or £25 per annum towards the support of poor scholars, on the fulfilment of certain conditions by the scholars and contributions by the locality. Then there are Royal Exhibitions of £50 per annum, and Whitworth Scholarships of £100, quite within the reach of students of the industrial classes, and other rewards and aids well known to every teacher of an inspected school.

With reference to the operation of the Education Act in this district, we may observe that previously to its introduction children, who are now compelled to attend school, were in the habit of running wild in the public streets (which, in fact, they made into play grounds), in course of training for vagrancy and crime. The absence of these "street Arabs" from public view is very apparent; and it is satisfactory to know that they are now properly cared for and are receiving the elements, at least, of an education which will fit them to become useful members of society, and not a terror to all who came into contact with them.

SCHOOL BOARD.

ESTABLISHMENT OF BOARD.

One of the main purposes of the Elementary Education Act of 1870 was to secure a sufficient amount of school accommodation, and in cases where the local authority fails, after due notice given, to supply any ascertained deficiency, the Education Department is empowered to cause a School Board to be formed for the district. In

the case of Rochdale, however, application was made
by the Town Council, September 1st, 1870, to the
Education Department, under the 12th section, and the
Department, in due course, issued an order for the
election of a Board of eleven members, which took place
on November 15th, 1870, when the following were
elected :—Edmund Ashworth, Esq., J.P., Oakenrod;
Joseph Brierley, Esq., J.P., Castleton; Henry Fishwick,
Esq., Carr Hill; Abraham Greenwood, Esq., Regent-
street; Rev. M. Moriarty, Watts-street; Jonathan
Nield, Esq., J.P., Dunster House; John Petrie, junior,
Esq., Broomfield; Joseph Rushworth, Esq., Sheriff-
street; William Whitworth Schofield, Esq., J.P.,
Buckley Hall; William Tuer Shawcross, Esq., Heybrook; Thomas Watson, Esq., Horse Carrs.

. Mr. Edmund Ashworth was appointed first Chairman,
and Mr. John Petrie, junior, Vice-chairman of the
Board.

SUPPLY OF SCHOOLS.

The Board having framed bye-laws to secure compulsory attendance, under the power given in section 74
of the Education Act, they directed an enquiry into the
school accommodation of the district which, taking into
account buildings and enlargements then in progress,
was found to be amply sufficient. On the extension of
the Borough another enquiry was necessary, which
resulted in showing that there were, in suitable and
efficient schools (existing or in course of being supplied),
places for 10,955 scholars, allowing not less than
8 square feet of area, and 80 cubic feet of space for
each child. The Education Department accepted this
as sufficient accommodation for the district, which was

estimated to contain about 10,000 children, from three to thirteen, for whom elementary school provision was required.

COMPULSORY ATTENDANCE.

The bye-laws framed by the Board, and sanctioned by Her Majesty in· Council, enact that every child in the Borough from six to thirteen shall attend school unless there be a reasonable excuse for non-attendance, such as is defined in the bye-laws. The Board's officers are authorised to visit parents and guardians, and to serve notices upon them requiring the attendance of their children at school. Provision is made for paying the school fees of children when the income of the parent falls below a certain scale, and also for remitting the same under like conditions in the Board Schools.

ATTENDANCE AT SCHOOL.

According to the last published report there were 11,223 scholars on the books of the various Elementary Schools, viz.:—under six years of age, 2,621; between six and thirteen, 5,602; and of these 10,087 were actually in attendance during the week when the returns were supplied by the schools.

SCHOOL BOARD.

The following is a list of the members of the Board elected November 15th, 1873:—Alderman W. T. Shaw-cross, J.P., Heybrook, Chairman; John Petrie, junior, Esq., Broomfield, Vice-chairman; Joseph Brierley, Esq., J.P., Castleton, Chairman of General Purposes and School Management Committee; Jonathan Nield, Esq., J.P., Dunster House, Chairman of School

Attendance Committee; John Albert Bright, Esq., One Ash; Lieut.-Col. Fishwick, J.P., Carr Hill; Rev. Edward O'Neill, S. John's; Rev. H. W. Parkinson, Drake-street (since deceased); Mr. Councillor Joseph Rushworth, Sheriff-street; Robert Schofield, Esq., Summerlease; Thomas Watson, Esq., Horse Carrs.

OFFICERS OF THE BOARD.

Mr. G. H. Wheeler, Clerk and Correspondent for the Board Schools; Mr. Joseph Heap, Legal Adviser; Mr. R. H. Brown, Treasurer; Mr. H. Goodhead, Mr. J. Reeve, Mr. M. L. Gallagher, Mr. T. Percival, Attendance Officers; and Mr. R. H. Huddlestone, Clerk's Assistant.

GOVERNMENT OFFICERS OF EDUCATION.

Her Majesty's Inspector of Schools for the Rochdale district is A. M. Watson, Esq., M.A., Fellow of Jesus College, Cambridge, and his Assistant, Mr. Sharpe, both residing at Bury.

THE GRAMMAR SCHOOL.
(FOUNDED 1565.)

This handsome brick building was erected in 1847. It is pleasantly situated on Sparrow Hill, in the midst of the " verdant lawns and flowery slopes " of the Public Park, which it also serves to ornament; and it is, in fact, a " cynosure of neighbouring eyes." A more agreeable and pleasant site for a school could not well be found; as the public recreation grounds close to its doors, afford a delightful means of healthful relaxation to the pupils during the intervals of study. Any one who remembers the former school building, near the Old Church, cannot fail to be struck with the advantageous change which has been made, alike in point of situation, architectural beauty, and necessary accommodation. The present master of the school is Mr. R. R. Grey, whose professional training, coupled with the experience which he has had in this and other schools, should give assurance that the boys placed under his charge ought to make satisfactory progress. Prior to his appointment it was customary to select a clergyman as head master, but we think it may be safely stated that the departure from the old practice, in the appointment of a layman, has not been prejudicial to the interests of the school as a public institution. The correct designation of the school is "*Archbishop Parker's Grammar School.*" It was founded by that most reverend prelate under indenture dated January 1st, in the seventh year of our "bright occidental star," Queen Elizabeth (1565), "out of the love and good will which he, the said Archbishop, bears towards all the inhabitants of the parish of Rochdale, and that their youth may be instructed in the learning of true piety and the knowledge of the Latin tongue." These subjects are taught free of charge; but as at the school the ordinary branches of learning are also taught, the pupils, except a few foundationers, are required to pay fees such as are usually charged in other middle-class schools. The course of study, therefore, embraces instruction in the Holy Scriptures, Greek, Latin, French, and other languages; Mathematics, and other subjects which go to form a sound and practical education. We believe the school is at present in a satisfactory condition;

13

and the gradual increase of pupils which has taken place is an indication that the inhabitants of Rochdale do not fail to appreciate the educational advantages which the school affords.

As to the history of this institution, it may be stated that the original school-house was built by the parish-ioners on a site near to the Old Church, which was given for the purpose by the Rev. Richard Midgley, the then Vicar of Rochdale, whence originated the name "School Lane;" and from this circumstance that locality may be regarded as classic ground. Judging from present appearances, however, we should be inclined to say that the place has sadly degenerated, and does not now give any indication of the savour of learning which must have pervaded it in the olden time. Three hundred years ago and more our ancestors probably chose the spot on account of its fine, open, and healthy situation, and they must have been gratified that a public seminary was placed in such close proximity to their ancient and venerated Parish Church. The beauty of the situation is now a thing of the past, and, "like an insubstantial pageant faded," has "left not a rack behind;" and it would be difficult to find on the spot where the building used to stand a breath of the pure air which gladdened the lungs of the "young idea" of ancient days.

On consulting "Baines's History of Lancashire" (1868), we find the following historical details, which may prove interesting to the reader. In a foot note referring to the school, it is stated that the "origin of this foundation is curious and little known; the rectories of ' Blacborne, Rachedale, and Whalley,'

erly appropriated to the Abbey of Whalley, together with the chapels (*sacellis*) annexed to them, having devolved upon Matthew (Parker), Archbishop of Canterbury, by exchange with Henry VIII. and his son Edward VI., on the dissolution of the monasteries, the rectorial tithes were leased to Sir John Byron who, amongst other conditions, engaged to pay the old annual stipend charged on the rectory by the Abbey of Whalley, to each of the ministers performing Divine service in each of the chapels attached to the churches of Blackburn, Whalley, and Rochdale. Being a zealous Roman Catholic, and having failed to fulfil this part of the agreement, and thereby reduced the ministers to great distress, the archbishop brought "the farmer," Sir John Byron, into court in 1561, who, after a protracted and costly litigation, under the fear of losing the tithes, cast himself upon the clemency of the archbishop, who adjudged that he should, over and above the rent agreed for in the lease, and in addition to the stipends to be paid to the ministers, pay £17 a-year for the maintenance of schoolmasters of a free grammar school to be founded in Rochdale in the archbishop's name. These conditions Sir John accepted with avidity, and hence the origin of the Rochdale Grammar School, which was rendered permanent by the sum of £17 per annum being charged upon the tithes of the parish in perpetuity."

The "avidity" referred to in the foregoing extract seems to be somewhat doubtful, as Canon Raines states that "Sir John" immediately consented, *though with an ill grace*," to comply with the primate's requirements. We are further informed by the Rev. Canon, in his admirable "Memorials of the Rochdale Grammar School," published in 1845, that the "indenture endowment was enrolled in chancery anno 13 Elizabeth, and there is a memorandum added, stating that the second counterpart of it, with the seal of the Archbishop annexed thereto, and confirmed by the Dean and Chapter of Canterbury, remained with the masters and fellows of Corpus Christi College, and that the said grant being decayed by water, was renewed under the seal of the Archbishop, and further stating that there remained in the same custody the original Grant of Richard Midgley, of the plot of ground, parcel of the Vicarage of Rochdale, for the building of the school house, with the confirmations already named."

The motto of Archbishop Parker, " *Mundus transit*," and his armorial bearings have been adopted as the motto and arms of the school, and are engraved on a stone above the porch.

Of the learned and pious founder it may be useful to add, that Queen Anne Boleyn, the second consort of Henry VIII., is said to have entertained for him a great and sincere regard. He was her chaplain, and shortly before her cruel execution, at the hands of her detestable and capricious husband, she commended her daughter Elizabeth to the pious care and instruction of her beloved spiritual adviser. He was afterwards chaplain to Henry VIII. and to his son Edward VI. On the accession of Queen Mary, of unblessed memory, he was deprived of his preferments, and had even to conceal himself. In "all the clouds that lowered upon his house" he preserved a calm and undisturbed mind, and could say with Milton—

———" I argue not
Against heaven's hand or will, nor bate a jot
Of heart or hope ; but still bear up and steer
Right onward."

He knew no "winter of discontent," for he trusted not
in an arm of flesh ; and when the "Maiden Queen"—
"the fair vestal throned by the west"—succeeded to
the Crown, the sun of prosperity shone upon him in
its fullest splendour, making "glorious summer," and
he was installed in the Archbishopric of Canterbury in
1559, being consecrated in Lambeth Cathedral on the
17th December in that year. He filled the see of
Canterbury for more than fifteen years, and died on the
17th May, 1575, in the seventy-first year of his age.

The tercentenary of the foundation of the school was
celebrated in February, 1865, by a very pleasing dramatic and musical entertainment, the school on the
occasion being filled with the principal gentry and other
patrons of the institution, including many of the old
scholars, some of whom took a prominent part in the
commemoratory proceedings.

We hope that the public spirit of the town will take
care that an institution so truly valuable, and possessing
such interesting associations, does not fall into decay,
but be always sustained and fostered as it undoubtedly
deserves to be.

MOSS SCHOOL.

The Rochdale Free English Endowed School—commonly called the "Moss School" on account of its being
built on a part of the parish formerly noted for its
mossy and swampy fields—is, so far as the number of
scholars to whom a free education is given is
concerned, the most important of the few educational
charities existing in Rochdale. It was founded in the
year 1769 by the late Mrs. Jane Hardman, whose

husband, Mr. John Hardman, had for a long time
previously, been known as one of the leading manufacturers of the staple woollen trade of the town, when
the trade was carried on all by hand in the homes of the
journeyman weavers and spinners. At his death, his
business was carried on for a few years by his son, who
often expressed a desire to see some provision made for
the education of the children of his workpeople and the
poorer classes generally, better than the dame schools
in cottage houses, which were, at that time, the only
ones accessible to the poor of Rochdale. But he did
not live to carry out this wish, for while away in London
on business, he was taken ill and died there. Mrs.
Hardman, now childless and a widow, derived some
consolation in carrying out her son's wishes, and
buying the land from the Vicar of the Parish, she
built the school and endowed it with certain lands and
tenements situated at Wardle, in all about sixty acres
of land, from which an annual income of about £120 is
now derived. Mrs. Hardman, who was herself a
Dissenter from the Established Church, desired to secure
the administration of the school on purely unsectarian
principles; and to secure this end she appointed a board
of fifteen trustees, eight of whom were dissenters, and
the remaining seven were members of the Established
Church, and this arrangement still exists. There are
forty boys and twenty girls receiving a free education in
the school, in addition to whom a limited number of
private pupils are received by the master. Free
scholars are admitted by personal application to the
Trustees at their annual meeting in June in each year.
The charity is free and open to all comers, but the

preference is usually given to orphans or the children of poor parents with large families. The course of instruction given in the school embraces Reading, Writing, Arithmetic, Geography, History, Grammar, Book-keeping, and Drawing, together with sewing for the girls.

SCIENCE AND ART CLASSES.

These Classes were originally established at the Lyceum, in October, 1867, but subsequently removed to the Board Schools, Baillie-street, where they are at present located. The object for which the classes were instituted was to afford the industrial and artisan classes in the town the means of obtaining instruction in the various branches of science and art at a nominally low fee, by means of grants from the Science and Art Department at South Kensington. Amongst those who took an active part in the inauguration of the classes and composed the first committee were Right Hon. John Bright, John Robinson (then mayor), John Tatham, Edward Taylor, James Brierley, Jonathan Nield, G. L. Ashworth, W. A. Scott, and W. Shaw, Esqrs., and the Rev. W. N. Molesworth. The following are the sciences in which instruction is given :—Practical, plane, and solid geometry, machine and building construction, theoretical and applied mechanics, steam, acoustics, light and heat, magnetism, chemistry, animal physiology, mathematics, and physical geography. In the art class students are taught freehand and model drawing, geometry, and perspective, the object being to educate persons in the art of inventing and executing patterns and designs, and designing for the various branches of orna-

mental manufacture. The whole of the subjects are of
real practical value to every working man, and are aided
by Government solely for the purpose of increasing the
skill of the artisan. The teachers are all competent,
and are paid by Government on the results of the
teaching, as tested by the examination in May. Those
pupils who succeed in passing the examination are
entitled to receive Queen's prizes, consisting of gold,
silver, and bronze medals, books, &c., and certificates
of merit. Through the liberality of several of the local
gentlemen, the committee have been able to offer
money prizes for competition. The prizes are distributed
to the students at the annual meeting in the Town Hall,
in September, the Mayor, for the time being, presiding.
In 1873 the prizes were distributed by the Bishop of
Manchester, and in 1874 by Jacob Bright, Esq. The
success that has attended the instruction given at these
classes may be gathered from the fact that many who
entered as students in 1867 have obtained their advanced
certificates, and are now engaged in teaching other
classes that have been formed in the town and neighbourhood. The Rochdale Equitable Pioneers, in their
educational department, are also turning their attention
to the subject of the introduction of science classes into
their scheme of instruction.

THE PUBLIC ELEMENTARY SCHOOLS.

The following is a list of the schools, the names of the teachers, the average attendance of scholars, and the amount of Government Grants paid to each school. It is an extract from the last published report of the Education Department :—

Name of School.	Teachers' Names.	Av. Atdc.	Gov. Grant. (1873-4.)
			£ s. d.
Parish Church ...	Mr. R. Stott, Miss E. Shepherd, and Miss R. Higgins	695	373 6 6
St. Alban's ...	Miss E. Alleson...	275	150 17 2
St. Clement's ...	Mr J. Oldham, Miss E. Hodgkinson	297	215 5 0
Oakenrod ...	Mr. G. Bountiff	116	126 3 1
St. Edmund's ...	Mr. S. Clegg	270	210 1 6
St. Mary's National	Mr. C. A. Pitts, Mrs. C. Ford... ...	249	154 5 5
St. James's ...	Mr. S. Green, Miss J. Wolfenden ...	337	193 10 7
St. Peter's ...	Mr. S. Morrill, Miss S. Booth, and Miss C. Booth	353	180 0 0
St. Mary's, Buersil ...	Mr. T. Oldham, Miss B. Holland, and Miss M. A. Kenworthy	421	265 18 9
Healey ...	Mr. T. Wolstenholme	229	164 18 0
All Saints' ...	Mr. J. Jackson, Miss A. Wharf, and Mrs. A. Armstrong...	336	216 5 0
Belfield ...	Mr. D Leach	92	81 0 0
British, Clover-st. ...	Mr. Whiteley and Miss S. Wharton...	256	181 10 0
Brimrod ...	Mr. J. Bloor and Miss S. Pilling ...	196	130 10 0
Wesleyan, Union-st.	Mr. R. Greenwood & Miss A. Nuttall	372	259 8 0
Wesleyan, L. Place...	Mr. A. E. Drury and Miss H. Heginbottom	260	176 9 0
St. Patrick's, R. C....	Miss M. J. Broughall and Miss Blackburne	326	201 0 0
St. John's, R. C. ...	Sister Euphrosine and Miss M. Mc. Carron	234	111 12 0
Nuttall-street ...	Miss E. Owen	103	58 12 5
Congregational, Smallbridge B. S.	Mr. W. Holt	154	117 9 7
Baillie-st B. S. ...	Mr. W. R. Shearer and Miss M. J. Rees	342	217 10 0
Milkstone B. S. ...	Miss M. E. Graham	163	37 19 0
Lowerplace B. S. ...	Mr. D. Rostron and Miss E. Leach...	113	59 12 10
			£3,883 3 10

THE RIGHT HON. JOHN BRIGHT, M.P.

T HE name of John Bright is of world-wide
reputation, and Rochdale is honoured in being
the birthplace of this distinguished statesman.

" How he lived, and toiled, and suffered,
That he might advance the people,"

are matters of history, and need not be fully entered
into in this brief notice. The son of Mr. Jacob Bright,
he was born at Greenbank, on the 16th November, 1811,
and is consequently in his sixty-fourth year. Mr.
Bright was one of the founders of the (long since
defunct) " Literary and Philosophical Society " in this
town, and frequently gave lectures in connection with
that society. His energetic efforts in the crusade
against church rates in this parish are well known ; and,
although at this early period in his public life, he was
subjected to considerable obloquy, he never shrunk
from the work with which he identified himself, but
laboured on amid good report and evil report until
success crowned the efforts of himself and his earnest
coadjutors. His more public life began in 1839, when
he became a member of the Anti-Corn Law League ;
and he was, with Mr. Cobden, one of the most brilliant
and important supporters of that great movement. He
gave himself to the work most completely, and ceased

THE RESIDENCE OF THE RT HON. JOHN BRIGHT.

not until the death-knell of the Corn Laws resounded
throughout the land, and the " cornfields rustled with
delight." In July, 1843, Mr. Bright was elected M.P.
for Durham, an earlier attempt made by him in the
spring of the same year having been unsuccessful. He
was subsequently, at the general election in 1847,
elected one of the members for Manchester, and continued so until the next general election, in 1852, when
he was again elected. He was a vigorous opponent of
the Russian war, and was one of the meeting
of the Society of Friends when a deputation from
that body was sent to St. Petersburg, to the
Emperor of Russia, to implore him to preserve the
peace. Mr. Bright's denunciations of that war were
powerfully energetic and uncompromising ; and the
course which he pursued on this question was exceedingly unpopular, and led to his being unseated for
Manchester. It is to be recorded, to the lasting disgrace
of that city, that at the time of his rejection he was ill
on the Continent, and consequently unable to defend his
seat.

Mr. Bright, however, did not long remain out of
Parliament, being elected, in 1857, for the important
constituency of Birmingham, of which borough he is
still the representative. Tenacity of purpose, and firm,
unyielding adherence to principle, are prominent traits
in Mr. Bright's character ; and he expounds and
enforces his opinions in language at once clear, forcible,
and appropriate. His copiousness and brilliancy of
speech are almost without parallel; and his acquaintance
with English literature is of the most intimate and
extensive kind. He is a born orator, and can sway an

audience as with the spell of an enchanter's wand. But his chief merit is his thorough patriotism, and it is essentially true of him, that

"He never sold the truth to serve the hour,
Nor paltered with Eternal God for power."

In the path of reform Mr. Bright has always been in the front rank, and has there borne the burden and heat of the day with hardihood and cool and patient magnanimity. He was one of those who sowed the seed whence has sprung the rich and luxuriant harvest of freedom which the people now enjoy. His confidence in the people has been unbounded, and he never had any misgiving that entrusting them with political power would result in the frightful disasters which the timid imaginations of the opponents of reform used to picture so vividly. He has worked heartily in helping to break down the barriers of exclusiveness which so long upreared themselves, and the people owe to their undaunted, and eloquent, and mighty tribune, a debt of gratitude and esteem which they can never repay.

The Right Hon. gentleman's efforts in the cause of Free Trade met with a hearty recognition from an extensive body of admirers throughout the kingdom. A public subscription was set on foot for the purpose of presenting him with a suitable testimonial, and a sum of £5,048. 8s. 1d. was raised on the occasion. On consultation with Mr. Bright, it was found that a library would be a form of testimonial agreeable to him, and, accordingly, £1,500 was expended upon more than 1,200 books, which were selected by himself. These volumes were placed in an appropriate oak case, costing

£400, specially designed for them, and it was at once an elegant and substantial piece of furniture, adorned with representations, in carved work, of the leading features of agriculture and commerce. The inscription, on a silver plate affixed, set forth that the gift was " an acknowledgment of his great services in the cause of free trade, in connection with the National Anti-Corn Law League."

This magnificent testimonial was presented to Mr. Bright in due course, in 1853, and the balance of the subscriptions, less expenses, was paid over to him. It may be interesting to add that the number of subscribers was 3,647, and the towns and villages which responded to the call of the committee amounted to 172.

Mr. Bright's intimate acquaintance with Indian affairs would have sufficed to obtain for him the high office of Secretary of State, if he had not preferred and accepted the less responsible post of President of the Board of Trade, on the return of the liberal party to power, after the passing of Mr. Disraeli's Reform Bill.

The late severe and protracted but now happily ended illness of Mr. Bright, necessarily occasioned his absence for a lengthened period from his place in Parliament; but Birmingham behaved nobly to their prostrate representative, not only deeply sympathising with him in his illness, but generously refusing to accept Mr. Bright's offer of retirement, in order that they might choose his successor. The kind consideration thus shown to him by his constituents has endeared Birmingham to him more closely than ever, and there can be little doubt that death only will sever the connection which exists between the great statesman and the noble and influential town which he has so long represented in Parliament. Mr. Bright's re-appearance in the House, and his appointment as Chancellor of the Duchy of Lancaster, failed to keep the Liberals in office, as was hoped, and he consequently, after the recent general election, which culminated in the return of Mr. Disraeli to power, resigned the seals as a cabinet minister.

The friendship which subsisted between Mr. Bright and Mr. Cobden was of the very closest and most affectionate character; and the death of the Apostle of Free Trade was a terrible blow for the former, from which, judging from his public utterances, we fear he will never recover. The love of David and Jonathan affords a parallel to the friendship which filled the hearts of Bright and Cobden; and the pathetic language of David can alone convey anything like the anguish which must have torn Mr. Bright's inmost being, when his dear companion and friend was taken from him for ever. "I am distressed for thee, my brother; very pleasant hast thou been unto me; thy love to me was wonderful, passing the love of women. How are the mighty fallen, and the weapons of war perished!" Rochdale also sustained a great loss when Mr. Cobden died; and this is a reason why we can more appropriately enter into the deep grief that fell upon our illustrious townsman. Mr. Bright's career has been most brilliant and eventful, and he can look back on a long life spent in good and honest work; no mean or self-seeking motives can be attributed to him; but thorough patriotism and love of his fellow-men have swayed all the public acts of his life. The path of duty lay clearly

defined before him, and he has trod it with firm and
unfaltering foot. He that walks that path,

> ——"Only thirsting
> For the right, and learns to deaden
> Love of self, before his journey closes,
> He shall find the stubborn thistle bursting
> Into glossy purples, which out-redden
> All voluptuous garden roses."

Our picture illustration of "One Ash," the residence
of Mr. Bright, is copied from a photograph taken by
Mr. Jackson, The Walk. "One Ash" is about half a
mile distant from the centre of the town, and not far
from the mills of the Messrs. Bright, at Cronkeyshaw.
The right hon. gentleman, though residing so close to
Rochdale, does not take any part in the town affairs,
and lives in comparative privacy. At election times,
when at home, he votes with his party; but, beyond
this, he does not identify himself with local politics.

We have, in the preceding remarks, referred to the
part which Mr. Bright took in the struggle for the
repeal of the Corn Laws. With regard to this subject,
and to Mr. Bright's subsequent success, and his illness,
we may be permitted to call the attention of our readers
to the following verses, which, amongst others, are
supposed to have been written by a "German who had
learned (he said) the English language." They are
quoted from "The Fijiad," Beeton's Christmas Annual,
1874. The entire poem is excellent, and full of humour,
and manifests great power on the part of the writer; and
on the whole, it is highly complimentary to the right
hon. gentleman :—

> "For once on a dime it happent
> Dat Justice hid her face,
> And dere were some would have starrf'd de poor
> In dere greed and dere prite of place;

Den mit his frent, good Cobden,
　John Brightmann he gained renown,
And he helped to raise fair Justice op,
　And to pull de corn laws down.

" But oh ! dere was Hande-ringen
　And shaking of many a head
Among de dukes and de nobel lorts
　At de tings John Brightmann said ;
Dey turned op dere eyes in horror
　When of landlords' greed he'd speak,
And dey said, but in politer words,
　' It was like John Brightmann's cheek.'

" And den de jolly farmers
　All in dere might arose,
And said John Brightmann would ruin dem
　Mit new-fangled ways like tose.
But John Brightmann laughed and told dem
　Dat he never could make out
Dey should want prodection, dose jolly men
　Who looked so dhick and stout.

" Bot right and justice triomphed
　For justice and right are strong,
And de poor man's bread no longer
　Was leavened by sense of wrong.
And de constitution lif'd still,
　And de dukes yet walked Pall Mall,
And de farmers John Brightmann ruined so
　Looked rich, and jolly, and well.

" John Brightmann rose to honour,
　As was bot right and fair,
And came to court, though great folk laughed
　To see dat Quaker dere.
Bot honour is a burden,
　Has made many backs to pow,
And fortune's wheel has turnt and turnt
　From ancient days till now.

" And so it came John Brightmann
　Was smit by sickness sore,
And de voice so brafe in council
　Was heard, for a time, no more ;
But all were glat when news came
　Dat John in de North was out,
Fishing for *Lachs* and *Forellen*
　Which, in English, is zalmon and drout."

ANCIENT FAMILIES.

WITH only a few exceptions, there are not any local ancient families of eminence now resident in the parish of Rochdale. Ancient mansions are to be found in which, in remote times, lived families of importance, but no descendants from these families now "live and move and have their being" amongst us; or, if any such exist, they have lost their distinguishable features, and can no longer be pointed out as possessing any peculiar marks of antiquity. We find, common enough, ancient names such as Buckley, Butterworth, Chadwick, Hamer, Healey, Holt, Howard, and so forth; but it would be an impossible task to trace up these names to the ancestors of past ages by whom, in some way or other, the names were rendered famous. We find Buckley Hall, Butterworth Hall, Hamer Hall, all of which have a specific history in relation to the olden time; but they have all passed into the hands of various owners who no longer represent the old families with whom the mansions originated.

THE BYRON FAMILY.
"CREDE BYRON."

The close connection in which the Byron family formerly stood to our ancient town, leads us, in the first instance, to make a few remarks on that noble House.

14

Its ancestry can be traced back to a period earlier than
the Conquest; and, in the twelfth century, we are
informed, the Byrons became connected with the County
of Lancaster; but it is more to our present purpose to
observe that it was not until 1643 that the family
became closely allied to Rochdale, when, on the 24th
October, in that year, Sir John Byron was created a
peer of the realm by the style and title of Baron Byron,
of Rochdale, in the County of Lancaster. This noble-
man greatly distinguished himself by his steady zeal
and devotedness to the cause of the unhappy King
Charles I., and was engaged on the royal side in the
memorable battle of Preston in 1649. His lordship
failed, however, to witness the restoration of the
Stuarts, and died in 1652. He was succeeded in the
title by his brother Richard, who thus became the
second baron. Passing over the latter's successor, we
come next to William, the fourth baron, to whom, in
1710, the Archbishop of Canterbury granted a lease of
his rectory of Rochdale for twenty-one years, for an
annual payment, in addition to a sum of £15 to the
schoolmaster, and £2 to the usher of the Grammar
School in Rochdale. His lordship was also under obligation to pay certain sums to the rector of Rochdale
and the curates of Saddleworth and Butterworth, and
to uphold the chancel of the Parish Church and the
chapels of ease of the other places above-mentioned.
The fifth baron is chiefly to be noticed on account of the
sad misfortune which befell him in causing the death
of William Chaworth, Esq., in a duel, in January, 1765,
and which led to his being tried before the House of
Lords on the capital charge of murder. Acquitted of

this crime, he was found guilty of manslaughter, but availing himself of the statute of Edward VI., he was set at liberty, and so escaped the consequences of his offence.   His lordship survived the trial for a period of thirty-three years, and died in May, 1798, without issue. There is almost an air of romance about the history of his lordship's brother, who, in early life, sailed with Commodore Anson, the celebrated circumnavigator, and was cast away on an uninhabited island in the Pacific Ocean, where he had to undergo privations and misery of the most painful kind.   Relieved from his dreadful situation he returned to England, and subsequently became a vice-admiral.   He died in 1786, leaving two sons, of whom John was married to Catharine Gordon, who was descended in a direct line from the Earl of Huntley and the Princess Jane Stuart.   From this union proceeded the sixth baron, George Gordon Lord Byron, the illustrious poet, whose name will live as long as the history of English literature endures.   His great efforts and the sacrifices which he made in the Greek war of independence, can never be forgotten, and in connection with his brilliant poetical powers throw a halo of splendour round his name which arrests the attention of all lovers of that land of ancient glory. Lord Byron died on the 19th April, 1824, at Missolonghi, in Greece, to the inexpressible grief of the entire Greek nation, in whose cause he suffered, and to whom he had devoted the best energies of his nature.   Their cause was his : his noble mind was filled with indignation at the wrongs inflicted on the Greeks, and he gave his mighty genius, his wealth, and his life in the cause of the nation which he loved so much.   Lord Byron's

marriage with Miss Anne Isabella Milbanke was a most
unfortunate one, and embittered the whole of his future
life. He contracted a great and invincible repugnance
to England; and the busy scenes which the war in
Greece daily presented afforded the liveliest occupation
to a mind which hated wrong and oppression, and
which delighted in aiding the weak against the strong.
As a poet, Lord Byron stands out prominently in the
first rank, and nearly all that came from his pen bears
marks of the transcendent power of a highly-gifted and
wonderful genius. Much that he wrote is no doubt
open to condemnation, and in some circles his works
are placed in the Index Expurgatorius ; but the literature of this country would be deprived of a most
splendid name, and of much brilliant writings,
if this narrow-minded exclusiveness were to be
generally adopted.   But happily this can never
be. It is an imperishable honour that Rochdale
can claim Lord Byron as its own; in this respect it
stands out among the famed towns of the kingdom.
True it is that in 1823 the close connection which
existed between the illustrious family of the Byrons
and our ancient town was severed, when the noble poet
parted with his vast manor to the late James Dearden,
Esq. Nevertheless, the memory of the connection will
ever remain, for time can neither dim its splendour nor
deprive us of the rich possession. The Byron family
had no residence in Rochdale; their seat was Newstead
Abbey, founded as a priory in the twelfth century, and
situated in the fertile district once known as Sherwood
Forest. The abbey has, however, passed into the hands
of new owners; but the associations connected with its

history are of an enduring character, and will always create a lively interest in the public mind. It is much resorted to by tourists from all parts, chiefly on account of its having been the dwelling-place of the great poet, whose genius has thrown a spell round the abbey and the pleasant neighbourhood of the once famous "merry green wood," wherein Robin Hood and his faithful bowmen performed so many note-worthy exploits in the days of yore.

THE ENTWISLE FAMILY,
OF FOXHOLES.

The Entwisles, of Foxholes, appear to have been orignally seated at Entwisle Hall, in the parish of Bolton. They are, undoubtedly, a very ancient and honourable family; and they have always been held in the highest esteem, both in the parish of Rochdale and in other parts of Lancashire. In the Parish Church of St. Chad's we find, in the chancel, a marble monument, erected in 1807, by John Entwisle, Esq., inscribed as follows:—
"To perpetuate a memorial erected in the church of St. Peter, at St. Albans (perished by time) this marble is here placed to the memory of a gallant and loyal man, Sir Bertine Entwisle, Knight, Viscount and Baron of Brybeke, in Normandy, and sometime Bailiffe of Constantine, in which office he succeeded his father-in-law, Sir John Ashton, whose daughter first married Sir Richard le Byron, an ancestor of the Lord Byrons, Barons of Rochdale; and, secondly, Sir Bertine Entwisle, who, after repeated acts of valour in the service of his sovereigns, Henry the 5th and 6th, more particularly at Agincourt, was killed in the first battle at St. Albans, and on his tombstone was recorded, in

brass, the following inscription:—'Here lyeth Sir
Bertin Entwisel, knight, who was born in Lancastershyre,
and was Viscount and Baron of Brybeke, in Normandy,
and Bailiffe of Constantine, who died fighting on King
Henry the Sixth party, the 27th May, 1455. On whose
sowl Jesus have mercy.'"

Of the above-named Sir Bertine Entwisle, we find in
Roby's "Traditions of Lancashire," a ballad relating
to him, wherein he is described as having gone forth
to "fight for England's weal," and mentions "his might
at Agincourt." He may not disregard the summons of
his king, who is in jeopardy, although his lady and his
daughter, in tears, endeavour to dissuade him from
going to the battle-field. Evil omens are observed
after the departure of Sir Bertine, which seem to show
that some calamity has happened to the right, trusty,
and valorous knight; when at length

> " An armed footstep on the stair
>   Clanked heavily and slow."

The " evil messenger " enters, and is told to show his
biddings to the dame and her daughter; but the " aged
man " vouchsafed neither look nor word. He is asked
by the lady and charged " by the rood " to say what he
brings, when

> " He drew a signet from his hand,
>   'Twas speckled o'er with blood;
>   Thy husband's grave is deep and wide:
>   In St. Alban's priory his body lies;
>   But on his soul Christ Jesu have mercy."

The ancient mansion of the Entwisles, at Foxholes,
has been held by the family for several centuries past;

and the present proprietor of the estates is the youthful son of the late owner, John Smith Entwisle, Esq., who died, after a short illness, a few years ago. The property of the Entwisles is situate in the township of Hundersfield, in this parish, and is very extensive and valuable. The late owner was a gentleman of a kind and genial disposition, fond of field sports, and was active and lively in his habits. He was, like many of his predecessors, a staunch and consistent Conservative. In late years he took an active part in politics; and at the time of his death he was the head of the Tory party in the borough. His father, the late John Entwisle, was member for the borough from 1835 to 1837; and his brother-in-law, Sir Alexander Ramsay, Baronet, has also represented the borough in Parliament; but Mr. John Smith Entwisle never sought to win the good graces of the electors on his own behalf. His father was High-Sheriff of Lancashire in 1824, and his departure to meet the judges at Lancaster, in discharge of his duties, was the occasion of a very imposing and effective public display. The death of the late Mr. Entwisle was quite unexpected at the time of its occurrence, and occasioned very great regret on the part of both Conservatives and Liberals. As the representative of an ancient family he was generally much respected, and his death rudely tore asunder the kindly relations which always existed between himself and the inhabitants of Rochdale. His name stands in honourable connection with the New Church at Hamer for which he generously gave the site, as well as contributing largely to the building fund.

Mr. John Entwisle, the father of the latter-named

gentleman, contested the Borough of Rochdale on the passing of the Reform Act in 1832. He was opposed on that occasion by Mr. John Fenton and by Mr. James Taylor, the election resulting in the return of Mr. Fenton. The numbers were:—Fenton, 277; Entwisle, 246; Taylor, 109. Nothing daunted by his defeat, Mr. Entwisle was again in the field as a candidate for Parliamentary honours, and on the 6th June, 1835, he was returned by a majority of 43 votes over his previously successful opponent, the numbers being :— Entwisle, 369, and Fenton, 326. Mr. Entwisle occupied his high position as member for Rochdale until his death, in April, 1837, when Mr. John Fenton was again elected, Mr. Clement Royds being the unsuccessful candidate.

The Entwisle family has had the honour of filling the great office of High Sheriff of the County of Lancaster on three separate occasions, namely, in 1798 (John Entwisle, Esq.); 1824, as before-mentioned; and, lastly, in 1849, when Mr. John Smith Entwisle was chosen by the Crown to discharge the functions of that much coveted and honourable post.

THE ROYDS FAMILY.
"SEMPER PARATUS."

Brown Hill, an ancient pile of buildings, is situate in the hamlet of Falinge, in Spotland, and was formerly the residence of Albert Hudson Royds, Esq., J.P., D.L.; afterwards, of H. H. Fishwick, Esq.; and it is now occupied by Edmund Albert Nuttall Royds, Esq., the second son of Albert Hudson Royds, Esq. Brown Hill is pleasantly situated, and commands a fine view of some parts of the adjoining country. It lies rather low

down, and thus does not appear so much to advantage
as does the not-distant mansion of Mount Falinge. The
latter place was built by the late James Royds, Esq.,
D.L., and is now occupied by John Robinson, Esq., J.P.;
it has been the residence, successively, of James Royds,
Esq.; Clement Royds, Esq., J.P., D.L.; and Albert
Hudson Royds, Esq. The mansion of Falinge is very
pleasantly situated on high, cultivated land, surrounded
by stately trees, and has a handsome appearance.
Green Hill is nearly opposite to Mount Falinge, and
is of more ancient date than Brown Hill. It was
formerly the residence of Clement Royds, Esq., subsequently of his third son, William Edward Royds, Esq.;
and now of Clement M. Royds, Esq. (the eldest son of
the latter), who is a banker, and a county and borough
magistrate. Green Hill is a fine brick edifice, and is
agreeably situated on flat meadow land. It is on a
field in front of the hall, by the kind permission of
Mr. C. M. Royds, that the Rochdale Agricultural
Society holds its annual exhibition, and the readiness
with which this gentleman thus places his grounds at
the disposal of the committee for this purpose is a
sufficient proof of the great interest which he takes in
this important yearly show, and of his desire that the
public should be well accommodated. It appears that
the family of the Royds' originally came from Yorkshire,
and settled at Marled Earth, near Wardlefold, in the
year 1600. In the will of John Royds, of Marled
Earth (born 1678), he is described as a cloth maker.
From that time to the year 1827 the family appears to
have been intimately connected with the woollen
trade, and carried on an extensive business. In

the year 1827 Clement Royds, Esq., bought the present banking business of "Clement Royds and Company" from Messrs. Rawson, who had previously carried on business in Rochdale. For generations many members of the family have been magistrates, and several of them deputy-lieutenants. A district and a village in Yorkshire are named after the Royds'. The present head of the family is Mr. A. H. Royds, formerly of Mount Falinge. He is a J.P. and Deputy-Lieutenant for Worcestershire, and has filled the dignified office of High Sheriff of that County.

. Mr. Clement Royds, the father of the last-named gentleman, was the son of James Royds, Esq., and from the year 1830 up to the time of his death, in 1854, he was an active, able, and energetic county magistrate. He was most regular and attentive to his magisterial duties, and his presence on the bench was always looked upon with satisfaction, as his great experience enabled him to discharge his official duties with efficiency and complete impartiality. He was a strong ally of the Conservative cause in the borough, and even presented himself as a candidate for the representation, but was unsuccessful. In 1850 he was appointed High Sheriff of Lancashire; and the 21st of March, in that year, was an eventful day in Rochdale, on the occasion of the High Sheriff's departure to meet the judges at Lancaster. A very imposing and attractive procession was formed, consisting of the public authorities, and of many friendly and other societies, together with a large number of the gentry and inhabitants of the town. There was a grand display of fireworks on the New Wall and in the Butts in the evening, a balloon was sent up, and the day was set apart as a general holiday, so as to afford all classes an opportunity of doing honour to the occasion, and as a mark of respect to the worthy High Sheriff. An ox was roasted whole and distributed, and unrestrained rejoicing was the order of the day. "Sheriff-street," in Spotland-road, takes its name from the fact that in the year mentioned, Mr. Clement Royds was Sheriff of the County.

Mr. Clement Molyneux Royds was appointed a County Magistrate in September, 1866; and he was placed on the Borough List of Magistrates immediately on the Borough Bench being formed. The family of the Royds' are much and deservedly respected; and the munificence and liberality of Mr. A. H. Royds have been recently conspicuously displayed in the erection, at his own cost, of the Church of St. Edmund's, in Spotland-road, which is particularly noticed in the preceding pages.

Oakenrod Hall is an ancient edifice, and was formerly the residence of the Gartsides, of Gartside. More recently it was the abode of two maiden ladies of the ancient family of the Butterworths, of Butterworth. In 1828 it had passed into the hands of the late James Royds, Esq. The ancient grandeur of the place has departed; and, like many other old mansions in various parts of the parish, it is, at present, occupied as cottage dwellings. The hall, farm, and other contiguous property, and much of the land in the immediate neighbourhood, form part of the possessions of Mr. A. H. Royds, the son and heir of Mr. Clement Royds, by whom they were inherited from his father, James Royds, Esq.

It will be seen on reference to our notice of St. Clement's Church, Spotland, that the land for that sacred edifice was the gift of Mr. Clement Royds; another proof, if such were wanting, of the spirit of liberality which characterises the family.

It is a singular circumstance, and worthy of record here, that for two successive years, viz., 1849 and 1850, the High Sheriff of Lancashire should have been chosen from the town of Rochdale; the late Mr. John Smith Entwisle, of Foxholes, in 1849; and Mr. Clement Royds, of Mount Falinge, in 1850.

THE MILNES,
OF BURNEDGE.

The Milnes, of Burnedge, are an ancient family having a residence at that place; and it is stated with, we believe, perfect truth, that they and their ancestors have been in possession of the estate for upwards of five centuries. We regret that we are not in possession of sufficient information with regard to this family to give particulars of their history, which, we have no doubt, would prove very interesting. We must, therefore, content ourselves with saying that the Milnes are held in great respect not only in this but also in adjoining parishes, where they are owners of extensive landed estates. In a part of their property at Burnedge, there is, we are told, a stone erected to denote that there the various parishes of Rochdale, Middleton, and Oldham converge. We believe that the present representative of the family is Mr. Joseph Milne, of Deane House, Buersil Head.

DISTINGUISHED MILITARY MEN.

LIEUTENANT HOPWOOD.

JOHN HOPWOOD was the son of James Hopwood, the worthy Host of the "King's Head," which used to be much frequented by the merchants of Rochdale. Our hero grew up into a smart and high-spirited young man, and was a clerk with the late John Elliott, Esq., but his military ideas becoming strong, great watchfulness was required to prevent him from enlisting as a soldier. Eventually his friends thought it best to humour the bent of his inclination, and a commission was obtained for him in one of the Lancashire Militia Regiments. The Government of the day being very much in want of men, in consequence of the requirements of the Peninsular War, offered a commission in the army to any militia officer who would raise a company of fifty men for foreign service. Young Hopwood was one of those who accepted the offer, and he sent round the town crier, with a promise of a liberal bounty. In two days, more than the number required was obtained, and it is stated that a finer body of recruits never left the country. Our young hero and his ardent followers were attached to the 95th or Rifle Regiment, and history informs us how this corps distinguished itself at the battles of Busaco, Salamanca, and Vittoria, and at the sieges of Cuidad Rodrigo and Badajos, in all of

which young Hopwood and his company were engaged.
He was wounded at Badajos, but recovering was present
at the battle of Arcangues, before Bayonne, on the 10th
of December, 1813, which was one of the last battles
fought prior to the abdication of Napoleon, and at
which young Hopwood was killed, while gallantly
leading on his devoted band.   His fellow-townsmen
showed their. esteem for his daring courage by erecting
a monument, in St. Chad's Church, to perpetuate his
memory.

CORNET AND ADJUTANT GRINDROD.

Other Rochdale heroes took part in the hard-fought
battles of the Peninsula, and some of them rose from
the ranks by means of indomitable perseverance and
personal bravery.   One of these was Timothy Grindrod,
whose father resided at Pinfold, and was an operative
stone mason.   Young Grindrod enlisted in the 11th
Light Dragoons, and being a smart and active fellow,
he was noticed by his superiors, and soon became a non-
commissioned officer.   His bold and dashing exploits
in several battles in the Peninsula, were rewarded with
a cornetcy in his chosen regiment.   In consequence of
his rapid promotion, a young relative of his, named
Dawson, became soldier-proud, and determined to enlist
in the same regiment.   He did so, and in a short time
embarked, with others, for the army in Spain.   The
day after his arrival at head-quarters he was attached
to his cousin's troop, and a speedy engagement was
expected.   This took place, and in the early part of
the contest a bullet from the enemy lodged itself in the
ear of the horse on which the raw soldier was mounted.

The animal, being in great pain, shook its head, and threw some of its blood on the rider, which alarmed Dawson, and caused him to rein back his horse; this being perceived by his relative, he immediately called out—"Dawson, to the front; if you flinch I will shoot you dead." He obeyed, and during the day proved himself like other Rochdale lads to be not wanting in valour. On seeing his cousin after the battle, he asked, "At what time do we start on 'em in the morning?" The reply was, "We don't work by Pilling's factory bell here." Adjutant Grindrod returned to Rochdale after the Battle of Waterloo. His constitution was entirely shattered by hard service, and he died in Whitehall-street, June 9th, 1820, aged forty-one. His remains were interred according to his request, near to the vault of the Rev. Dr. Drake, in the New Burial Ground. Military honours were paid to his memory, and the clergy, gentry, and merchants attended his funeral.

LIEUTENANT (or CAPTAIN) BUTTERWORTH.

Henry Butterworth was a younger son of Mr. Edmd. Butterworth, of Green, near Rochdale, yeoman, one of whose ancestors distinguished himself in Flanders, under the command of the Duke of Cumberland. Henry was born on the 18th March, 1783, and at an early age was sent to one of the West India Islands, as assistant superintendant of a sugar plantation there. Finding this occupation to be uncongenial, and having an ardent desire for a military life, he implored his elder brother, Edmund, who was an officer in the 3rd Lancashire Militia, to use his influence and procure him a commission. This was done, and young Butterworth was appointed ensign in the 1st Lancashire Militia, which were then embodied for permanent duty. His martial spirit being still unsatisfied, he, like young Hopwood, volunteered for foreign service, and fifty ardent Lancashire lads joined him, to take part in the glories of the battle-field. The young ensign was appointed to the 32nd Foot, and his fellow-townsmen are well acquainted with his thorough devotedness to his country. He took part in most of the battles during the sanguinary war in Spain, as his Peninsular medal of eight bars testified, viz. :—Rolera, Vimiera, Salamanca, Talavera, Pyrenees, Nivelle, Nive, and Orthes. At Salamanca he was seriously wounded, and one of the devoted men of his regiment, named Ashworth, from Smallbridge, carried the wounded hero on his back three miles, to the rear of the army; on recovering he again engaged in active service, and was present at the Battle of Waterloo, receiving a medal for that glorious victory. After the peace, in 1815, he retired from the army and returned to Rochdale, and ere long was honoured by being appointed a county magistrate and a deputy-lieutenant. He enjoyed tolerable health until the early part of 1860, when he sickened and died, on June 8th, in that year, aged seventy-seven. He was carried to his last resting place at St. John's Church, Smallbridge, by eight Waterloo veterans, whom he had named previously to his death, and to whom he had proved a generous friend.

THE OLD VOLUNTEERS.

ABOUT one hundred years ago a military spirit pervaded the minds of a number of the inhabitants of Rochdale, but there was a great reluctance to leave their cosy hearth-stones. A volunteer corps, of a fine body of men, was then in existence, and they had a band of wind instruments. There were also clubs for paying bounty to a substitute for any member who might have been balloted into the militia, and these clubs were held at the "King's Head," Lord-street, "Blue Ball," Yorkshire-street, "Roebuck," and other public-houses, and the subscription was 10s. a-year. A well-remembered incident occurred on the occasion of finding a substitute for one of those whom the destinies were anxious to drag to the battle-field. It was made known that a proxy was required, whereupon a stalwart Bagsladian put in an appearance, and upon being questioned as to the bounty he would require to fill the place of the recreant native, and defend his beloved land in his stead, replied:—"That he was sixty-three inches high, and his price was a guinea an inch." As he was the only substitute who was forthcoming, sixty-three guineas were willingly given to save his principal from the horror of meeting the foe in the deadly strife of war. The class of men of whom the Bagslate substitute was a type, were not, as a rule, actuated by patriotic feelings, "filthy lucre" being the attraction; and, in times of

15

need, they were not always at hand, and even when so, were but poor and indifferent soldiers.   Thus—

> " Raw in fields the rude militia swarms;
> Mouths without hands; maintained at vast expense,
> In peace a charge, in war, a weak defence;
> Stout once a month, they march, a blustering band,
> And ever, but in times of need, at hand."

On the 3rd of August, 1795, there was a disturbance in Rochdale respecting the high price of flour and potatoes, an old woman named Fenton, *alias* " Sparey Springer's wife," being the ringleader. The Volunteers were called out by the authorities, and, unfortunately, they misunderstood the command of the Rev. Dr. Drake " to shoot o'er 'em," and two old-men named Robert Crompton and James Fletcher, who were standing in the Old Market Place, were killed. An inquest was held upon them the following day, and the jury returned the verdict that " they were killed of necessity in defence of his majesty's subjects."   When the Rev. Dr. gave the command, it is said, a Mr. Oram, a manufacturer from Bury, came up on horseback, and fancying that the orders were to "shoot Oram," he rapidly turned his horse round and beat a precipitate retreat. The death of the two old men brought the corps into great odium, and a few years after they were disbanded. After the battle of Waterloo the invasion fever—" Suspicion all stuck full of eyes "—subsided, and the clubs at the public-houses fell into a moribund condition through the " sinews of war " being dried up, and in the course of a short time they gave up the ghost; and from that time to the present the clubs have been conspicuous by their absence—a "consummation devoutly to be wished" by really patriotic persons who had the welfare of the country at heart, for no doubt such clubs tended very much to create a craven and contemptible spirit.

24TH LANCASHIRE RIFLE VOLUNTEERS.

"DEFENCE, NOT DEFIANCE."

THIS corps was formed in 1859. The volunteer forces were organised in consequence of a rumour that England was about to be invaded by the French. The rumour was unfounded; but there was a general feeling that the island was not secure from invasion; and the existence of volunteer regiments in other countries was held by many to warrant the propriety of forming in England a force which, whilst hoping for the best, might be prepared for the worst. The loyalty of the people was readily displayed by numerous organisations in the leading towns of the kingdom; and Rochdale people took a lively view of the "situation," and became infected with what was derisively termed the "volunteer epidemic." A large meeting was held in the Public Hall, November 29th, 1859, Henry Fishwick, Esq., occupying the chair. He stated that there were fifty names of intended volunteers, and that the promoters were ready to enrol others and elect officers. The "roll" was called, and forty men were sworn in by Mr. Nield, J.P., who was present at the meeting. At the adjourned meeting on 2nd December, twenty more men were sworn in, and Mr. Joseph Fenton was appointed captain; Mr. Fishwick, lieutenant; and Mr. T. B. Philippi, ensign. A vote of thanks was given by the meeting to Lieut. Tweedale (of the militia) for his assistance in forming the corps. The Mayor, upon a requisition, convened a town's meeting in the Public

Hall, on December 7th, "to consider the propriety of establishing a publicly recognised rifle corps," and there was a numerous attendance. Dr. Molesworth moved "That this meeting cordially approves of the establishment of volunteer rifle corps;" and a letter was read from Mr. Joseph Fenton in favour of the establishment of a corps in Rochdale. A lively discussion followed, and Messrs. John Ashworth, Edward Taylor, Edmund Ashworth, and others, offered a determined opposition. An amendment was carried that the formation of the corps should be deferred; but the corps had been already formed, and Captain Fenton met the volunteers for the first time at a meeting held in the Public Hall, December 20th, 1859. It was then announced that the public subscriptions in aid of the corps amounted to £240; and up to January 14th, 1860, almost £350 had been raised. In February, 1860, the Lord Lieutenant notified that "Her Majesty had been graciously pleased to accept their services;" and the corps was numbered the 24th Lancashire. The corps was gazetted, 6th March, 1860, and on the following day Captain Fenton, Lieutenant Fishwick, and Ensign Philippi, attended the levee specially given to volunteer officers, and were presented to Her Majesty. The non-commissioned officers were appointed on the 10th March, and drilling was vigorously taken up. The corps appeared on parade, for the first time, on 17th April, and presented a very creditable appearance. There was a church parade on the following Sunday, and the volunteers attended Divine Service at St. Clement's, Spotland.

The following are the names of the several commanding officers, and dates of enrolment:—Joseph Fenton,

Esq., who had the first command of the corps (then consisting of one company), with rank of captain; enrolled in December, 1859, and resigned the following year. Henry Fishwick, Esq. (the first volunteer enrolled), subsequently took the command, and on the formation of additional companies he received a commission as major. In 1868 it was decided to increase the strength of the corps to six companies so that the commanding officer would have the rank of lieut.-col., and on the requisite increased strength being obtained, Jonathan Nield, Esq., in 1869, took command as lieut.-col. Major Fishwick resigned in October, 1869, and the following month Captain Philippi was gazetted to the vacancy. On the resignation of Lieut.-Col. Nield, in December, 1870, Captain James Fenton became commanding officer; which rank he still holds, with great credit to himself and to the corps. Mr. Nield was, in September, 1871, enrolled as honorary colonel, the other members of the honorary staff being Quarter-Master (and previously Captain) James Schofield (who has since resigned), Assistant Quarter-Master (previously Ensign) E. A. Clegg, and the honorary chaplain, the Rev. Dr. Molesworth. The following are the names and ranks of the present officers (in addition to the honorary staff):—James Fenton, lieut.-col.; T. B. Philippi, major; W. E. Richardson, surgeon; T. S. Russell, adjutant; Captains Healey, Schwabe, Colley, Brooks, Beverley, and Howard Healey; Lieutenants Molesworth and Pooley; and Sub-Lieutenant Backhouse. The corps has recently lost two of its officers, Lieutenants Mattley and Williams, their deaths occurring in July and October, respectively, in 1874.

THE YEOMANRY CAVALRY.

THE Rochdale troop of Yeomanry Cavalry was embodied in the year 1844, chiefly through the instrumentality of Albert Hudson Royds, Esq., who was appointed captain of the troop. Thomas A. Crook, Esq., was made lieutenant, and W. E. Royds, Esq., cornet. About seven years after Mr. A. H. Royds resigned, and the captaincy was then conferred on Mr. Crook; Mr. W. E. Royds being promoted to be lieutenant. After the death of Mr. Crook, Mr. W. E. Royds was elevated to the vacant office of captain, and C. Patrick, Esq., was appointed lieutenant. A few years after, owing to the resignation, on account of failing health, of Mr. W. E. Royds, the command devolved on Mr. Patrick, and he was appointed captain, which post he still occupies. C. M. Royds, Esq., is now the lieutenant, and Ernest E. M. Royds, Esq., the cornet. There are fifty men in the troop, all of whom are very soldier-like in their bearing. As usual they provide their own horses and uniform, in consideration of which they receive annually a clothing and contingent allowance of £2 a man; are exempt from the tax in respect of the horses employed on duty, and draw, during the annual training, two shillings for forage, besides a subsistence allowance of seven shillings a day. The yeomanry are available in aid of the civil powers; and in time of invasion, or apprehended invasion, the Sovereign may embody them for service in any part of Great Britain, under the provisions of the Mutiny Act. Once a year they are summoned to Lancaster for ten days, to go through a course of training. They travel the distance on horseback in two days; the first day's march is to Preston, and on the second day they arrive in Lancaster. We believe it is a fact that the troop have not been called upon to perform active duty on any occasion, but we feel certain that if the emergency should arise the men would be found thoroughly efficient, and fully competent to deal with any foe with whom they might come in contact. To have the resource of such aid, in case of need, is no doubt of much value to the public authorities.

ECCENTRIC CHARACTERS.

"Strange are the tricks of human kind;
Some queer examples here you'll find;
Laugh at their follies as you will,
The whole would quite a volume fill."

CCENTRICITY is a phase of character to be heard of and seen in other towns besides Rochdale, but the few examples that have existed here are worthy of notice for their jocularity, native wit, and amusing personal oddities. Many years ago it was the custom amongst the labouring classes to designate each other with curious, and in some instances, characteristic appellations, such as "Abey o' Pinders," "Adam o' Rappers," "George o' Jammys," "Joan o' Bucklers," "Jem o' Bradleys," "Thrump o' Dollys," "Cheetham o' Castleton," and the like. As local ideas expanded under the progressive spirit of manufacturing industry, the habit gradually sank into disuse, yet it lingers in some of the lower parts of the town, and especially in the surrounding villages, and there are many poor families whose real name is totally eclipsed by the fictitious appellation. *Apropos* of this we may mention an anecdote which we have lately met with. A stranger, in a village not far from Rochdale, was one day enquiring from " a native " for a person of whom he was in search, but whose local cognomen he did not know. He enquired for the object of his quest by the name bestòwed on him in the polite world, but no such person was known to the acute (?) native. The stranger was about to give up his search in despair, when there came up another "native" who was asked if he knew the person wanted. He at once set his wits to work and speedily settled the difficulty by informing the stranger and native No. 1, that he, the latter, was the identical individual that was being so diligently "sperred for." "Then, whoy th' dickens," said he, "doesn't he ax for me by my gradely name, and not by that as noather mysel' nor nobody else knaws me by. If he'd nobbut axed me for 'Jack o' Bills o' Ned o' Tummas's' I should ha' knawn in a crack as it wur me as he wanted. He mun ca' folk by their reet names, else he'll ne'er get on i' this world."

DONCASTER RACES AND "BULL HOLE."

Mr. William Holland, a very respectable malt and hop merchant of this town, although a shrewd trades-man, fell once a victim to the designs of an oily-tongued vendor of property. Mr. Holland was induced to inspect an old woollen mill, in Birtle, which had been offered for sale, and found the reservoir full of water, the machinery in perfect action, and the workpeople in great activity as if a splendid trade was being carried on. The vendor described all in glowing terms, putting in the shade even the descriptive language of the noted London auctioneer, Robins, and when the cunning maltster was inclined to examine the boggy land, the vendor immediately lifted his eyes heavenward and dilated on the weather and the probability of rain, but as soon as they got over a fence and into better pasture he was again wonderfully eloquent on the excellent quality of the soil, and poor Holland was induced to part with three thousand guineas for the purchase of the old mill and the land. However, when Mr. Holland became the owner, and acquainted himself with the nature of the property, he found that the water in the reservoir had vanished, the trade was insignificant, the workpeople few, and the land marshy and unproductive; in fact, to use a homely expression, he was "regularly sold." This valuable property was appropriately named "Bull Hole." The unfortunate transaction so preyed upon the purchaser, that he, to some extent, became demented, and was often heard anathematising "Bull Hole." Eventually he staked "Bull Hole" against three thousand guineas upon a race at Doncaster, and when the contest was coming off, Mr. Holland stood on a prominent position, ejaculating at the top of his voice "Bull Hole or no Bull Hole," to the great amusement of the crowd whose attention was diverted from the race to his strange antics and mysterious ejaculations, knowing that no horse running bore such an undignified name. At last, as the race was terminating, his feelings seemed to be wound up to the highest pitch, and as his favourite horse reached the winning post, he changed his expression, with great animation, to "Bull Hole, by Jove," and won his three thousand guineas, and thus the forebodings of the unprofitableness of the "Bull Hole" transaction were, fortunately, not verified, although the water supply, the trade, and the boggy earth were comparatively worthless.

A NOVEL MODE OF BORROWING MONEY IN THE OLDEN TIMES.

The following amusing story is another evidence, among many others that might be cited, that modern money lenders are not as roughly handled as some of their more ancient brethren used to be. John Stott, who was better known by the name of "Tappet," was the maker of a wheel which bore that name, and which is used by fulling millers. Having commenced the building of some houses in Yorkshire-street, he found to his great annoyance and dismay that he was short of £200 to complete them. He was greatly perplexed and almost in despair as to where he could borrow the money, and at last he sought inspiration in St. Chad's Churchyard. Having ascended with much deliberation the famous steps, he beheld, with rapture, the goodly prospect which presented itself, like a vast panorama spread before him, and pondered as to the likeliest resident in all the scene on which he gazed who would favour him with the sum of which he stood in so much need. With the eye of a hawk he scanned the various dwellings, and at length fixed his gaze keenly on the residence of Mr. Simeon Dearden, in the Orchard, and mentally fluttering over his intended victim for a time, at last determined to pounce on the golden treasure which he believed to be carefully kept in the dwelling so closely nestled by the banks of the Roach. Inspired with new-born courage, he descended from his eyrie, and proceeded to the scene of action. Knocking at the door of the manor house, Mr. Dearden opened it and exclaimed:—" Ah ! is that thee,

Táppet ?" Stott replied "aye, and I want to borrow
——" No sooner had the word "borrow" escaped
"Tappet's" lips, than the doubting money lender seized
hold of him, and attempted to bundle him out of doors,
declining to listen to any explanation. "Tappet"
struggled in resistance, for his case was desperate, and
in a determined voice declared that the lawyer should
hear his tale. Both came to the floor in the struggle,
"Tappet" being uppermost, exclaiming that he would
not strike, but he insisted on finishing his tale. The
man of parchments finding himself helpless in such a
grip, consented to listen, and was then allowed to rise.
He listened attentively to the pathetic tale of "Tappet,"
and then exclaimed :—"Tappet, if thou art as determined
to pay it back as thou art to borrow it, thou shalt have
it." A gleam of intense and lively satisfaction spread
itself over Tappet's countenance, and the promise was
given, the money exchanged hands, was duly repaid
with all costs and charges thereon, and in the course of
time Tappet died a rich man.

"JONE O' BRADSHAW."

"Revenge is sweet," saith the proverb, and so it
would appear to be judging from an incident that took
place between a lawyer and his client. Many years ago
a Rochdalian, known to fame as "Jone o' Bradshaw,"
felt much aggrieved at the way his lawyer, Mr. Simeon
Dearden, had treated him, and he was determined to
"feed fat the grudge" he bore the man of law. He
sent the bellman round the town to announce that his
health was much impaired by recent persecutions,
and that he had determined to sail down the Roach

from Rochdale to Liverpool for the benefit of his health. On the day appointed thousands of persons flocked into Rochdale to witness the departure of the intrepid sailor. It was hay time, and the lawyer was the owner of some fine meadows of grass which were ready for the scythe, and which lay along the banks of the Roach. Jone appeared at the time appointed, and embarked in a large tub, armed with a pole to use as an oar, and down the river he floated with "streamers floating in the wind," to the great delight and amusement of a vast concourse of persons who rushed through the lawyer's meadows, treading down and spoiling the grass, and along the river banks to witness the strange spectacle and the progress of the journey. When Jone got as far as Town Mill, he was satisfied with the injury he had caused to be inflicted upon the lawyer's grass, which became unfit for the scythe of the mower in consequence of the incursions of the populace on the occasion. Jone disembarked, and chuckled at the sweetness of the revenge he had tasted; but the history fails to record whether the lawyer submitted peaceably to the wrong done to him, as a Christian man should, or whether he took proceedings against the arch delinquent, according to the statute in that case made and provided.

"JOHNNY BAA-LAMB AND ST. CRISPIN."

John Lord, better known as "Johnny Baa-Lamb," was not favoured by nature with straight legs, and he was always thirsty. In fact, he never objected to consume a pint of ale while standing on his head out of his clog if it was given free, and such were the conditions. He would repeat the saying with a sigh and a relish about

Christmas, that "New yer's days keep'n comin reawn,
like old Ratcher's cream-jug, 'ut never stopt till some-
b'dy wur laid under th' table." And speaking of a
deceased "pal" he would say, "He's ta'en his reed
and geirs in lang sin."

John Mills, a follower of St. Crispin, had also a
dry throat, and his eyes used to glisten over a pot of
beer. Likenesses of these two strange mortals were
once exhibited in the window of Mr. Holden, stationer,
whose shop used to stand at the top of The Walk, but
the artist had sketched Lord holding a pint of ale in
his hand, whilst Mills was made to assume a neutral
posture. Mills was so much annoyed that he smashed
the stationer's window. Mr. Holden asked for an
explanation, when Mills called his attention to the
fact that Lord had been represented with a pint of
ale in his hand, while he, who could drink a good
"saup," was not so favoured, and he would break the
windows again if the insult was to be continued. The ·
artist introduced the desired pint pot in the sketch
to the great satisfaction of Mills, who felt himself highly
honoured. One could easily fancy these followers of
Bacchus conversing in this style when carousing over
some fine nut brown ale :—"Noan o' yor brew'd besoms
this, bo' gradely stingo. A quart o' this o' th' top ov
a beefstake 'ud mak' a chap's ribs feel do'some, would
nor it? Well, here's luck! That's what aw co' milk
o' paradise, or natyer's pap. Yo' may seawk at it till
yo're blynt, an' ne'er be satisfied." At the burial of
Dolly, Mills's wife, her sister, it was noticed, was
very much affected, and stood on one side of the grave,
—hen the newly-made widower, who stood on the other

side, enquired, "What's to do with thee, lass?" She replied, "There's nought but trouble on this side of the grave." The widower cheerfully remarked, "Come to this side, then?" Soliloquising on Dolly, he said, "Owd woman, yo desarv'n a comfitable sattlement i' th' top shop." Mills was always backward in paying his rent, and his landlord being determined to get quit of him, gave him notice to leave. Mills, with an air of astonishment, asked his landlord for an explanation. The latter replied that he never could get any rent from him, and that was the reason. Mills persuasively remarked, "Of course I do not pay you rent, but I *owe* it you."

"Johnny Baa-Lamb," who was ever on the look out for "summat to sup," entering the "White Lion Inn," Yorkshire-street, one day, was pleased to find that some acquaintance had just ordered a quart of ale, and having only a penny in his possession, and anxious to quench his thirst by a "gradely" good swig, he said to his friends, "I'll bet you a penny that I can drink one gill out of that quart of ale, and neither less nor more." The friends wishing to witness such a marvellous feat, and to test his ability as to such exact measurement, readily consented. "Johnny" swigged off the entire quart of ale with intense gusto and without winking, and then coolly remarked, "Chaps, I've lost;" thus securing a "stunning" draught for a penny, to the great amusement of the company, and the disgust of the "verdant" owners of the ale, who declared that Johnny was a "false owd boggart" who'd live to be hanged some day, if he didn't get drowned first.

OLD " DOCTOR."

An eccentric character named Taylor, but who was better known as " Old Doctor," used to gain a livelihood by the occupation of a porter, with donkeys. He used to reside in a cellar under the shop which is now kept by Mr. Standring, boot and shoe dealer, in Yorkshire-street, and the donkeys shared his dwelling with him, and were able to ascend and descend the cellar steps with alacrity. " Doctor" prided himself on his pugilistic skill and strength, and his fellow-lodgers seemed to have imbued him with their spirit. His nasal organ was highly coloured with a bluish tint, as if the temperature of it was at a freezing point, and his countenance seemed to say to a beholder, " It's some o' a cowd neet. Meh nose fair. sweats again." On the 5th day of May, in 1829, " Doctor" came to a tragical end. He led up a mob to attempt to rescue some rioters who were being taken to the New Bailey, calling out " come on lads, never mind, it's only blank shot." He had in his hands stones at the time. The military fired, and he was shot dead.

"THE REPUBLICAN TINKER."

Briggs, a tinner, in Lowergates, was supposed to be a " Jacobin," but was really a republican. He used to display in his shop window verses of his own composition which were regarded as treasonable, but he was not prosecuted as he was considered to be a lunatic.

> " For forms of government let fools contest ;
> Whate'er is best administered is best."

At times he would go through the streets with tin ware on his back, with a large white hat, bordered with green, on his head, proclaiming republican principles. On one of these occasions he met the Rev. Dr. Drake, the vicar of the parish, on the Bridge, and seizing him by the collar and his nether garment, he attempted to throw the worthy Doctor into the river, remarking, "Ducks swim and so should Drakes." Some time after, Briggs emigrated to South America. Mr. Morton, a confectioner, who used to keep a shop on South Parade, went to South America twenty-five years after, and while residing in the backwoods, information was received one evening that a man was dying from exhaustion, and he was found to be Briggs of Rochdale.

"BULL ROBIN."

" Bull Robin," whose proper name was John Cropper, although of a simple nature had the courage to enlist, and during the American War of Independence he "smelt powder" on a battle-field for the first time. As soon as the engagement began, he instinctively illustrated the first law of nature—self-preservation— very forcibly, by hurriedly taking shelter behind a tree, and calling out to his comrades, "Now, chaps, get behind the trees or somebody will be kil't or lam't." Having served the allotted period, he returned home unharmed to his native town, and enjoyed a pension. When "Robin" used to go to the "Eagle and Child" on pension days, the landlady, Mally Lee, was assiduous in her attention to his comfort, always pressing him to partake of a pint of warm ale, but when Robin's "brass" had disappeared his presence was no longer welcome, and she used to say, with indignation, "get out of the gate, Robin; thou art always in the way."

16

When "Robin" got into the "sear leaf," he was once
heard to deplore his waning vitality by repeating a
familiar Lancashire simile :—"Aw're u'st that I could
ha' swallut it iv it had bin as cowd as snowbos ; bo' mi
clock-wark's gettin' like owd Gimp's cart shaft—rayther
temporary."

"OLD BARNISH."

Old Barnish, a clock maker, who made St. Chad's
clock, was a jocular character, and went through innumerable scrapes. "He'd sit a fire cawt ony time,
tellin' his bits o' tales." Wishing to do a good turn
for a friend, who, through imprudence during his courtship, had good reason to hasten the marriage ceremony,
he called at the house of Mr. Bellis, the curate of St. Chad's
Church, about four o'clock one fine, bright morning, and
pressed him to perform the service. Mr. Bellis declined
to do so until the clock struck eight. A short time after
Barnish ascended the tower of the church, and made
the clock strike eight. The curate hearing the bell,
and being unaware of the deception, proceeded to the
vestry and went through the service, and within a short
time the reasons for the bridegroom's haste were
apparent by the merging of a husband's into a father's
cares. Barnish recommended the bridegroom to be
" as patient as Willy Wood's horse, ut died one day in
a fit of patience, waitin' for fodder." " Old Barnish,"
much against his will, having been once taken into
custody by a portly parochial constable of the olden
type, for a trivial offence, he point blank refused to
walk to the Manchester prison unless the corpulent
officer of justice allowed him to share in the allowance

usually paid for the journey. This the officer sternly
refused, and insisted on Barnish starting; but the
tempter, in the shape of a hedge in the neighbourhood
of Slattocks, incited Barnish to make an effort for freedom, and over the hedge he jumped with the vigour of
a hunter. Alarmed at the escape of his prisoner,
"Dogberry" gathered up his corpulency, after the
manner of Sir John Falstaff, and followed the fugitive
with all the agility he could muster; but the fates were
against him, and he sank on the other side up to the
hips in a treacherous bog, greatly to the amusement of
Barnish, who immediately made his way with all speed
to Bolton, and spent several days there in following his
own trade. The term of imprisonment which he was
adjudged to undergo, and from which he had escaped
having expired, Barnish presented himself at the prison
gates in Manchester, and insisted on being locked up,
saying that he came from "Rachda." The governor
declining to believe the statement that he was the man
who had escaped, refused to admit him within the
charmed domain over which he ruled supreme; whereon
Barnish, much elated at his successful escapade and
inwardly chuckling thereat, returned to his native domi-
cile, boasting of the way he had served "Dogberry,"
and "interviewed" the governor. If the eccentric
clock maker had lived in these "degenerate" days of
ours, the probability is he would not have escaped the
punishment awarded as easily as the story shows, for
immediately on his re-appearance, he would have been
pounced upon and carried off to "durance vile," with
small chance of repeating his "little game," so vigilant
are our police officials at the present day.

"CRAZY MICHAEL."

Michael Butterworth, who was distinguished by the appellation of "Crazy Michael," used to reside in his "baronial mansion," in Cheetham-street, in a cellar, and had often aimed at Parliamentary honours. During Parliamentary elections it was his practice to offer himself as a candidate, and his address bore the aristocratic signature of "Michael Adolphus Butterworth, of Cheetham-street Hall," but senatorial fortune never smiled upon him. As there was no chance of a seat in St. Stephen's, Michael next aimed at military honours. When a company of yeomanry was being formed in Rochdale, he feeling chagrined at the command not being offered to him, inaugurated a troop of doffers, whom he mounted on highly trained and carefully selected Jerusalem ponies, and he rejoiced in the title of the "Commander of the Donkey Troop." When the yeomanry went through their drill, in the Butts, Michael, with his grotesque supernumeraries, went through their burlesque military performances in front of the "Wellington," he mounted upon an ass, with his legs trailing on the ground, in the presence of a large concourse of persons. Michael was a fine, stout fellow, but he was troubled with an appetite he could never satisfy. On one occasion a gentleman, by way of a joke, sent him, as his representative, to a tenant's dinner, at Manchester. He demolished no less than a dozen plates of meat, and the waiter at last, losing all hope of being able to saisfy his cravings, called his employer, and informed him of the hopelessness of the undertaking, as "he was a man of an unbounded stomach;" and five shillings were readily given to Michael to adjourn elsewhere for the remainder of his dinner. In point of appetite it may, therefore, be concluded, that the Dragon of Wantley was a fool to Michael:—

> "He'd eat more meat than three score men ;
> He'd eat a cow ; he'd eat a calf ;
> He'd eat a bullock and a half."

But this, we fear, is mere romance, but peace to his memory ; like good, old Polonius, whom Hamlet slew, "He is now at supper, not where he eats, but where he is eaten ; a certain convocation of politic worms are e'en at him." Alas, poor Michael !

"GEORGE O'PINDERS."

George Taylor, who was styled by his "pals" "George O'Pinders," was concerned in the riot at the New Bailey, on the 5th of May, 1829, and was taken into custody, and committed to the Lancaster Assizes to undergo his trial. For the defence, evidence was brought forward in order to prove that he was not of sound mind. The judge wished to know what symptoms of insanity the prisoner had ever exhibited. A witness informed his lordship that "Pinder" had once carried a donkey from Heywood to Manchester for a wager of a gallon of ale, and he thought that was a very strong proof of insanity. "Pinders" kept up a perpetual grin during the trial, and the jury thinking that

> "Eternal smiles his emptiness betray
> As shallow streams run dimpling all the way,"

and coupling the fact with the evidence about the donkey came to the conclusion that he was *non compos mentis*, and he was acquitted.

"CRAZY DAVID."

A lazy fellow, known only by the name of "Crazy David," was not so crazy as he professed to be. He was of a corpulent figure, and often darkened the doorways of shopkeepers, to whom he was a complete nuisance. He was, moreover, remarkable for his impudent solicitations for alms—an occupation which he found to be much more agreeable than working. On one occasion being advised to go to work and earn an honest livelihood, he replied, "Well, it is summat if the town cannot keep *one* gentleman." "David," on another occasion, when going his begging rounds, called at a gentleman's residence, whose back-door step he often visited, and the servants, anxious to discourage his visits, warmed up some old stew which had not improved with the keeping. "David," after taking a few mouthfuls exclaimed, "Every man to his likin', but no moor o' yon stew for me, as Cakey Joe said when he found th' ratton bwones in his stew." He added, "Aw'st keep comin' ogeean, yo' may depend, like Clegg Ho' boggart." When living, his relations gave him the cold shoulder, but when dead their affection for him was galvanised into sudden warmth, and they surrounded him like locusts for a share of the money he had hoarded in the course of a not unsuccessful career as an unabashed and indolent mendicant.

"BAREFOOT SAM."

It was the custom in days of yore for the faithful who had fallen from duty to walk to the shrine of saints barefooted, by way of penance; the character, however, we are going to pourtray did not fall within the description given, and did not go about barefooted on that account, but more as a matter of necessity than choice, and thus the name of "Barefoot Sam" stuck to him through life as the limpet sticks to the rock. The leather covering for his pedal extremities being absent, as a matter of course, there was no necessity for stockings, so here was a three-fold saving—buying, washing, and darning—and by adopting the costume of knee-breeches, Sam curtailed expenditure in fustian as well. The feet and legs being thus kept cool, it was thought unwise to heat the other extremity of the body with a covering, therefore, the cost of a cap was saved, and his expenditure in clothing reduced to a minimum. Although exposed to wind and rain, Sam could boast of a fine figure, and of legs that even footmen envied. Sam's chief occupation was to dodge carts about the streets, and weak-kneed carters used to reward him with coppers for giving them a lift. His strength was proverbial—equal almost to Samson's—and his drinking propensities great. For a pint of ale he would lift a sack of flour off the ground with his teeth. The jaw-bone of a long-eared quadruped in the hands of the hero who spoiled the Philistines worked wonders; but this feat of Sam's, which ought to have been a jaw-breaker, surely entitled him to share the laurels. He must, indeed, have been a strong man, and might have competed in feats of strength with the "very strong man," Kwasind, the friend of "Hiawatha," whose praises are duly recorded by the poet Longfellow in imperishable verse, but we can't for the life of us be flowery about Sam.

"PAUL PRY."

"Octavius Augustus Lee,"—

"Phœbus, what a name,
To fill the sounding trump of fame!"—

was a "*leetle*" fat tomb-stone engraver of "infinite jest," and he bore his "sponsorial and patronymic appellations," as Ingoldsby says, with the greatest pride and complacency. "Octavius Augustus" was not a Roman emperor, and although following a decidedly "grave" occupation, he was of a thoroughly jovial and eccentric temperament. Besides recording the names, ages, virtues, and achievement of the "dear departed," he provided entertainment for his droughty fellow-countrymen who had not yet "shuffled off this mortal coil" at a celebrated hostelry in the classical regions of School-lane, and known by the name or sign of "Paul Pry." On his sign board he gave an invitation to all passers by in the following doggerel verse:—

"Just pop in, you won't intrude,
The beer is good, so don't be rude;
Friends to meet, he is glad to see,
Your humble servant, O. A. Lee."

If the beer which "Octavius Augustus" brewed was not a good deal better than his rhymes, we are inclined to compassionate the lieges who swallowed it, and if he did not prosper in life, it might be owing to his having combined too many occupations—stone engraver, publican, and poet! "A Jack of all trades," the adage says, "is master of none." But let us not be hard on poor "Octavius Augustus;" he has gone where neither beer, poetry, nor grave stones are required. Alas! that the paths of glory which "Octavius Augustus" trod should lead but to the grave,

"JANE CLOUGH,"

OF BAGSLATE.

Jane Clough, a coarse, masculine-looking woman, whose voice did not remind one of the music of the spheres, and who used to reside at Bagslate, gave up part of her time to the study of botany, and the cultivation of "monster gooseberries" and carnations. Jane was not by any means a counterpart of the "Jane" so highly eulogised in the delightful song so charmingly sung by Sims Reeves as "pretty" and "shy," and there was no prim gallant in those days who had the courage to invite her to meet him in the evening "when the bloom was on the rye." Nor was there any young Lochinvar in these parts sufficiently daring in love to whisk off our heroine on a milk-white charger, and bear her away to his home. Jane was in her element if only permitted to join a group of the wisemen who upheld the state at a street corner, and take part with them in discussing politics, cock-fights, and a "gradely" dog fight. As to politics, it would appear as if she had been a fore-runner of the strong-minded women of the present generation, as she took the liveliest interest in that absorbing science. She preferred the society of the masculine sex, and, as a rule, shunned that of woman kind in general. Jane was a staunch Conservative, and would always insist on heading that party's processions on great and stirring occasions, but we have not been able to find that the friends of the cause to which she allied herself ever went to the expense of dressing her on such eventful occasions in the "blue" colours which usually distinguish the Conservatives,

"MALTOOT."

Another strange character, who died early in 1873, named Shaw, *alias* "Maltoot," is worthy of notice. Shaw was a noted wrestler. He started business with a donkey and cart, as a carter, and he used to ornament his person with military attire on some days, and on others was to be seen with an old college student's cap, and garments of many colours, but his wooden leg gave a flat contradiction to his military assumption, and his red proboscis to his collegiate pretentions. Although some thought him to be weak-minded, he possessed native wit of no ordinary character. Passing the residence of a " limb of the law " one day, he was asked if he could " sup " a pint of ale. Shaw replied that he could if he had the chance. He was invited within doors, and a pint of nut-brown ale gave an impetus to his loquacity. The lawyer, proud of his possessions, showed Shaw into his library, and, amongst other pictures, drew his attention to a portrait of himself, and invited comment. Shaw, after surveying it with as much attention as a connoisseur, remarked that the attitude was not correct. The lawyer assured him that all his friends had pronounced it a remarkably good likeness, and wished to know what was the fault he had noticed. Shaw gravely remarked that the portrait represented his host with his hands in his pockets, whereas he was in the habit of having them in other people's. On one occasion, when a company of soldiers arrived in town on their way to Manchester, Maltoot dressed himse up in all the military attire he could find in his wardrobe, and strutted through the streets with the air of a commander-in-chief, with his head erect, as if he

had a stiff-neck. Some privates, who were strolling up
Drake-street, and must have been raw recruits, saluted
him with the profoundest respect, evidently thinking,
from by his gay attire and peacock appearance, that he
must be a field marshal or general who had unfortunately lost his leg in some disastrous engagement in
defence of the liberties of his beloved country. The
"general" condescended to recognise, in the usual
manner of warlike chiefs, the military honour paid to
him, and, in addition, graciously smiled upon his sub-
ordinates. Appearances are apt to mislead, and our
great dramatist has informed us that "the world is still
deceived with ornament," and so it was here, for if
these warriors had been better acquainted with Rochdale, and its celebrities, they would not have mistaken
"Maltoot" for a general or field marshal, but would
have known that he was simply a driver of asses.
Shaw had some little experience of prison life, and on
one occasion, being questioned on the internal arrangements, remarked that they were excellent, and that he
held the strong opinion that every Englishman ought
to be confined once so that he might thoroughly appreciate the admirable arrangements which were made for
the good of those who sometimes did ill. Although
this man had a rough exterior, and played the fool, he
was not destitute of better sentiments in his latter days.
"Maltoot" was loyal to the back-bone, for he was
once heard to repeat, "Don yo' knaw what we ha' opo'
th' throne o' Englan' just meet neaw? A mother an'
her childer, mon! And a gradely dacent little woman,
too, as ever bote off th' edge o' a moufin." When the
new Town Hall was opened he joined the procession in

his donkey-cart; and it is stated that in the evening he sought admission to the banquet given on the occasion, having his wood leg highly ornamented in *blue and gold*, and tied round with the gayest of blue ribbon; for he was a "true blue," and had a great contempt for Radical opinions and doings. It is right to say that the "Blues" were not, however, very proud of their odd acquisition. By the favour of a literary friend we are enabled to place before our readers *Maltoot's Epitaph* :—

> "Here lies ' Maltoot,'
> Who in pursuit
> Of business lost his leg:
> He then became
> 'An imp of fame,'
> And onward used to 'peg.'
> He carted coal, stone, cinders, dust;
> He liked cash down and not much trust.
> His leg of flesh and leg of wood
> Were active and much toil withstood,
> And now he rests where all men must,
> With earth heaped on him for a crust.
> Noisy in life, he lies quite still,
> And can no longer shout or swill;
> For pity's sake, let's drop a tear,
> And say ' Poor Mal. is buried here.' "

RUSH-BEARING.

THE annual ceremony of rush-bearing, in Rochdale, which commences on the third Sunday in August, is of great antiquity, probably as remote as the age of Pope Gregory IV. (A.D. 827). About sixty years ago its celebration was performed with much pomp and circumstance. The rush-carts were skilfully built in a conical shape, rising to a sharp ridge at the top, and on the summit was a bower in the form of a crown, made of holly, laurel, and other evergreens, round which were twined garlands of the gayest flowers. About thirty young men with white smocks, profusely adorned with gaudy ribbons, and with floral wreaths on their heads, were yoked in couples before the rush-cart. Each couple held a stave fastened to the ropes attached to the cart shafts, and at intervals the young men engaged in a sort of "morrice dance." A strong horse drew the cart, and the merry strains of music served to increase the hilarity of the occasion, whilst crowds of people collected and followed the procession as it went through the streets. The rush-carts generally came from the neighbouring villages, and fights of a desperate character used often to take place between the owners of rival rush-carts. Of late years rush-carts have not often made their appearance in Rochdale, and it would seem that the custom is dying out. In ancient times the

ceremony used to terminate at the Parish Church, and
the rushes were spread on the clay-floor under the
benches, to serve as a comfortable winter carpet, and
there they remained until the arrival of warmer weather;
but within the last forty years the "church is frequently
the last place thought of in this festival, which has
degenerated into a mere rustic saturnalia." The money
collected as the carts made their progress through the
streets was generally spent in mere drunkenness and
folly.

The rush-cart banner, or flag, was always a most conspicuous object in the public procession of the carts.
Great taste and large expense were usually bestowed on
this gorgeous and indispensable adjunct, which was
raised on stout poles, and carried by two or more men
in front of the cart. It was a point of pride with the
builders of every rush-cart to strive to outvie all com-
petitors in this particular respect; and it was generally
considered that the "Marland lads" were mostly
successful in providing and displaying the banner *par
excellence* and so frequently was this the case, that it
has become almost a proverb, when speaking highly of
anything, to say, "It's as bonny as Marland banner."
When the banners were not in active use, they often
found a resting place at the pawnbrokers, where they
remained until the rush-bearing of the following year,
when, of necessity, funds were scraped together by
great effort, and the banners left my "uncle's" custody.
No doubt the current coin of the realm was more
acceptable to that worthy individual than the grandest
banner that ever flaunted in the breeze.

THE OLD MARKET OR TOWN CROSS.

ROCHDALE, like most ancient towns, was once ornamented with a "Market or Town Cross." Crosses of this description were usually erected in some conspicuous place, either to mark boundaries, or to keep in mind certain important local occurrences, which it was considered desirable to commemorate, and the idea of the cross itself was doubtless that in the busy transactions of life it should be remembered that the Christian religion, of which the cross was the sacred symbol, was that which the people professed to love and follow. The Rochdale Cross stood on a plot of ground in front of where the extensive premises of Mr. J. H. King, ironmonger, Yorkshire-street, now stand. About one hundred years ago, Mr. Edmund Lord (grandfather of the late high bailiff of the County Court) and a number of frolicksome comrades of his, one night pulled the cross down in a joke, and the authorities of the day, who might have no love for such an ornament in that particular place, or from a notion that such memorials tended to superstition rather than usefulness, did not consider it necessary to take means for its re-erection, or to punish the persons who had meddled with it so unceremoniously. For years it disappeared from the public gaze, and slept in mother earth. When the new road was being made to Manchester, it was found embedded

underneath a foot-path near Goose Lane, and the late
Mr. Lancashire, who would no doubt regard it as a
most interesting relic of ancient days, considerately gave
it a standing place in his garden at Willow Bank.
When Mr. Lancashire left Willow Bank, he gave it
into the care of the late Mr. Samuel Lomax, of Castle-
Hill, and this memorial of antiquity is still kept in
private in Castle Hill garden, although solicitations
have been made to restore it to its natural guardians,
who wished to give it a resting place in the Public Park.
In olden times, no doubt, this cross was looked upon
with considerable respect and veneration; and it may
have been the rendezvous of lovers who have long
passed from earthly scenes, and are mouldering now
in the dust. Many tales of romantic interest are associated with these primitive crosses in various parts of
the country; and the Rochdale Cross, we have every
reason to believe, had its legend also. "Meet me at
the Cross" was no uncommon phrase in the days of our
forefathers, and to make vows at such spots was not
unusual, and gave additional solemnity and binding
obligation to the vows themselves. To injure or deface
the crosses in any way was regarded as a serious offence,
which carried with it a considerable amount of odium
and disgrace, and the depredators above referred to
would have been dealt with very severely if their offence
had been committed in earlier times.

THE ROCHDALE MARKET.

> " The place where people most do congregate
>   To buy their butchers' meat, their fish, and game;
> Where eager dealers for their patrons wait,
>   To fill their coffers being all their aim."

ABOUT sixty years ago, the market was held at the bottom of Yorkshire-street, in that part of the town which is still denominated the "Old Market Place." The vendors had to stand in the open air, exposed to all kinds of weather; and were seen muffled to the ears in winter, and scorched by the "sun's meridian ray" in summer. The presence of so large a number of hucksters, dealers, and chapmen in such an important thoroughfare, caused a most inconvenient interruption, not only to pedestrians, but also to the passage of horses, carts, and carriages, as the street at that time was, at this point, only 15 feet wide. In consequence of the royal mail-coach being interrupted on one occasion in its passage through the town, the Government made a complaint to the local authorities, who gave orders that the market business was to be removed to Cheetham-street, but it was only partially successful. This brought about the formation of a Market Company, who applied to Parliament for an Act to establish a Market Hall, on the site of the present building. The property owners on the Castleton side of the river, opposed the application, as they were in favour of the Market Hall being erected in the neighbourhood of Packer-street. Lord Stanley (the late Earl Derby) was the chairman of the committee on the passage of the Bill through Parliament, and he stated

17

that he had once passed through Rochdale, and had been detained a considerable time in consequence of Yorkshire-street being blocked up by the market stalls and carts ;-he strongly advocated a plan for widening the street, which he considered to be absolutely necessary, in order that the ordinary traffic along the street might not be impeded.   The company agreed to widen the street, as required, on receiving the promise of £500 from the inhabitants of Wardleworth, and the Act was passed in 1823. The land, 7,000 yards, and buildings thereon, cost about £23,000, and the erection of the hall and shops about £30,000. The hall was opened fifty years ago.   The original shares were £50 each, but they were necessarily increased to £90.   For twelve or fourteen years no profit was realised, but at the present time (1874) the annual dividends are about £8 a share. The shares number 360.

Before the Market Act was obtained, the then lord of the manor, Lord Byron, the poet, received the market tolls through his agent, Mr. Kershaw, solicitor, and the Market Company had to purchase these manorial rights. Joseph Brierley, Esq., J.P., is the present chairman of the Company, and Mr. Charles Collier is the superintendent.   The Corporation has obtained Parliamentary powers to purchase the Market Hall, and the property connected with it; but it does not at present appear how soon the contemplated purchase can be carried into effect.   No doubt it is important that the Corporation should acquire the Market property in the same manner that it has possessed itself of the Water Works and the Gas Works, which were formerly in the hands of private shareholders.

THE INFIRMARY.

"'Tis not enough that we with sorrow sigh,
That we the wants of pleading man supply;
That we in sympathy with sufferers feel,
Nor hear a grief without a wish to heal:
Not these suffice—to sickness, pain, and woe,
The Christian spirit loves with aid to go,
Will not be sought, waits not for man to plead,
But seeks the duty—nay, prevents the need;
Her utmost aid to every ill applies,
And plans relief for coming miseries.
Here all have kindness, most relief, for some
Is cure complete—it is the sufferer's home;
Fevers and chronic ills, corroding pains,
Each accidental mischief man sustains,
Have here attention—here the sufferers lie,
(Where love and science every aid apply),
And healed, with rapture live; or, soothed by comfort, die."

THIS benevolent institution claims, and is entitled to, the warmest sympathy and support alike of the opulent and the working classes in our midst, its aim being to help and succour the afflicted poor in the time of their greatest need. Its primary or more important object is to mitigate bodily suffering, arising either from disease or accidental causes, in which respect it is indispensable to all who are not able to pay for private medical or surgical aid, or as a necessary means of assistance in cases of emergency. For such purposes the institution is absolutely essential to the well-being of the dense community which exists in Rochdale. By its prompt and humane action it interposes to stem diseases which, if unchecked in their outbreak, would spare neither rich

nor poor, for disease, like death, is most indiscriminate
in its operations, and is no respecter of persons. In
October, 1831, the late Clement Royds, Esq., and other
worthy gentlemen, amongst whom were Messrs. John
Entwisle, John Howard, junior, J. Roby, William
Littlewood, O. H. Redfern, Thomas Booth, James
Midgley, and the Revs. W. R. Hay, W. H. Twemlow,
W. J. ffarington, J. Ely, and F. Haworth, founded this
system of charitable treatment, at a meeting held at the
Wellington Hotel; and the "Dispensary" was situate
in South Parade, in the premises now occupied by Mr.
Jackson, solicitor. The building subsequently proving
to be inconvenient, more suitable accommodation was
provided near the end of Lord-street, facing Manchester-
road, and there, from 1831-2 to 1871, the work of the
charity was carried on. Up to this time a medical
officer resided on the premises, and it was his duty to
visit poor patients, who were recommended by the subscribers, at their homes, and supply them with medicines
free of cost, but there was no provision made for indoor
patients. In 1871 the committee found that it was
absolutely necessary to remove into larger premises,
and make provision for indoor patients, and the present
building in Yorkshire-street, corner of Elliott-street,
was rented, and received the name of "The Infirmary."
There are two wards in it, one for the females, and the
other for the males. There are four beds in each ward,
and on some occasions patients have had to wait for an
empty bed, the number of applicants being so numerous. The committee now complain of the unsuitable-
ness of the building, owing to its limited size, deficient
drainage, and its close proximity to the street, and

propose to erect a new and more commodious Infirmary, to be devoted entirely to surgical purposes. The cost is estimated at £10,000, which it is intended to raise by canvassing the inhabitants, and opening subscription lists at the various banks, to be supplemented by a bazaar, intended to be held in 1875, and for which much preparation is being made at the time we write. After the death of the Rev. W. R. Hay, the Rev. Dr. Molesworth was appointed president, and he has held the office ever since with credit. The late George Howorth, of the Savings' Bank, was the first secretary; Joseph Wood, Esq., banker, next occupied this post; and Mr. Peter Lee, grocer, Yorkshire-street, filled the office of hon. secretary from 1866 to 1872, at which date he was succeeded by Mr. Councillor Ernest E. M. Royds, who, like his predecessor in office, is most zealous in the noble cause of providing for the sick and needy. The other officers who are carrying on this good work at present are, G. T. Kemp, Esq., J.P., vice-president; Albert Hudson Royds, Esq., J.P., treasurer. Committee:—Messrs. John Ashworth, C. M. Royds, Wm. Shaw, Colonel Fishwick, George Mansell, Ralph Robinson, Thomas Schofield, Peter Lee, W. Woolley, R. S. Rowan, E. A. N. Royds, Joseph Handley. Medical Officers:—Dr. March, Mr. Richardson, Mr. Bland, Mr. Charles Ogden. Resident Medical Officer:—Mr. Wm. M. Turner. We sincerely hope that the response of the public to the urgent appeal of the committee for funds, for the new erection, will be of the most liberal character; and that we shall soon have the happiness of seeing such a building provided as will meet the necessities of this great parish of Rochdale.

PACK-HORSES, THE WAGGON, STAGE COACH, AND RAILWAY.

THE Rochdalians, in primitive days, laboured under many disadvantages in their rather uncouth system of travelling, as well as in the conveyance of goods. If an inhabitant had to travel a considerable distance, and was not the owner of a horse, he had either to resort to "shank's-pony," or mount one of a string of "gals," which were often in a poor and half-starved condition. They were generally led by one or two old stage horses accustomed to the road, and seldom attended by more than one driver. They travelled at the slow pace of about two miles an hour in a long, straggling, and broken string, and browsed on the fells, moorlands, and lane sides. The leading horse carried a bell or pair of bells suspended to his head gear, and the tinkling of these bells guided the "gals" in the dark, or in the turnings of narrow lanes, and warned passengers of their approach. They were occasionally seen quenching their thirst in the midst of a mountain stream in the heat of a sultry noon, and taking a temporary shelter under the branches of wide-spreading trees; and in winter facing the driving rain and wind, the biting frosts, and the puzzling mists, over hills and mountains. On these long journeys they were seldom met by any pedestrians except rustics, who resided in the immediate neighbourhood, such as a shepherd farmer, a rude quarryman, or collier, cattle jobber, or the vagabond on tramp with his starving wife and children, eagerly

devouring crusts of bread which charity had afforded
them. The transit of goods and the conveyance of
passengers by pack-horses, are remembered by some of
the oldest inhabitants of Rochdale; and it is well known
that hand-loom weavers were often under the necesssity
of carrying their pieces to Manchester on their backs,
and amongst the number, the late Mr. Holt, of Chamber
House, who, when a young man, experienced such
days of real hard labour, but by his industry he amassed
a large fortune, and, in advanced life, was often seen
riding through the town with the air of a fine old
English gentleman. It was a custom in the surrounding
country, especially in the neighbourhood of Saddleworth,
for those on matrimonial pleasures bent to be married
at the Rochdale Parish Church. As many as twenty
or thirty couples, on horseback, used to accompany the
bridegroom. The "happy pair" headed the procession,
the lady sitting on a cushion behind her lover on the
best horse that could be obtained for the occasion.
These "wedding marches" always created a large
amount of interest, and met with pleasant recognition
and hearty congratulation as they passed along the road
to the church where the twain were to be made one flesh.
From the fact of these swains seeking matrimony, it
would appear they must have discovered that it was
"not good for man to be alone." Solitude is all very
well in its way, but some of these dwellers in remote
regions would appear to have shared the opinion of the
poet who expressed his experience of a solitary life after
this fashion :—

> "How sweet, how passing sweet, is solitude !
> But grant me still a friend in my retreat,
> Whom I may whisper solitude is sweet."

THE WAGGONS.

With the improvements of the roads, waggons made their appearance about the year 1775, and were used as public conveyances between distant places, but they travelled at a miserably slow pace, and their passengers, in addition to being thus carried, received a good shaking free of any extra charge. A few post-chaises were provided for the use of the upper class. Some of the wholesale houses in Rochdale employed farmers' carts to carry goods from the Calder over Blackstone Edge that came from London *via* Hull. Travelling by the old lumbering waggons was by no means pleasant, as they were not provided with springs, and "Jolt, jolt, all the way, served to make more sad the day."

THE STAGE COACH.

" Long time elapsed or e'er our rugged sires
Complained, though incommodiously pent in,
And ill at ease behind. * * * *
Ingenious fancy, never better pleased
Than when employed to accommodate the fair,"

devised the stage-coach, about ninety years ago, which superseded the jolting waggon, and it was certainly a great improvement upon the previous modes of travelling. The coaches used to start from the Butts to Manchester twice a-week, and at first the mail-coach was the only one that travelled into Yorkshire. It was named the "High Flyer," driven by Robin Grey in 1790, but very soon private enterprise also entered upon that route, and two coaches ran from Rochdale to Leeds over Blackstone Edge. It may appear somewhat marvellous, in the eyes of this generation, that the meagre communication between the West Riding and Lancashire should have given rise at times to a fierce competition. The most famous of the opposition coaches was the "Duke of Leeds," which was brought out against the "Defiance." For the first weeks of its running it exhibited a brush to signify that it would sweep the "Defiance" off the road. The route of the day mail was over Blackstone Edge, and the night mail through the vale of Todmorden. Rochdale became the dividing station to Yorkshire, and the coaches increased to six, and four local coaches to Manchester. The fare to Manchester was 1s. 6d. outside and 2s. 6d. in; but the charge of the mail-coach was 4s. inside and 2s. out. Next a coach named the "Neptune" travelled from Rochdale to Liverpool, through Bolton and Wigan, and before the railway was established it was found necessary to add another. It was customary for intending travellers to book a week before the appointed day, if they wished to secure seats to Yorkshire, and two days before their journey to Manchester.

THE RAILWAY.

The giant power of steam being at length discovered, it was soon employed to "drive the rapid car." In 1837 a company was formed to make a railway between Leeds and Manchester, which is now known as the "Lancashire and Yorkshire Railway." At that period railways were regarded as a nuisance if the lines ran through towns, and this feeling was so strong that not only public authorities but private individuals opposed the making of railways in close proximity to towns. At one time a line was surveyed, and it was intended that it should run on the south side of Rochdale and go through Lowerplace, that being the nearest point to the town, but the owners of property in that neighbourhood sternly opposed the scheme. A little light kept gleaming into the minds of the projectors and the public, and at last it was thought desirable that the railway should run as close to the town as possible, and the present line was made. The building off Milnrow-road which has a horse-shoe shaped yard before it, and close under part of the present station, on the left hand side, was the first railway station erected in Rochdale. Additions were made to it piece-meal until it has assumed a fair length, but it is by no means a convenient or handsome structure. The line was opened in 1838 as far as Littleborough, and the carriages consisted of first, second, and third classes, but the latter were not provided with seats, and were called "stand-ups" on account of the occupants being compelled to stand. The fares were fixed after the standard of the Yorkshire coaches, namely, 4s. first class to Manchester, 2s. 6d. second class, and 1s. 6d. third class. The public resisted these charges, as some other coaches which travelled between Rochdale and Manchester ran at lower rates, and for some time the local coaches ran in opposition to the railway. All classes opposed the high rates and determined to travel only by the "stand-ups," and to the honour of the rich they and the poor flocked together in these trucks only suitable for cattle, for the sole purpose of lowering the fares. At last Parliament interfered with all the railways, and compelled the companies to provide covered carriages with seats, and the third class at a fixed rate. It may be interesting to state that the number of passengers in the month of May, 1840, was 12,063, the total receipts amounting to £554 11s. For parcels, &c., the amount paid did not exceed £41 19s. 7d. The passengers in the month of May, 1874, numbered 92,390, and the receipts were £4,377 12s. 1d. Now no less than 186 trains pass through the Rochdale station in a day. A new line has been opened to Oldham, and is a a great convenience to the inhabitants of Milnrow, Newhey, and Shaw. In 1867 a single line was opened to Facit, and not before it was much needed. At the present time there are great complaints that this line does not extend to Bacup and Burnley, and there is an agitation for a new line from Colne, through Burnley, Bacup, and Rochdale, to Manchester. Mr. Cross is the station master at Rochdale, Mr. C. Marsh and Mr. John Wrigley, inspectors; Mr. David Buff, main line inspector; Mr. Busby, goods agent, and Mr. Joseph Wild, goods inspector.

THE CANAL.

CENTURY and a half ago merchandise had to be conveyed over Blackstone Edge and other approaches to the town by gangs of pack-horses, and at that time it was difficult for carriages to travel by the road over the hill into Yorkshire. In 1765 a worthy magistrate, of Belfield, Mr. Richard Townley, was impressed with the great disadvantages which the merchants and manufacturers of Rochdale laboured under, through being compelled to use land-carriage, and he employed an engineer of fame, Mr. Brindley, who was in the service of the Duke of Bridgewater, together with his steward, Mr. Whitaker, to survey and make a plan of the best line of canal to Rochdale. After many years of agitation, an Act of Parliament was passed on the 4th of April, 1794, empowering the making of a canal, and on the 21st of December, 1804, it was opened with a pleasing ceremony. Two elegant yachts, containing the committee of the Canal Company, and other proprietors, proceeded by ice boats from Rochdale to Manchester, a distance of upwards of twelve miles. At Failsworth, about four miles from Manchester, a band of music belonging to the first battalion of the Manchester and Salford Independent Volunteers, entered the leading yacht, and played popular airs. On approaching Manchester the banks of the canal were

lined on both sides with many thousand people, and the
roofs of factories, houses, balconies, and all the elevated
situations were crowded, and the church bells rang out
merry peals, and the multitude welcomed the approach
with reiterated cheers. This canal commences in the
Calder Navigation at Sowerby Bridge Wharf, and runs
westward up the vale of Calder, close to that river and
turnpike road, passing in its course Mytholmroyd,
Hebden Bridge, and Todmorden; and bending south-
wards, it proceeds past Gauxholme to the Summit, the
ascent having been from the feeders of the Humber,
and the descent is now to the Mersey level, passing
Littleborough, to what is locally known as "Lock
Bridge," whence a branch to the Central Basin,
Vicar's Moss, Rochdale, between Oldham-road and
Drake-street. Here the extensive warehousing and
canal yard of the company are situate. The main line
still pursuing a southerly direction, passes Bluepits, a
short distance from which place there is a branch to
Heywood, the canal continuing its course to Failsworth,
whence it bends a little westward of south, passing
Newton, Ancoats, to the Duke of Bridgewater's Canal,
into which it locks at Castlefield, Manchester. Ashton-
under-Lyne, and Oldham Canal, can be joined at the
Piccadilly Wharf. According to the levels taken by
Mr. Rennie, the engineer of this work, the rise from
Sowerby to where he proposed the Summit level to
commence, near Travis Mill, is 275 feet in a distance of
about eleven miles and a quarter, and the fall from the
Summit to the Duke of Bridgewater's Canal is 438½ feet.
The level of the Rochdale Canal Basin is 400 feet. This
canal is one of the main links in the chain of inland

navigation between the east and west seas, being made for vessels of such a size as enables them to navigate in the tideway, and to pass between Liverpool and Hull without the expense of re-shipping their cargoes, thus affording great advantages to the populous towns of Manchester, Rochdale, Halifax, Wakefield, and others, on the banks of the intermediate rivers. The canal cost about £471,950. W. Fenton, Esq., J.P., of Beaumonds, was the chairman for a great number of years, and C. M. Royds, Esq., is the present chairman; and we find the names of J. Butterworth, Esq., J.P.; James Brierley, Esq., J.P.; J. Nield, Esq., J.P.; Henry Newall, Esq., J.P.; E. A. N. Royds, Esq., J.P.; William Fenton, jun., Esq.; Joseph Fenton, Esq., J.P.; and other Rochdale gentlemen on the board of directors.

THE RIVER ROACH AND ITS TRIBUTARIES.

MANY of the present inhabitants of Rochdale remember that this now polluted river, not thirty years ago, flowed through the town in a state of comparative purity, and "above the golden gravel" they have seen—

> "Here and there a lusty trout,
> And here and there a grayling."

The minnow, the loach, and the eel were caught as late as the year 1835, and, no doubt, the eel much later; but the nauseous matter now poured into the river from manufactories and sewers has made it a nuisance. It is true that in the year 1869 the Royal Commissioners enquired into the cause of the pollution of rivers, and held a solemn investigation as to the state of the Roach, and hopes were entertained of a speedy remedy; and if their report had been adopted, and the means recommended carried out, the nuisance would have been abated, but it still exists. The Roach rises on the north-westerly side of Blackstone Edge in 50 degrees, 40 minutes, 25 seconds north latitude, and 2 degrees, 3 minutes, 7 seconds west longitude; and as it proceeds receives the Castle Clough Brook, the Town House Brook, near Town House; the Featherstall Brook, near Stubley Hall; the Ash Brook, near to Holme Mill; the river Beal, at Belfield; and at a

place familiarly known as the "Meetings," the Heybrook; thence it flows in a serpentine manner through
the centre of Rochdale. At the Holme, near to Mitchell
Hey Mills, the Spodden enters the Roach. This tributary rises near High House, in the township of Spotland,
and passes through Shawforth, Tongend, Hall Fold,
and Healey, dividing the hamlets of Catley Lane and
Falinge. The valley of the Spodden has been, and at
some points still is, most picturesque; and near to
Healey Hall, the residence of Robert Tweedale, Esq.,
the scenery is very beautiful. The "Thrutch," a
narrow gorge, is an interesting feature, and was still
more so before the great flood of July 4th, 1838, which
destroyed what was known as the "Fairy Chapel," a
cavern in the rock, which had a pulpit, reading desk,
and seats, formed out of the rock by the action of the
water. This flood rose to the height of 15 feet at Spotland Bridge, which it washed away, as well as other
bridges. The fall of rain and ice was chiefly on Rooley
Moor, where, on the following day, pieces were found
weighing as much as twelve ounces. The storm was
one of the most violent ever known in this neighbourhood, and its ravages were excessive in the Spodden
valley, the works at Broadley, Healey Hall, Foot Mill,
and Mr. John Whitaker's dye works, at Spotland
Bridge, being almost demolished. The hail storm
passed over the southerly side of Rochdale, breaking
all the skylights of the houses, and windows in its course,
and also some weaving sheds, and particularly at Mr.
King's factory, at Moss Mill, where it was popularly
said to have broken 1,000 panes. At Gibson Row the
cradles containing the children were swimming about in

the houses. At the top of Toad Lane, at Water House, the residence of a Mr. Henry, the flood was so sudden that the clothes which were drying before the fire were . washed out of the house. In the Old Market Place the water was one yard deep in five minutes, but the Roach was scarcely affected by the rainfall. Referring to the Spodden, Drayton writes :—

" First Roach, a dainty rill, from Rochdale, her dear dame,
  Who, honoured with the half of her stern mother's name,
  Grew proud, yet glad herself into my banks to get,
  Which Spodden from her springs, a pretty rivulet,
  As her attendant brings."

The Red Brook, which flows through Coptrod Estate, the residence of Mr. Mellor, is the next tributary on the north, and on the south the Sudden Brook is the last tributary of the Roach, within the boundary of the borough. About a mile and three-quarters further down, at Hooley Clough, the Naden water enters the Roach whence it flows along to Bury, and discharges itself into the Irwell, at Radcliffe, having had a flow in a direct line of thirteen miles, and in its meandering a flow of eighteen miles. The Roach is characteristically little more than a mountain stream, and were it not for the reservoirs at its sources would be frequently nearly dry; but Parliament has granted powers to the Rochdale Canal Company, the Rochdale Water Works Company, and the Oldham Corporation to impound its waters. Parliament has required that a given quantity of water be sent down the stream in the twelve working hours. The river is subject to sudden floods; the highest in the Roach being in 1798, and known as the "Rushbearing Flood," when it rose to the

18

height of 10 feet 8 inches above its usual level; another great flood was that known as the Holmfirth Flood; and another, in 1866, when the height was 7 feet 2 inches. The river now receives some attention from the Health Committee of the Corporation, and we may hope that in another edition of this work we may have to record that it has ceased to be a sewage and has become a trout stream.

THE RAINFALL.

The proximity of the town to the range of hills known as the Back-bone of England, which divides Lancashire from Yorkshire, and to the hills bordering on the Forest of Rossendale, makes the drainage to be rapid, and this is compensated by a very large rainfall. Unfortunately there is not an official observatory, and we are, therefore, not able to give a statement on official authority; but, it so happens, there have been private observers, and from this source we learn that for the last eleven years the rainfall has averaged $38\frac{1}{2}$ inches, which has fallen in 191 days. For nine years of this period the statement is as follows:—

Year.	Rain in inches.	Wet Days.
1866	47·2	190
1867	41·0	222
1868	33·6	198
1869	44·0	206
1870	35·3	165
1871	30·0	197
1872	45·1	254
1873	32·4	215
1874	38.4	206

These figures are reduced from the publication of Mr.
T. H. Hayle's observations in the *Rochdale Observer*.
Notes of the weather had been taken some thirty years ago
by Mr. John Ecroyd, and from a lecture, published in
1848, on the sanitary condition of Rochdale, by Mr.
Edward Taylor, we learn that the rainfall in 1847 was
44 inches, the wet days 136 ; and, in 1848, 58 inches,
the wet days 159. In the two years the highest state
of the thermometer was 82, and the lowest 12 in 1846-7 ;
and the highest 81 and lowest 12 in 1847-8, the average
highest being 62, and lowest 27 in 1846-7 ; and in
1847-8, 65 and 30, so that the mean difference was 35
for both years, which showed favourably for the climate
of Rochdale, for in a comparison with London and
Durham the mean difference is 1½ degrees in favour of
Rochdale. The rainfall on the surrounding hills is
said to average 42 inches.

HEALTH OF THE TOWN.

We are aware how fallacious a statement may be
as to the salubrity or healthiness of a locality, and how
inclined all natives are to exalt their own neighbourhood. To prevent such a fallacy and leaning, we give
the Registrar General's returns for the last year ending
September 30th, 1874 :—Rochdale, 23·7 ; Stockport, 30·9 ;
Wigan, 35·8 ; Bolton, 26·5 ; Bury, 22·6 ; Ashton, 30·6 ;
Blackburn, 31·6 ; Preston, 38·4 ; Oldham, 27·6 ; Salford, 28·5 ; and we also give the death rate of Rochdale
for the last ten years, which will be found to compare
well with other towns :—1865, 24·93 ; 1866, 30·04 ;
1867, 22·96 ; 1868, 24·59 ; 1869, 29·48 ; 1870, 26·49 ;
1871, 23·76 ; 1872, 24·87 ; 1873, 21·11 ; 1874, 20·83.

EQUITABLE PIONEERS' SOCIETY, LIMITED.

" For we doubt not through the ages one increasing
purpose runs,
And the thoughts of men are widen'd with the process
of the suns."

THIS society was established in 1844 by a few
poor working men. The immediate cause of
its formation was the unsatisfactory result of
a strike of the woollen weavers, in consequence
of some dispute between them and their
employers. A more remote cause was that some of
the men, who were leaders, had imbibed certain notions
respecting co-operative effort which led them to hope
for happier days for themselves and families if these
notions could assume practical shape. Efforts of co-
operative trading had been attempted years before, but
the idea of equality had been too prominent. Every
member had equal shares and equal profit, and no
premium of any kind was offered to members for
bringing in business or capital. The result was that
the shares were in most cases purchased by enterprising
members, and the business continued for their individual
benefit. These early pioneers considered that by carrying out a principle of equity, as opposed to equality,
success would be more likely to be attained; and they

agreed that the net profits, after paying expenses, and interest on capital, at £5 per cent. per annum, should be divided amongst the members in proportion to the purchases each had made during the period in which the profit arose. They also carried out another idea which has materially helped to secure success. Knowing that the bulk of the labouring population were weighed down by debt in consequence of the great facility offered by the credit system, it was resolved that all business should be transacted for ready money only. Their plans being matured, the promoters took the shop in Toad Lane, which is now occupied by the tailoring department, and let off a portion. Having secured twenty-eight members, who had managed to subscribe amongst them as many pounds, they commenced business in the grocery and provision line, on December 21st, 1844, the shop, at first, being open in the evening only. The members were their own shopmen, each assisting as he could until constant hands were rendered necessary, and the shop kept open daily. In this manner was planted the little seed of co-operation which has become such a mighty tree. The members and business of the society increased, more premises were required, and butchering, drapery, and tailoring were added, until, in 1856, it was found necessary to open a branch in Oldham-road. A second was provided by purchasing the business of another society in School-lane. Whitworth-road and Pinfold branches rapidly followed, and, at intervals, others have been added in and near the town, till the number now amounts to fifteen. The best idea of the society's progress can be obtained by a perusal of the table published

in the society's almanack for each year.   The last table
we reprint :—

Year.	Members.	Funds.	Business.	Profits.
		£	£	£
1844	28	28		
1845	74	181	710	22
1846	86	252	1146	80
1847	110	286	1924	72
1848	149	397	2276	117
1849	390	1193	6611	561
1850	600	2289	13179	880
1851	630	2785	17633	990
1852	680	3471	16352	1206
1853	720	5848	22700	1674
1854	900	7172	33364	1763
1855	1400	11032	44902	3109
1856	1600	12920	63197	3921
1857	1850	15142	76789	5470
1858	1950	18160	74680	6284
1859	2703	27060	104012	10739
1860	3450	37710	152063	15906
1861	3900	42925	176206	18020
1862	3501	38465	141074	17564
1863	4013	49361	158632	19671
1864	4747	62105	174937	22717
1865	5326	78778	196234	25156
1866	6246	99989	249122	31931
1867	6823	128435	284910	41619
1868	6731	123233	290900	37459
1869	5809	93423	236438	28542
1870	5560	80291	223021	25209
1871	6021	107500	246522	29026
1872	6444	132912	267577	33640
1873	7021	160886	287212	38749
1874	7639	192814	298888	40679

Our notice would be incomplete if the great and
successful educational efforts of the society were not
mentioned.   Very early in its history a fortieth part of
the profits was applied in providing a news-room and
library for members and their families.   The fund is

managed by a separate committee. Notwithstanding that for many years the educational department was really illegal, it was continued until sanctioned by law, and it has now assumed somewhat colossal dimensions. The money spent on news-rooms (of which there are thirteen branches), libraries, lectures, classes, and other educational agencies, has, for many years past, amounted to upwards of £1,000 per annum. The society has seldom placed itself in antagonism to other tradesmen. It has won its way slowly but surely until it has become of world-wide celebrity, and it cannot be doubted but that its success has inaugurated a new era for the labouring classes of this and other countries. The anticipations of its founders are not all realised, but the hitherto attained success has no parallel in the history of industrial effort. Its capital is now nearly £200,000. It is dividing interest and profit at the rate of £40,000 per annum, and gives encouragement and assistance to the social, economical, and educational improvement of its members, and affords a model for hundreds of similar societies throughout the civilized world.

The educational department has 10,504 volumes in the circulating and reference libraries; 9,807 are in the lending library, and have an annual circulation of 30,000. There is, in connection with the library, an excepted class which contains local newspapers and literature, and rare and valuable works, such as "Simpson's War in the East," "Hogarth's Works," "Whitaker's History of Whalley," "The Herbarium" of the late James Molineux, of Rochdale; a complete copy of the *Rochdale Recorder*,

1827-8; *Rochdale Standard*, complete, 1856-7 ; *Rochdale Observer*, complete, except four numbers; *Rochdale Times*, complete, etc. These works are not allowed to circulate, but can be consulted at the library.

The central premises, in Toad-lane, at the corner of St. Mary's Gate, are imposing and handsome in appearance, and substantial in structure. They can be prominently seen from most parts of the town, and consist of three shops upon the ground floor, with store rooms beneath. The second storey is fitted up as a show room for drapery, a store room for grocery, and with commodious offices. The third storey contains the library, which has an area of 150 square yards ; a well-lighted news room (area 150 square yards); and two committee rooms. The fourth storey is used for meetings and lectures, and is capable of seating 1,500 persons. Mr. Councillor James Cheetham was the architect of this fine edifice, which reflects credit upon him, and it is a very important addition to the useful and ornamental buildings of the town, and one of which the inhabitants may well feel proud.

> See what results from smallest actions flow;
> See how united efforts daily grow;
> See how the seed has multiplied and spread
> Unnumbered blessings on the poor man's head.
> Union is strength, and they who once were small
> Have grown like giants and are stout and tall!
> Then honour those by whom these things were planned,
> Whose genius spread itself from land to land.
> They saw with eye, keen as the eagle's glance,
> How constant effort would man's good enhance;
> Nor gave up hope though things were sometimes dark,
> And though the fire gave sometimes but a spark.
> Hope on ! their motto was ; the day must dawn,

They knew, when man to man would close be drawn.
Each hour beheld the prospect grow more bright,
And hearts once sad were filled with new delight;
For, from on high, a blessing seemed to fall
On those held long by care and want in thrall.
How kind, beneficent, and wise has been
The work thus done, and how sublime the scene
Which now appears before the astonished eye,
Proof of how much results from industry !
Material blessings crowd on every hand,
And inward blessings which all understand.
Still may the work go on till o'er the world
Co-operation's banner stands unfurled ;
And till mankind may everywhere behold
A sight more grand than vast upheaped gold.
The work must spread—time can but help it on,
But let us not forget the friends who're gone;
Theirs was the scheme—the vast design was theirs ;
They knew the toil, and they long felt its cares ;
They saw the triumph, and they sank to rest
Well pleased, and why? they knew that men were blest !

THE THEATRES.

"The players . . . . . . they are the abstract and brief
chronicle of the time: after your death you were better have a
bad epitaph than their ill report while you live."

THE inhabitants of Rochdale were accustomed to
be entertained with theatrical performances as
early as the year 1766, and they seem to have
thoroughly appreciated them. No doubt these
performances had an educating and beneficial
effect upon the people, as well as being a means of
recreation and amusement. "The drama," Bacon declares, "is as history brought before the eyes. It
presents the images of things as if they were present,
while history treats of them as things past." At the
same time, theatrical performances may have a perni-
cious effect by a misapplication of the moral. As history
brings before our mind's eye characters of various
kinds, so, also, does the drama; and if individuals
among the audiences at theatres prefer to imitate the
vices rather than the virtues of the *dramatis personæ*,
the actor is no more to be blamed than is the graphic
historian or the brilliant novelist; and to be consistent
in the indiscriminate condemnation of theatrical performances, it becomes almost necessary that the reading
of history, and of the works of Shakespeare, Dickens,
Thackeray, and other writers of the same class should

also be condemned and forbidden; for, in the works of these eminent authors, we find not only examples of virtue and goodness, but also of vice and moral deformity in their most hateful form. Misery and vice abound in the world, and the works of the dramatist and the novelist do but put these things before the spectator and the reader in a vivid shape, not from any wrong or improper motive, but to illustrate human life and conduct, as well as to "point a moral and adorn a tale." But while we make these remarks on theatrical representations in general, it is to be understood that we rigidly condemn and view with the utmost abhorrence everything of a lewd, indecent, or improper character, for we consider that the true end of the drama is "to hold as 'twere the mirror up to nature, to show virtue her own feature, scorn her own image, and the very age and body of the time his form and pressure." Any gross pandering to the evil passions of the people cannot be too strongly deprecated, and he is an enemy to his species who seeks by the aid of the theatre to disseminate and portray sentiments and characters which tend to vitiate, or warp the moral sense of the people. It is then that the theatre becomes a plague-spot, and a hideous pest-house.

After the Wesleyans gave up the warehouse at Waterside, near the river, on which site a part of the Town Hall now stands, which was used as a preaching room in 1760, it was leased as a theatre. This place would accommodate about 600 people. A Mr. Howard was the lessee for a number of years, and the performances were largely attended, not only by the inhabitants, but also by persons residing in the country for

miles round. After the Wesleyan body left their
chapel in Toad Lane, which stood on the present site
of the central stores, the society established by the late
Countess of Huntingdon occupied it about the year 1790,
for a short time, and then it became a theatre. The
first lessee was Mr. Howard, next Mr. Corbett Cook, then
Mr. Edmund Falconer, and Mr. James Rodgers, the
present owner and manager of the Prince of Wales
at Birmingham, was the lessee for five seasons. Most
of the "star" actors of those days played at these two
theatres, and amongst them the Kembles, Young,
Liston, Miss Foote, Miss Farren (who afterwards became
the Countess of Derby, and was grandmother of the
present Earl of Derby), Grimaldi, Mrs. Jordan, G. V.
Brooke, Barry Sullivan, Vandenhoff and his daughter
and son Henry, W. Ellerton, Rickards, John Sloane,
Mrs. Weston, and George Preston. As many as twenty
carriages have been seen in Toad Lane waiting to
convey the gentry home from the theatre after the
performances. Those were the palmy days of the
drama in Rochdale, and old play goers used to refer with
great pride to those times and to the fact that the above-
named celebrities had "fretted" their hour on the stage
in Rochdale. George Vandenhoff, in his "Dramatic
Reminiscences," relates an amusing practical joke
which was once played upon a tragedian by a comedian
in the Rochdale theatre in Toad Lane. Dick Hoskins,
was the low comedian referred to, and "when he came in
contact with a tragedian for whose talents he entertained
a contempt, or whose person or manners displeased
him, woe to the unhappy subject of his fun! All his
tragedy was turned into farce, when Dick was in the

humorous vein. Thus, he played the Grave-digger, one night at the Rochdale Theatre, to the Hamlet of a Mr. C——, a most solemn and mysterious tragedian of the cloak-and-dagger school. This gentleman's tragedy was in Dick's eyes much more intensely comic than his own broadest strokes of farce; accordingly, Dick held no terms with it, and showed the unfortunate object of his merriment no quarter on the stage. When, therefore, Hamlet approached the grave to hold his dialogue with Dick in it, the latter began his antics, and extemporised all sorts of absurd interpolations in the text—which he spoke in his own broad Lancashire dialect. There was not a great house, and Dick allowed himself full license. Mr. C—— scowled fearfully; but Dick was unabashed. At length he put a climax on his audacity, that 'topp'd the infinite of insult.'

" The theatre was built on the site of an old dissenting chapel, which had formerly stood there, in which a preacher named Banks had held forth, and in the small graveyard attached to which the Doctor—for he was popularly dubbed Doctor Banks—had been buried some twenty years ago; and his name was familiar yet. So, after answering Hamlet's question—

" ' How long will a man lie in the earth ere he rot?'

" Dick proceeded in due course to illustrate his answer by Yórick's skull; and taking it up, he said, in the words of the text—

" ' Now here's a skull that hath lain you in the earth three-and-twenty years. Whose do you think it was?'

" ' Nay, I know not,' replied Hamlet, in his sepulchral, tragedy-tone.

" ' This skull, sir,' said Dick, pursuing the text thus far, and then making a sudden and most unlooked for alteration—

" ' This was Doctor Banks's skull!'

" And the word skull he pronounced like bull.

" Of course the house was in an uproar of laughter and confusion. The victimised tragedian stamped and fumed about the stage, as well he might, exclaiming, 'Yorick's, sir, Yorick's!'

" ' No,' said Dick, coolly, when the tumult had subsided, taking up another skull, and resuming the text—

" ' *This* is Yorick's skull, the king's jester ; but (going off again) t'other's Doctor Banks's, as I *told* you.'

" This was too much ; this was the last straw on the tragedian's back! He jumped into the grave, seized the (very) low-comedian by the throat, and a most fearful contest, never before—or since, I hope—introduced into the play, ensued, in which Dick held his own bravely, and succeeded at length in overpowering, in a double sense, the worsted tragedian, whom he held down in the grave with one hand, while he flourished ' Doctor Banks's skull' in triumph above his head!

" The curtain was dropped, amidst roars and shrieks of laughter, in which king, queen, monk, and courtiers, who, in the vain hope of arresting the row, had been sent on with Ophelia's empty coffin, were compelled to join, forming a tableau, which finished the play for that night."

In 1865 the "Theatre Royal" in Toad Lane was pulled down, and the present central co-operative stores were built on part of the site. Mr. Pickles, an itinerant theatrical manager, erected a commodious wooden building in Newgate, and here, for several years, the public were nightly entertained with dramatic performances.

A limited liability company was next formed to build a theatre off Manchester-road, near Holland-street, in £1 shares, and 6,000 shares were taken up. In November, 1867, the building was completed at a cost of £9,000, and was named "The Prince of Wales Theatre." It is built of brick, and its outside appearance is heavy and inelegant; but the internal arrangements are excellent and comfortable, and the *coup d'œil* is certainly extremely pretty. The model is very much like the "Prince's Theatre," Manchester, but this may be accounted for by the fact that Mr. Edward Salomons was the architect for both theatres. Ascending the principal stair-case we pass through folding doors into the fozer, behind the dress circle, a roomy lounge, with an open fire-place, and with ladies' retiring room, and all necessary conveniences. There are no boxes provided on the dress circle tier, so that the whole space commands an uninterrupted view of the stage. The only boxes erected are on the pit level. The gallery is very spacious, and the front of it recedes a little behind that of the dress circle, so as to reduce the shadows which generally fall so strongly under the ceilings. The lighting is effected by means of a powerful sun-burner in the centre of the ceiling, above which is a ventilating shaft carried high above the roof. In the ceiling of the pit and dress circle extracting flues are provided communicating by means of trunks with the main shaft, where, of course, there is an immense accelerating power provided drawing off the vitiated air. The box fronts and proscenium are decorated in *carton-piene* enrichment, well moulded, and with a very effective composition of *resaissance* forms in relief, harmoniously arranged. There is a general inclination of the level of the dress circle down towards the proscenium, which prevents those in the back seats from being incommoded by those sitting in the front. The opening of the proscenium is 25 feet. The stage measures in width 55 feet 6 inches, and in length from the curtain line to the back wall 47 feet, the stage having a projection into the auditorium of 6 feet. The front of the dress circle is about 35 feet from the curtain line, and the height from the ceiling to the pit floor is 36 feet. The pit will accommodate 700 persons; dress circle and boxes, 230; gallery, 670; total 1,600.

Owing to the building costing £9,000 the original shareholders had to borrow £4,000 from a club in the town to discharge the liabilities in the construction and fitting up of the theatre, and the result was that ultimately through the theatre not being the profitable speculation which many of the promoters and supporters of the undertaking fondly imagined it would be, proceedings in chancery were taken for winding up the company, so that the club took possession, and the shareholders lost all the money they had invested, and the creditors of the company sustained considerable loss. This misfortune brought sorrow into many a family which had scraped money together in the hope of realising a good dividend by investing in the company's shares.

> " As ships that sailed for sunny isles,
> But never came to shore,"

so, unfortunately, it has been with the shareholders

and the money which they in a foolish hour risked in a speculation which at one time promised to be highly advantageous. Loud and bitter were the lamentations and denunciations when the crash came, and angry complaints of recklessness and mismanagement were hurled at the devoted heads of the directors, and it will be long, indeed, before the unhappy and disastrous business will be buried in oblivion.

The practice of " hat-dropping " at the theatre, from the gallery into the pit, which one so frequently witnesses, recalls to mind the following lines from the " Rejected Addresses."

> " Pat Jennings in the upper gallery sat;
> But, leaning forward, Jennings lost his hat;
> Down from the gallery the beaver flew,
> And spurned the one, to settle in the two.
> How shall he act ? Pay at the gallery door
> Two shillings for what cost when new but four ?
> Or till half-price, to save his shilling, wait,
> And gain his hat again at half-past eight ?
> Now, while his fears anticipate a thief,
> John Mullins whispers, take my handkerchief.
> Thank you, cries Pat, but one won't make a line ;
> Take mine, cried Wilson ; and, cried Stokes, take mine.
> A motley cable soon Pat Jennings tied,
> Where Spitalfields with real India vies.
> Like Iris' bow, down darts the painted hue,
> Starred, striped, and spotted, yellow, red, and blue,
> Old calico, torn silk, and muslin new.
> George Green below, with palpitating hand,
> Loops the last 'kerchief to the beaver's band ;
> Upsoars the prize; the youth, with joy unfeigned,
> Regained the felt, and felt what he regained,
> While to the applauding galleries grateful Pat
> Made a low bow, and touched the ransomed hat."

19

ST. ALBAN'S NURSING INSTITUTION AND BOYS' SCHOOL.

"There is that scattereth, and yet increaseth; and there is that withholdeth more than is meet, but it tendeth to poverty. There is that maketh himself rich, yet hath nothing; there is that maketh himself poor, yet hath great riches."

THIS extensive, beautiful, and attractive pile of buildings has been erected principally for the use of the parish of St. Alban's, and at the sole expense of Mr. Jonathan Nield, of Dunster. It stands on a plot of land between Drake-street and the Public Park, and the school is completed and open. In the year 1858, a commodious girls' school and school-house were erected on the opposite side of Latin-street, in connection with St. Alban's Church, and the nursing institution and the boys' school, which we are about to describe, complete a range of handsome and useful buildings, of which the parish of St. Alban's, and the town of Rochdale, may well be proud. The building covers an area of 14,014 feet, and is built of Summit stone, in pure Gothic style. The ornamental tile-ridges, and fancy gutter and down pipes, enhance its appearance. The Drake-street frontage is 84 feet long, and the building runs back 182 feet. Entering the main porch from Drake-street brings the visitor into the hall. On the right hand side there is a well-lighted and ventilated room

22 feet by 16 feet in size, which is intended for a library. It has a fine bay window, with panelled ceiling, and the main front of the building is supported by a splendid granite column, with a carved cap. On the left of the hall is a lavatory, which is nicely fitted up. Beyond this he enters the lecture hall, intended for parochial meetings or lectures, and its area is 40 feet by 27 feet. It has a fine bay window 11 feet by 6 feet, and the dressings are in Bath stone. The most attractive piece of workmanship in this hall is the massive stone chimney-piece, on which are sculptured wool sacks to represent the staple trade of the town. The next attractive feature is the arcade and gallery over the lavatory and entrance hall. The pillars are in terra-cotta, and the caps are in Bath stone. The gallery will be used as an orchestra. The lecture hall is wainscoted with pitch pine, and the roof is also of pitch pine, in the Gothic style. The whole building is heated with hot water on Bacon and Company's improved principle. Behind the lecture hall there is a coffee bar, 11 feet by 10 feet in size, for the supply of refreshments; and at the back of the library stands a kitchen, 14 feet square, over which is a sitting-room and bed-room for the use of the attendants of the establishment, with scullery and outbuildings. The space between this building and St. Alban's girls' school and school-house, is now named Latin-street, and leads from Drake-street into the Park. By the Latin-street door the visitor enters the boys' school-room, which is 64 feet long by 30 feet. It is lofty and well-lighted, having, besides six mullion windows on each side, two dormer windows above made to open for ventilation, as well as the "hit

and miss" gratings between each window. It is warmed by hot water, and has also open firegrates at each end. The walls are plastered in stucco, and are finished round to the height of five feet with Keen's cement, "Dado," which has a very hard surface and is as fine as marble. The roof is of pitch pine and surmounted by a small bell-turret. At one end of the school-room there is a class-room, 23 feet 6 inches by 17 feet. The desks, which have been made by Messrs. Sidebottom and Co., of Manchester, answer the three-fold purpose of desks, seats, and tables. The entrance to the nursing institution leads out of St. Alban's-street, and in the lobby there are two beautiful screens, in pitch pine, with ornamental glazing, by Pepper, of London. On the right is a room 14 feet by 10 feet, ornamented by two painted windows, by Bell, of London. There is a beautiful room 15 feet long and 11 feet wide, but its use has not yet been decided upon. The arched doorway is in Bath stone, beautifully carved. Adjoining this is a sitting-room. On the left of the entrance there is a small room, with painted glass windows, which will be used for a writing-room; and leading from that is the dining-room, 21 feet 6 inches by 14 feet wide. There are kitchen, scullery, laundry, and two bath-rooms, fitted up with the latest improvements. On the first floor there are six rooms for sitting-rooms and bed-rooms for the nurses, and four rooms set apart for reception of males and females who have met with accidents. The architect who designed this extensive building is Mr. Joseph Clarke, F.S.A., of Stratford Place, London; and Messrs. Neill and Sons, of Manchester, were the builders.

GEOLOGY AND MINERALOGY.

LTHOUGH "the heavens above," which we have so few opportunities of seeing unobscured, are hardly so precisely mapped out as to give us a local astronomy, yet we must not omit a few words on "the earth beneath" in a district which, perhaps, owes its material progress to its mineral riches. Rochdale is almost embosomed in an amphitheatre of hills, connected with the Pennine chain which runs from the moorlands of Derbyshire and Staffordshire to the borders of Scotland, and, possibly, we owe some share of the undoubted healthiness of the town to the protection afforded by the elevations north and east of us, and the pure air which is wafted thence to us. The Lancashire and Cheshire coal field, which extends under the town, underlies the bulk of that portion of the county lying south and east of a line drawn from Colne to Liverpool, constituting an area of about 250 square miles, with a total average thickness of over 100 feet of coal beds. The series of strata being usually considered as divided into upper, middle, and lower, the latter or gannister beds only are worked in this neighbourhood. The production is not comparable in quantity to the middle series of beds which prevail towards Wigan and other places, but that known as the Mountain Mine, the lowest except the Rock Mine, is of the very best quality. According to the geological survey, a small out-lying portion of the middle strata containing the Arley Mine seam lies near to the south-eastern portion of the borough, and a small patch at Belfield. Again, our lower coal strata bring up the valuable beds of flagstone worked at Whitworth, Facit, etc., and which are distributed far and wide. The fine clay seams wrought near Littleborough and Dearnley are also associated with the same strata and give employment in the manufacture of pipes, fire bricks, gas retorts, etc. Iron stone has also been found in small quantities; at Tunshill, Iron Works were formed some sixty years ago, but the iron had much sulphur combined with it, and at that time its separation was not so well understood. Common clay and sand are abundant, and the finer sand stone, suitable for building and paving, is quarried on the north-eastern side of the borough. It is a curious fact that the millstone grit crowning the heights of Blackstone Edge, "Robin Hood's Bed," as it is fancifully termed, is invariably found to underlie the coal beds. How then has it got to its present elevation in the world? Probably by the operation of two agencies *upheaval* from below, of which there are abundant evidences in the numerous faults in the carboniferous strata hereabouts, and *denudation* or wearing off afterwards by the long-continued action of frost, rain, etc. There is evidence that the coal fields of Lancashire and Yorkshire were at one time connected and continuous, and probably also the Welsh coal field, so that we may fairly assume the neighbouring hills to have been covered with hundreds of feet of coal bearing beds, and, if so, where are they now? Partly in the sand and gravel deposits which the retreating sea beach

has left behind, and partly buried beneath the waters
of the Irish Sea and German Ocean. The same causes
have operated to scoop out, as it were, the cloughs and
ravines which bring their tribute of waters to the Roach,
and are undoubtedly still doing the same work silently
and slowly, but surely. At the foot of Sparrow Hill,
within the Park railings, lies a huge boulder stone,
which deserves a word here, and which, if there were
"sermons in stones" could, no doubt, tell a wonderful
tale. A fragment burst by the frost from a glacier
valley in the hills, it was probably carried away, embedded in an iceberg which wore and scarred its sides
in an erratic voyage, and finally melted and deposited
its burden in the depths of the ancient sea which then
rolled its waves above our country. The character of
the stone is of the same kind as now found on the
Norwegian Coast, but boulders of all sizes and sorts are
found over the whole district, brought as well from the
Cumberland or Welsh range as from Norway.

> Within the bowels of the earth there lie
> Abundant treasures fit for man's supply;
> By patient labour they are brought to light,
> And torn from beds where long they'd slept in night.
> They yield us comfort, and without their aid
> Small were the progress which mankind had made.
> Coal, stone, and slate, clay, sand, and shale
> Assist us in our passage through this vale;
> And if deprived of these essential things,
> Where were the bliss of which the poet sings?
> Doomed to a state of hardship and despair,
> Man would be wretched—life too sad to bear.

ROCHDALE UNION.

PREVIOUSLY to 1837 paupers were relieved by the overseers. In January, of that year, an order of the Poor Law Commissioners, acting under the Poor Law Amendment Act, was issued, forming the Rochdale Union, comprising Blatchinworth and Calderbrook, Butterworth, Castleton, Spotland, Wardleworth, and Wuerdle and Wardle, and the following persons were elected guardians:—Blatchinworth and Calderbrook: Hugh Race, James Hudson. Butterworth: William Meadowcroft, Alexander Richardson. Castleton: James Hoyle, Benjamin Heape, John Samuel Wood, John Howard. Spotland: Robert Kelsall, John Whitworth, John Holt, James Dearden, James Lord. Wardleworth: James Littlewood, John Petrie, Thomas Shaw. Wuerdle and Wardle: John Lord, William Barlow. The Ex-officio Guardians were:—The Rev. Robert William Hay, John Entwisle, Esq., M.P.; Clement Royds, Esq.; John Holland, Esq.; William Chadwick, Esq.

The first meeting of the guardians was held on 15th February, 1837; and in July, 1845, the laws relating to the relief of the poor, under the Commissioners, were put in force, and the Rochdale Union was then divided into three districts for the purpose of relief, viz.:— Spotland, consisting of the Township of Spotland; Wardleworth, consisting of Wardleworth, Wuerdle and Wardle, and Blatchinworth and Calderbrook; Castleton, consisting of the Townships of Castleton ahd Butterworth. There were six medical officers' districts, viz. :—Castleton, Butterworth, Spotland, Whitworth and Brandwood, Wardleworth, and Wuerdle and Blatchinworth. The workhouses were capable of accommodating the following inmates, viz. :—Hollingworth, 58; Calf Hey, 30; Marland, 50; Spotland, 100; and Wardleworth, 24. In 1865, Calf Hey and the old Marland workhouses were closed. The guardians, in the same year, erected a new workhouse, at Marland, capable of accommodating about 260 inmates (including sick cases), and about 40 children. In 1868 the subject of workhouse accommodation underwent full inquiry, and the guardians decided to erect one workhouse for the whole union, as it was considered that the classification requisite for the comfort of the inmates would be better secured, the whole official management concentrated, and a great saving of cost effected. A site at Dearnley, containing twenty-four acres, was purchased for the sum of £2,500; and another adjacent plot, of about seven acres, was afterwards purchased. The Union Workhouse is now being erected from the design, and under the superintendence, of Mr. George Woodhouse, of Bolton. The new buildings will afford accommodation as follows —

	First Erection. Inmates.	When Extended. Inmates.
Main Building	408	504
Imbecile Wards	128	152
Infirmary	62	89
Fever, &c., Hospital	34	46
	632	782

The contract for the erection of the first buildings is £41,312 2s. 9d.; the contractor is Mr. Bickerstaff, of Preston. It is expected that in the course of another year the buildings will be ready for use, and Rochdale will then possess a workhouse which will bear favourable comparison with any in the kingdom. When the union was formed, in 1837, the rateable value was £134,440; in 1874, it was £409,398. Mr. William Roberts, solicitor, was the first clerk; but on his receiving the appointment of Poor Law Auditor, in 1858, his partner, Mr. Holgate, became, and has since continued, clerk.

Elected guardians for the year ending April, 1875. Chairman, Fletcher Bolton; Vice-Chairmen, James Whitworth, Abraham Hill. Blatchinworth and Calderbrook: John Tetlow, Charles Rigg. Butterworth: William Clegg, James Whitworth, Edmund Milne. Castleton: Fletcher Bolton, James Sharrocks, Samuel Lord, John Parker, Thomas Holt. Spotland: William Barrowclough, Jas. Grandidge, John Scowcroft, James H. Scholfield, James Lord, John Butterworth, Abraham Hill. Wardleworth: Thomas Schofield, William Brocklehurst, James Maden, George Handley. Wuerdle and Wardle: John Heap, Edmund Leach, senior.

REMARKABLE CRIMES.

"Foul deeds will rise
Though all the earth o'erwhelms them to men's eyes;
For murder, though it have no tongue, will speak
With most miraculous organ."

ROCHDALE, fortunately, has not been the scene of much bloodshed, but some few atrocities of this nature which have occurred possess remarkable features, and strengthen the impression that the crimes that have been committed do not hide themselves, and that neither "cell, nor chain, nor dungeon, speaks to the murderer like the voice of solitude." An outline of the most startling of these deplorable occurrences we subjoin.

THE HALF-MOON INN MURDER

Heads the list of notorious crimes in this locality within the past twenty years. The details of this tragedy may be briefly narrated. On Saturday evening, 21st July, 1855, a man took lodgings for the night at the above-named public-house. He had with him a woman, whom he represented to be his wife, but they were both unknown to the innkeeper. The man was Jonathan Heywood, a foundry labourer, and the woman was Margaret Jones, a widow, with whom Heywood had been cohabiting. The two retired to a bedroom provided for them, and no disturbance was heard by the

inmates in the course of the night. As the man and
woman did not come down stairs the following morning,
the bedroom was entered, and a horrible sight presented
itself. The woman had been brutally murdered, and
the man had escaped, probably at daybreak. A reward
was offered for the apprehension of the murderer, and
a man was apprehended as having been last seen in the
deceased's company, and strong evidence was given
against him. It, however, proved to be a case of
mistaken identity, and the man was released after being
in custody about a fortnight. It appears that soon after
the murder, Heywood went to his sister's house and
asked her to wash his clothes which were besmeared
with blood, and on her refusal he attempted to remove
the stains himself. He then obtained work at Bamford
as a farm labourer, and it was there that a clue was
obtained to the real criminal. Whilst his fellow-work-
men were discussing the all-absorbing topic, he seemed
much disturbed, and the fact of his being conversant
with the whole of the details aroused suspicion, and he
was brought before the magistrates and committed for
trial. He was executed at Kirkdale shortly afterwards.

THE HOLLINGWORTH MURDER

Occurred on the 11th June, 1865. The murderer was
James Kelly, a musician, who lived at Three Lane Ends,
in a house now occupied as part of the Royal Oak Inn,
in the lane leading from Smithy Bridge to Hollingworth
Lake. He was of very intemperate habits, and occasionally conducted himself strangely, but was reputed
to be generally sane, and he lived upon excellent terms
with his wife. On the day named he suddenly attacked

his wife whilst alone in the house with her, and cut her throat, the head being almost severed from the body. He was observed by a neighbour to wash his hands at a well across the road, and on the house being entered the woman was found dead in a large pool of blood. Kelly was apprehended, and it being proved on his trial that he was of unsound mind, he was ordered to be confined during her Majesty's pleasure.

THE SLATTOCKS MURDER

(21st August, 1866) was one of the most cold-blooded and horrible occurrences in the annals of crime. An Irish labourer, named John Brennan, a peaceable, well-disposed person, was employed by an innkeeper and farmer named Burrows, whose son, James, having demanded money from Brennan, was refused, whereupon the miscreant struck deceased a fatal blow on the head with a crowbar. Burrows was apprehended, and the crowbar was found secreted in the wall of one of the farm buildings. He was executed at the New Bailey, Salford.

THE MURDER OF THE REV. A. J. PLOW AND JANE SMITH.

On the 2nd March, 1868, there occurred, at Todmorden, a most atrocious crime, viz.:—A young man, named Miles Weatherhill, had become acquainted with a servant girl, about sixteen years of age, at the Todmorden Vicarage. The Rev. A. J. Plow, the vicar (formerly curate at St. James's, Rochdale), objected to the attentions of Weatherhill towards the girl, on account of her youth, and forbade his visiting her at the house.

Having ascertained from another servant named Smith
that Weatherhill had visited the girl whilst the vicar was
at church, Mr. Plow sent her home to her parents. In
consequence of this procedure, Weatherhill conceived and
deliberately carried out a terrible revenge upon the
vicar and other inmates of the vicarage. Arming himself with pistols and a hatchet, he proceeded to the
vicarage and there inflicted dreadful injuries upon
Mr. Plow, and shot the servant Smith dead. The
murderer then deliberately re-loaded his pistol, and proceeding upstairs to Mrs. Plow's bedroom, he fired at
her as she lay in bed. He had also taken upstairs the
kitchen poker, and as the shot did not take effect, he
struck Mrs. Plow upon the head and face with the
poker, fracturing her nose and inflicting other severe
injuries. Her death occurred in about twelve months
after, and no doubt resulted from the violence and its
attendant circumstances. Mr. Plow survived his injuries only a few days, and died on the 12th March,
1868. Weatherhill was tried at the Manchester Assizes,
and, being found guilty of both murders, was executed
a few weeks later in front of the Salford New Bailey.

THE BURNEDGE TRAGEDY.

Ezra Whiteoak, an industrious, sober, and quiet man,
who originally came from Craven, in Yorkshire, married
a respectable young woman from Buersil Head, and in
August, 1868, they kept a small farm at Calf Hole, a
place about three-quarters of a mile from Buersil Head,
and he worked as an out-door labourer. They had two
children, the elder, James, aged eight years, and the
younger, Sarah Ann, aged three. They all lived quite

happily together, but brooding over his wife's illness, and fearing pecuniary embarrassment, he was induced, in a fit of temporary derangement, to murder his two children, and from the wounds he inflicted upon his own throat with the razor, he died in a week after.

MURDER AT PINFOLD.

In December, 1870, the death of Mr. Reuben Bottomley occurred from violence by Samuel Smith. Bottomley was near to the Castle Inn, Pinfold, on the night of the 20th November, 1870, when he was attacked by Smith, and received several violent kicks which resulted in death six days later. Smith was convicted at the assizes, and sentenced to twenty years' penal servitude.

LOBDEN COINERS AND THEIR TRAGICAL END.

About sixty years ago a gang of men set to work in a lonely miner's hovel, on Lobden, near Whitworth, to forge £1 notes and make base coin. For a time they were successful and evaded the vigilance of the officers of the law. Mr. James Whitehead, who was better known by the bye-name of "Jem o' Peters," and who at that time was the landlord of the "Flying Horse," Rochdale, betrayed them, and three out of the six were executed at Lancaster. One was buried by his relatives in Hallfold Chapel yard, and the corpse of a second named Cudworth, of Dearden Yard, Rochdale, was restored to his relatives for burial.

MERCHANTS' AND TRADESMEN'S ASSOCIATION.

ON the 5th of May, 1863, this association was established in Rochdale. Its objects are "to promote measures calculated to benefit and protect the mercantile and trading interests of its members, and of the town and neighbourhood of Rochdale generally; to represent and express their sentiments on commercial affairs; to undertake the settlement of questions and disputes arising out of trade by arbitration, or otherwise, when submitted to it for decision; and generally the attainment of such commercial advantages as the exertions of individuals may be less adequate to accomplish." This association has conferred many benefits upon the town, such as reducing the railway fares between Rochdale and Manchester, procuring fortnightly instead of monthly County Courts, more rapid delivery of letters, removed the liability of landlords to pay the gas rates of defaulting tenants, assisted in obtaining the new Post Office, and other minor local improvements, and also took part in the prevention of fancied improvements in commercial law. Every July an opportunity is afforded to the inhabitants of visiting, by a cheap trip, some place of interest. The first excursion was to the famed English Lake district, Windermere, in 1866; the second to Ripon and Fountains Abbey; "The Queen of English

Watering Places," Scarborough, was visited in 1868; the princely residence of the Duke of Devonshire, Chatsworth, and the venerable pile of Haddon Hall were seen in 1869; Alton Towers, the residence of the Earl of Shrewsbury, was visited in 1870; and the grounds which had been cultivated out of barren soil and a clough, were most picturesque, and fully warranted the encomium bestowed on the late Earl, that "he made the desert smile;" the ancient seat of the Wynns, Wynnstay Hall, and Chirk Castle, the noble residence of Col. Myddleton Biddulph, and the sweet vale of Llangollen were inspected in 1871; the romantic Castle of Kenilworth; the birth-place of the prince of poets, Stratford-upon-Avon; Warwick Castle, and the aristocratic town of Leamington were seen in 1872; Belvoir Castle, the seat of the Duke of Rutland, with its rare objects of grandeur, was inspected in 1873; and last year Ludlow Castle, of historical renown, which is surrounded by exquisite scenery, was visited. Mr. George Miller, merchant, late of Rochdale, but now of Manchester, was the president of this association for ten years, and Mr. Councillor Benjamin Butterworth, for many years, served as vice-president. Mr. Councillor James Tomlinson was elected president for the year 1874, and Mr. William Brocklehurst, of Yorkshire-street, vice-president. Mr. Fletcher, accountant, was the first secretary, and Mr. J. A. Wood next filled the post for several years, and Mr. William Robertson, accountant, &c., 98, Yorkshire-street, has discharged the duties of secretary for the last six years.

20

CHAMBER OF COMMERCE.

"It is delightful to see a body of men thriving in their own fortunes, and, at the same time, promoting the public stock."

THE Rochdale Chamber of Commerce was formed in February, 1866, and owes its origin chiefly to the exertions of T. B. Willans, Esq., J.P. In that month a meeting was held at the Wellington Hotel, at which James Heap, Esq., of Milnrow, presided. It was convened for the purpose of affording the manufacturers of Milnrow reliable information in reference to the scale of charges paid in Rochdale and neighbourhood for certain classes of work, in the process of manufacture, so as to enable these manufacturers to adjust their wages accordingly. Mr. Willans was present at the meeting, and suggested the desirability of forming a Chamber of Commerce in Rochdale, and expressed his belief that such an association would prove of great value to the commercial interests of the town and neighbourhood, and he considered it rather a reflection that Rochdale had been so long apathetic in the matter, while other towns of less importance possessed Chambers of Commerce, which watched measures affecting the trading interests of the country, and he concluded by moving the establishment of a Chamber of Commerce for Rochdale. The motion met with the unanimous approbation and support of the numerous influential manufacturers present at the meeting, and the Chamber was accordingly formed.

The Chamber is composed of merchants, manufacturers, bankers, and tradesmen. It has always taken a lively interest in commercial treaties with a view to the removal of restrictions on the import of English goods into foreign countries. Wm. Fenton, Esq., banker, was elected first president, in 1866, and retained office until 1869, when the Chamber found a most energetic successor in Mr. T. B. Willans, woollen manufacturer. Mr. Willans devoted great attention to the intricacies of the French commercial treaty, and in 1870 he was placed on the Foreign Tariff's Committee of the Associated Chambers of Commerce. The treaties with Austria, the Zolverein, and Spain and Portugal were carefully considered, and the abolition of duties on cotton goods to India, and the development of the agricultural resources of British India were advocated by the Chamber. In 1872, John Tweedale, Esq., of Healey Hall, succeeded Mr. Willans, and during his term of office the Chamber advocated many subjects of local and general interest, and made considerable advance as a useful public institution. Mr. Tweedale was a strong advocate of compulsory registration of trade marks, and gave valuable evidence before a select committee of the House of Commons. In 1869, Mr. Edmund Ashworth, who has for many years occupied a prominent position in local matters, was elected, and still continues to be president. The present vice-presidents are Messrs. R. Schofield, woollen manufacturer, and E. E. M. Royds, banker. Mr. C. J. Roberts, solicitor, was secretary for

the first three years; Mr. William Hoyle occupied the
post for the next two years; and Mr. J. M. L. Chadwick
has been the secretary ever since. When commercial
matters were withdrawn from the cognizance of the
Board of Trade, the Chamber of Commerce, with the
other associated chambers, warmly advocated the establishment of a department for commercial affairs in the
foreign office to be presided over by a cabinet minister.
On the formation of the Chamber the question of direct
railway communication with London was taken up; and,
as a consequence, through carriages have for some time
been run from Rochdale *via* Oldham and Guide Bridge
to London. The Chamber induced the Lancashire and
Yorkshire Railway Company to improve the means of
ingress and egress for passengers at the Rochdale Station,
the collection of tickets for express trains at Manchester,
and the running of the 5.50 train in the morning to Manchester to catch the early London train at London Road
Station. Special service and extra trains are to a great
extent owing to the efforts of the Council, and, in 1869, we
find them pressing upon the Lancashire and Yorkshire
Railway Co. to adopt the principle between Rochdale and
Manchester, so successfully inaugurated by the Midland,
of attaching third class carriages to every train. The
persistent efforts of the Chamber from 1869, in conjunc-
tion with other public bodies in the town, to obtain
postal and telegraphic accommodation in accordance
with the wants of the town, received partial recognition,
and many important improvements were conceded in
the shape of accelerated deliveries, additional officers,
and other matters. When, in 1867, the insurance
offices raised the tariff on woollen mills nearly fifty per

cent., the Chamber promptly joined issue with the offices, and collected statistics showing that the losses to the offices were not incurred in this district; but, on the contrary, that only one-third of the premiums paid had been claimed by the millowners for losses by fire. Although the offices seemed determined to adhere to their increase, the Chamber persisted in their efforts until July, 1873, when the rate was reduced from 21s. to 16s. per cent. The Lancashire and Yorkshire Railway Company enjoys a very unfortunate monopoly of traffic accommodation, highly prejudicial to the commercial interests of the town. From the opening of the Chamber to the present time every effort has been strained to obtain an independent line or improved accommodation, but as yet without success.

THE IMPORTANT TRADES OF THE TOWN.

"For I dipt into the future, far as human eye could see,
  Saw the vision of the world, and all the wonder that would be;
Saw the heavens fill with commerce, argosies of magic sails,
  Pilots of the purple twilight, dropping down with costly bales."

HAND-LOOM WEAVING.

AS early as the year 1558 flannel was the staple trade of Rochdale, and these goods were renowned for their durability and excellence. In the reign of Queen Elizabeth, Her Majesty's alnager had a deputy here for the stamping of woollen cloths, under the authority of the Act passed in the eighth year of her reign. At the beginning of the present century, great improvements were made in looms and jennies, and the greater part of the population were employed in spinning and hand-loom weaving, but the remuneration was poor, their labour hard, and their hours long, for they worked fourteen hours a-day. These hard-working people, consequently, did not suffer from being

"Stretched on the rack of a too easy chair,
  Where everlasting yawns confess
  The pains and penalties of idleness."

The weavers used to earn on an average 9s. or 10s. a-week, and the spinners about 6s. or 7s. a-week. The rents of their cottages, which usually contained only two rooms, were £4 or £5 a-year; these rooms had one pair of looms, and one jenny in them, and the practice was to place the beds underneath the machinery, and here repose was found for weary limbs in

"Tired Nature's sweet restorer, balmy sleep."

Many possessed that useful article of furniture—-

"The chest contrived a double debt to pay,
A bed by night, a chest of drawers by day."

The men wore corduroy, and the women bed-gowns. If a woman possessed a gown, it was considered a novelty, and special care was taken of it. The bonnets had a coal-scuttle appearance. Fortunately food was cheap, and thus small earnings "went a long way." The children also worked during these fourteen hours at winding bobbins, and their remuneration was small indeed. They were poorly clad, and their education entirely neglected. There were "drones" then as there are now, but they were more numerous, and their habits are described in an old hand-loom weaver's song of that period, which used to be sung in beer-houses :—

"To work on Monday I think it is not right,
That day should be spent in some other delight,
Either pitching, or tossing, or some other sport,
And at night to the ale-house we all do resort."

The song goes on to relate that the carousing continued on Tuesday, Wednesday, and Thursday, and

"On Friday morning I'll whistle and sing,
And go to my looms as content as a king;
And out of the house you'll scarce see my face,
For all the night o'er I must stare through the blaze.

On Saturday noon when my work it is done,
Then I am the lad that must carry it home;
Then over my left shoulder my piece I'll fling,
And at night o'er a jug of strong beer I'll sing."

About eighty years ago the principal employers of
hand-loom weavers were Mr. William Midgley, of
Buersil; Mr. James Royds, of Falinge Fold; Mr. Jas.
Midgley, top of Wardleworth Brow; Messrs. Leach
and Tweedale, of Shawclough; Mr. Clement Royds;
Mr. Robert Holt, of Well-o'-th' Lane; Mr. Gould, of
Wardleworth; and Mr. James Fenton, of Bamford.
Spinning at one time was done on one spindle, and
then increased to sixty spindles, next to seventy, eighty,
ninety, and, ultimately, up to one hundred and twenty;
but as soon as the spindles got over one hundred they
were found difficult to turn by hand labour. Forty or fifty
years ago steam power was introduced instead of hand-
loom spinning and weaving, and competition began
between hand labour and steam, and gradually the
latter made headway, but was viewed with jealousy by
the work people. The first carding mills that can be
remembered were " Jone o' Dan's," at Caldershaw, in
Spotland, and Mr. Whitehead's factory, which stood
on the plot of ground near to the present residence of
Thomas Bright, Esq. There was also a stone factory
on the present site of Messrs. Petrie's foundry in
Whitehall-street, and in these old mills the work carried
on consisted of carding and slubbing, which were previously done by hand up to about ninety years ago.

SHUTTLE GATHERING AND THE DESTRUC-
TION OF THE NEW BAILEY.

In May, 1808, there was a dispute between the hand-
loom weavers and their employers about wages, and
shuttles were gathered in order to stop the weaving of
goods, and a serious riot ensued. Prior to this the

employers had agreed to a standard list, and the dispute occurred through some of the masters departing from the list. Two or three cart loads of shuttles were put into a house at the top of Blackwater-street, but the authorities had them removed to the New Bailey, in Rope-street. The mob was so exasperated that they attempted to take possession of the town and break open the prison, and failing, they burnt down the latter. The Rochdale Volunteers being at that time disbanded, and the " regulars " engaged in the Peninsular War, the Halifax Volunteers, numbering 1,100, were ordered to Rochdale, and came in the dead of night. A large number were billeted in St. Mary's Church, others in the Cloth Hall, and the remainder in the various public-houses. The mob broke nearly every window in Yorkshire-street, except Mr. Ralph Taylor's, which were spared in consequence of one of the crowd shouting out, " He was always a good felley to the poor." The rioters attacked and ill-treated the late Mr. Clement Royds, J.P., at the top of Toad-lane, on his way home. The operatives did not succeed in getting their demand settled, and resumed work, but some time after their employers agreed to another scale of prices. For a time these prices were adhered to, but in consequence of several manufacturers doing work in their own houses, and underselling others in the trade, some of the employers again deviated from the list of prices. At that time Mr. Turner, of Haslingden, and Mr. Rostron, of Edenfield, visited Rochdale, and adopted the practice of putting their work out here as they could get it done one-third cheaper and did not pay the standard price. In 1824 another list of prices was agreed

to between the manufacturers and their work people.
The work was to be done in certain reeds, and Messrs.
Turner and Rostron were not to be allowed to give out
work in Rochdale. This agreement was adhered to up
to 1827, but at times previously to this there was great
dissatisfaction respecting a species of " truck system."

DISPUTES AND STRIKES.

In 1827 a dispute took place between the late Mr. H.
Kelsall and his weavers because he made grey goods
and did not pay according to the standard list. A
strike ensued which lasted a month, when Mr. Kelsall
agreed to adhere to the list in future, and to repay £367
which the Hand-loom Weavers' Union had expended in
maintaining the men ; but it is alleged that some time
after he induced his work people to refund the £367.
The Union, for some years, had in vogue a "ratting"
system, which was called "Old Betty," or "window
smashing." If a person refused to join and contribute
to the Union, his windows were smashed. In 1827
Mr. Tweedale, of Healey Hall, began to introduce
machinery into his works, and there was a strike about
this, which lasted nearly three months, but it was
settled by a compromise that certain specified prices
should be paid for work done on machinery.

THE POWER-LOOMS.

Shortly afterwards the late G. Ashworth, Esq., J.P.,
of Sunny Bank, commenced establishing the power-
loom, which, being successfully started, resulted in his
erecting the first woollen power-loom shed about
1831. Notwithstanding the large number of hand-

loom weavers, and their strenuous opposition to the
introduction of machinery, such has been the rapid
strides of the latter as almost to exterminate the race of
hand-loom weaving itself. The rate of remuneration
to those employed upon power-looms is considerably
higher than the earnings under the old hand-loom
system, and the character of the manufacture is not
only unimpaired but absolutely improved; and the
cheapness of production, has in face of the enhanced
cost of the raw material, not interfered either with the
production or diminished the demand.

ANOTHER RIOT: TWO PERSONS KILLED.

In 1829 there was a severe struggle about wages,
and it appeared to be general, and shuttles were
gathered. Mr. Chadwick's factory, in Water-street,
was broken into by the rioters, and the shuttles removed.
Mr. Pilling's factory, at the top of Drake-street, was also
entered and Mr. Robinson's, at the top of Drake-street,
and the shuttles were carried away. In the evening
horse and foot soldiers arrived, and when a large
number of workpeople heard of the fact at a public
meeting on Cronkeyshaw, they squandered in all
directions. About twenty of the principal rioters were
captured. The Hand-loom Weavers' cash box, containing £137, was seized at the "Coach and Horses,"
Lord-street, and deposited in the New Bailey. The
rioters were committed for trial, and were taken from
the Police Court to the New Bailey, tied to a rope, an
infuriated mob following. A guard was left in charge
of the prison, and as soon as the main body of the
military had left, the rioters began to attack the building,

headed by a man who went by the name of "Old
Doctor." The soldiers then began to fire, when
"Doctor" exclaimed "Come on lads, never mind, it's
only blank shot," and while in the act of throwing a
stone he was shot dead, several other persons being
killed and wounded. A youth, brother to Mr. Alderman
Stott, late of Rochdale, was in a window in a corn
mill on Corn Mill Brow, and was killed by a stray bullet.
A person named Thomas Kershaw was one of the ring-
leaders. He was apprehended at Liverpool, having
paid his passage to America, and committed to the
Assizes, and transported for life; the rest of the prisoners
were incarcerated—some for four months, others for
twelve months, and some were discharged.

PAROCHIAL CONSTABLES REWARDING THEM-
SELVES FROM THE UNION CASH BOX.

A few days after the trial above-named, three constables named Benjamin Taylor, James Taylor, and
Stott, broke open the hand-loom weavers' cash box, containing £137, which was deposited in the New Bailey,
and repaired to the White Lion Inn, Yorkshire-street,

> "To swallow gudgeons ere they're catched,
> And count their chickens ere they're hatched,"

and here they were pounced upon while dividing the
spoil, and were sent to prison. It was Mrs. Pilling,
the turnkey's wife, who, by peeping through the key-
hole of the prison, observed the constables committing
the felony, and it was her information which led to the
conviction of these dishonest representatives of the law.
In 1830 Mr. James Schofield, manufacturer, of Heybrook, who had previously agreed to pay his work

people at the rate of 16s. in the pound, reduced the
sum to 12s. in the pound, and the result was a turn out
of all the weavers, and most of the other manufacturers
followed the example of Mr. Schofield, and the strikes
lasted thirteen weeks.

THIRTY WEAVERS SENT TO PRISON.

The weavers of Messrs. Barnes (Milnrow) refused
to take their work in, and thirty of the offenders were
sent to prison, but after they had been in a few days,
they gladly promised to finish their work, and pay all
the expenses.

PLUG DRAWING AND THE CHARTER.

In 1842 another disturbance took place, and plug
drawing became general for the purpose of stopping
all trades. It was a political movement, connected with
Fergus O'Connor's Chartist Scheme, and the idea entertained was to cause all work to cease until the charter
became the law of the land. The disturbance lasted
only a few days in Rochdale, owing to the judicious
conduct of the then acting magistrate, who, as the
rioters entered the town, prevented the shedding of
blood and injury to property, and secured the speedy
restoration of order. The course adopted in suppressing
this riot caused angry discontent amongst some partisans,
and, ultimately, occasioned a strict investigation and
lengthy correspondence with the Government authorities. Eventually the conduct impugned was justified,
and, after the strictest enquiry, it was gratifying to
receive the highest commendation for the policy pursued
in the critical circumstances.

The access to statistical information is so meagre and unreliable, that we are prevented making faithful comparisons of the immense progress which has been made in the flannel manufacture from the period at which we commence our observations down to the present, but it must be patent to common observers, from the almost countless numbers now employed in the numerous extensive manufactures within the borough, that the strides have been not less great than gratifying to contemplate, and, doubtless, there is a no less magnificent future for those engaged in this branch of industry.

"Human experience, like the stern-lights of a ship at sea, illumines only the path which we have passed over;" and so it has been in the struggle between employers and employed in Rochdale, and riots are now things of the past. In contrasting the condition of the working classes eighty years ago with their position at the present time, it is indisputable that they have advanced socially, morally, and educationally. Instead of working fourteen hours a-day, they are now employed ten hours. Instead of their homes being blocked up with machinery, they are, in many cases, provided with pianos or harmoniums, and peaceful evening is welcomed in by cessation from labour, and rest of mind and body.

> " Blest be those feasts with simple plenty crowned,
> Where all the merry family around
> Laugh at the jests or pranks that never fail,
> Or sigh with pity at some mournful tale;
> Or press the bashful stranger to his food,
> And learn the luxury of doing good."

THE COTTON TRADE.

The manufacture of cotton was introduced into Rochdale about eighty-five years ago, and the first manufacturer was Mr. J. Pilling, the grandfather of Messrs. Joseph Brierley, J.P., and James Brierley, J.P. He commenced business in premises in Holland-street, where not only carding and spinning but hand-loom weaving were done. The machinery was turned by a gin, with horse-power. About ten years after an extensive mill was erected in College-street, and here the first power-loom in this neighbourhood made its appearance in the year 1820. About eighty years ago a Mr. Lodge built a factory at Oakenrod, and the machinery was worked by water-power. Carding was done on the premises, and the work people did the spinning and weaving at their own homes by hand. Town Mill, at the top of Holland-street, was erected soon after the opening of Mr. Pilling's mill in Holland-street, and Mr. Whitehead, the occupier, carded for other manufacturers. This mill was also worked by water-power. Hanging Road Manufactory is also of ancient date, and the founders of two or three of the most celebrated firms in this town were originally employés at one time in this mill. The steam engine was the product of the famed engine factory of Messrs. Bolton and Watt. The commencement of cotton weaving was of much more recent date than the flannel trade, and has made very rapid progress for the short period it has existed, and has become a formidable competitor with surrounding towns. It would too much increase the dimensions of this work to enumerate the various important and extensive establishments which now adorn the town, and contribute so largely to its wealth.

In 1861, when the news reached this country of the civil war in America, great distress arose amongst the operatives through the cotton famine and the cessation of work in the mills, and these events will ever be remembered as among the most memorable occurrences in the history of this borough. The opportune and indefatigable services rendered by the late G. L. Ashworth, Esq., J.P., in his charitable efforts to meliorate the distress of the cotton operatives, and preserve them from pauperism, as well as for the future continuance of the industry, will not soon be forgotten. We are now happily enjoying the beneficial effects of this timely intervention, after the reorganisation of labour in the American States ; and the order which has been re-established has produced a condition of things which cannot fail to contribute to a prosperity never surpassed.

THE CARPET TRADE.

The only carpet manufactory in Rochdale is that of Messrs. Bright & Co., on Cronkeyshaw. In 1849 this now extensive manufactory was commenced with sixteen looms to weave tapestry, and gradually the premises had to be extended to make room for the increasing machinery, in order to keep up with the demand for carpets manufactured by this firm. In 1861 an action was brought by Messrs. Crossley, of Halifax, against Messrs. Bright, for an alleged infringement of a patent. The dispute was decided in favour of Messrs. Bright, and Messrs. Crossley had to pay the expenses which amounted to about £90,000. Messrs. Bright now employ in the carpet department about 400 work people, and, from 108 looms, 26,000 yards of carpet ʼre turned out weekly.

SILK MANUFACTURE.

The manufacture of silk, was introduced into Rochdale about 35 years ago by Mr. Edward Briggs, from Kent. The manufactory was at Sudden in the building which was lately occupied by Mr. Tucker, deceased. Mr. Briggs commenced with manufacturing felts, next silk hatting, then raised silk for hats, and ultimately silk velvets, silk dresses, and handkerchiefs. Mr. Joseph Porter shortly after commenced weaving silk with hand-looms in a building in Rope-street, which is now occupied by Mr. Jewison, chandler. Messrs. James Taylor, George Healey, and Thomas Watson next opened a small hat manufactory in St. James's Place, Whitworth Road, and in 1851, they get up a woven fabric with a cotton ground, and spun silk weft, and exhibited a specimen at the exhibition of 1851, along with coloured yarns, &c. They were awarded a medal, and this was the starting point of this firm's successful career.

HAT MANUFACTURE.

Hat manufacture up to sixty years ago was one of the most important trades of Rochdale, and was then in its prime. The principal manufacturers were Messrs. John Taylor and Robert Taylor, John Kenyon, Thomas Kenion, J. & J. Fildes, and Abraham Barlow. The hats that were made consisted of felt, fur, beaver, and silk. Strikes and disputes were so frequent between the workmen and their employers that this special trade was driven out of the town to Oldham, Denton, and Stockport. The last felt hat manufacturer was Mr. Edward Briggs, of Sudden, and the last silk hat makers Messrs. George Healey and James Taylor.

21

FOUNDRIES AND MACHINE WORKS.

The first iron foundry in Rochdale was that of Mr. Jeremiah Meanley, which stood on the ground between Packer-street and the site of the Town Hall Tower. Mr. Charles Meredith took the business in 1815, and carried on the manufacture of ovens and cottage boilers for many years. Mr. John Petrie started a foundry next in High-street, and first made engine sides which previously were composed of wood, and he did other hand work. Messrs. David Howorth, Skinner, and Halstead next opened a foundry on Foundry Brow, off Drake-street, and made all kinds of machinery. Mr. John Ashworth some time after commenced a foundry in Oldham-road, on the premises in which Mr. Councillor Tomlinson carries on the business of a machinist at the present time. One of the earliest machinists was Mr. John Ogden, whose works were at the top of College-street, and he was the first to make carding engines and teasing machinery for wool. Mr. John Clegg, whose premises were situated in Union-street, was the first jenny maker, and Mr. Edmund Leach, of Summer Castle, was noted for his power-looms. Mr. John Mason, in his foundry off Drake-street, made "mules," "throstles," and "billeys." Messrs. John Ackroyd and Wilkinson were the first who made nails by machinery, and their works were at the Bottom-o'-th'-Lane. Before this period there was not a single foundry or machine shop in the town, and all the work had to be done in Bury; but at last when this particular branch of industry was introduced into Rochdale, it made rapid progress, and now nearly all the machinery for fabrics is manufactured here.

LITERATURE, PUBLICATIONS, AND PERIODICALS.

Books to amuse us, books to make us wise,
Books to kill time as time on slow wing flies;
Books on polemics, and small books of song,
Books which to science's fair realm belong;
Books full of satire, and books dull as lead,
Books of all kinds before the eye are spread.
And our short list attempts to keep in view
The names of books which Rochdale knows or knew.
For fame the authors sought but most I ween,
Have but a glimpse of her fair features seen;
Some stand out brightly—Roby, Collier, Waugh—
On these Oblivion ne'er her veil shall draw.
Others have dropped quite " dead-born from the press,"
And whelmed their authors in dire wretchedness;
Some few we turn to with intense delight,
And some 'tis wished had never seen the light.
Of making books there surely is no end,
For all men think that they can all men mend;
And thus it is that scribbling still prevails,
Who wins is happy, he who loses, rails.

LEAVING to antiquarian research the precise dates and circumstances of the rise of literature in Rochdale, it may be stated that prior to the last century there was no local literature. John Collier ("Tim Bobbin"), in 1745, published the *Blackbird*, a short satirical poem on a local justice; and, in 1750, "A View of the Lancashire Dialect by way of dialogue between Tummus and Meary," etc., which, with his other works are, though coarse, a capital satirical and humourous comment on the manners, customs, and politics of the day.

In 1810 an introduction to an intended history of Rochdale was published by W. Nuttall, who was a schoolmaster, and lived opposite to St. James's Church, Whitworth Road. He came to an untimely end.

Mr. Aston, in 1827, commenced the first periodical—a newspaper—the *Rochdale Recorder*. In politics, it was according to the phrase of the day, a "Church and King paper." The price was 7d., there being a stamp duty of 4d. on each paper.

The era of the Reform Bill agitation, and the elections which followed in 1832 and 1836, were prolific in the production of squibs, songs, etc., and good specimens were reprinted in book form by W. Butterworth.

Mr. Roby's "Traditions of Lancashire" appeared in 1829, in two vols., beautifully illustrated. It was printed by Spottiswoode & Co. Mr. Roby, in after years, wrote several other works, and amongst them a "Tour in Switzerland and the Rhine." Critics have spoken in the very highest terms of Roby's "Traditions." Certain it is, that for brilliancy of writing, and the expert manner in which tradition is woven into the very texture of the story, Mr. Roby had not many equals; and almost all his stories bear undoubted marks of the power and genius of the writer, and all are perfect specimens of the romancist's art. They at once arrest and chain the attention; and the reader feels that he is under the spell of a potent and friendly enchanter.

The Rev. Canon Raines, of Milnrow, has been, and is, a contributor of eminence to the Chetham Society's publications. As an antiquarian his reputation stands deservedly high; and we know few who are more entitled to the respect which his name commands as an able writer in the particular department over which this admirable society keeps "watch and ward." The untiring industry of the worthy Canon is well known and appreciated by his professional brethren.

In 1842 *Common Sense; or, Everybody's Magazine*, edited by Dr. Molesworth and the Rev. William N. Molesworth, was issued. This periodical was in favour of the continuance of Church Rates, and antagonistic to Dissent. It was quickly followed by *The Vicar's Lantern*, edited and supported, according to rumour, by Messrs. John Bright, Thomas Booth, John Coates, Oliver Ormerod, and Alderman Edward Taylor. These gentlemen strenuously and ably advocated the separation of Church and State, and voluntaryism in religion. The printers, respectively, were Samuel Ashworth and Jesse Hall.

The *Spectator*, a monthly periodical, which contained the well-known "Yeomanry Papers," by Mr. Oliver Ormerod, appeared in 1844.

The *Pilot*, also a monthly periodical, appeared in 1844, amongst the reputed conductors being Mr. John Petrie, Mr. Thomas Schofield, and Mr. Edward Taylor.

The *Beacon*, another monthly periodical, reputed to be edited by Dr. J. Elliott Wood and Mr. J. Nield, was printed by J. & J. Mills.

The *Looking Glass*, said to be conducted by Mr. Edward Taylor, had an existence of twelve months.

Ikey, said to be edited by Mr. William Todd, and printed by W. Prince, came out for three or four months The price of all the above periodicals was one penny.

Mr. Edwin Waugh's writings may be said to have become generally famous. His Lancashire songs and tales stand at the head of the literature of this class; and his works abound in pathos and humour.

Mr. John Ashworth published "Wesley's Ghost," and a few years afterwards his "Strange Tales" and "Walks in Canaan" appeared. Mr. Ashworth has been eminently successful as a writer of short stories, illustrative of incidents in the lives of the poor and destitute ; and it is commonly reported that "Strange Tales," in their collected form, have had an immense circulation.

In 1851, the second weekly newspaper, the *Rochdale Sentinel*, was commenced by Mr. Edward Taylor and Mr. John Phillips. The price was 4d., the stamp duty having been reduced to 1d. It was eight pages. Like all newspapers at that time, it had but a limited circulation as compared to the untaxed papers of our day, the circulation being about 800.

"A Rachde Felley's Visit too the Greyt Eggishibishun," by Mr. Oliver Ormerod, was published in 1851. It contains : "O Ful, Tru, un Pertikler Okeawnt o bwoth wat aw seed un wat aw yerd, we gooin too the Greyt Eggishibishun, e Lundun, Un o greyt deyle o Hinfurmashun besoide, wele Kalkilated fur to giv thoose foke o gradely hinseet into things, us hassant ad nothur 'toime nur brass for to goo un see fur thersels; kontaining loikewise O Dikshunary manefakturt fare o'purpus for thoose us ur noan fur larn't. Be O Felley fro Rachde. O Fur Sixpunze. Furst Edishun. 61 pages. *Rachde : Printud un Sowd be H. M. Crosskill ; un o Booksellers.*"

In 1856, a third weekly newspaper, the *Rochdale Observer*, was published by Messrs. Robert and Joseph Lawton.

A fourth newspaper, the *Standard*, came out in 1857, published by Messrs. Robert and Joseph Lawton, but some time after the *Observer* and *Standard* were amalgamated, and in the course of years the name *Standard* was discontinued, and that of *Observer* retained. Mr. W. A. Scott is now the proprietor of the journal thus united.

In 1859 " Owd Neddy Fitton's Visit to th' Earl o' Derby," by Miss M. R. Lahee, was published by Mr. J. Heap, of Bury, and in December, 1865, by the same authoress, " Life and Times of the late Alderman T. Livsey." At least a dozen works have been written by Miss Lahee, and many of them have gone through several editions. She is a very pleasing and able writer.

Mr. John Bright published, in 1840, an address on the late Church Rate Contests. Several years ago he wrote an introduction to the " Prize Essay on the Game Laws."

The Rev. W. N. Molesworth wrote the " Prize Essay on the English and French Alliance " in 1860; the " History of the Reform Bill " in 1865; and the " History of England " from the years 1830 to 1871-73. The last-named history has been favourably received by the public, and in our opinion it is a highly meritorious publication. The work has been recently re-issued in a cheaper form.

In 1869 a book of poems by Mr. James Holden, entitled " Poetic Zephyrs," was published by Mr. John Heap, of Bury.

In 1870, " A Wicked Woman," a novel, by Gertrude Fenton, was published.

In 1871 "The History of the Chapelry of Goosnargh," by Lieut.-Col. Fishwick, of Carr Hill, was published; and, in 1873, the "History of Kirkham; and, in 1875, "The Lancashire Library," were also published by this gentleman. The gallant colonel is most indefatigable in his antiquarian researches; and the books which he has issued are of the greatest value to those who are interested in such subjects.

In 1872 "The D'Eyncourts of Fairlegh," by Mr. T. Rowland Skemp, in three vols., was issued.

"The Water Way to London" was published by Messrs. Schofield and Grindrod.

A sixth newspaper, the *Spectator*, was published by Mr. W. Clegg, in 1859.

The *Pilot*, a newspaper, was published by Mr. White, in 1858, and discontinued in 1871, after 671 numbers had been issued. Its tone was Conservative.

A newspaper, the *Rochdale Times*, was brought out by a limited company in 1871, and is still in existence.

In January, 1874, there appeared the first number of a fortnightly satirical and humourous journal, entitled the *Rochdale Chimes,* projected and edited by Mr. W. Swift. The journal changed hands after the eighth number, and was discontinued with the twelfth.

The history of the above papers, the causes of the discontinuance of some, their politics and peculiarities, it is not our province to dilate upon. It may be sufficient to say that local rivalries, party politics, and personal interest, had all their special influence, and we may express the hope that the *Rochdale Observer*, now published by Mr. W. A. Scott, which represents Liberal measures and progress, and the

Rochdale Times, which devotes itself to the Conservative interest, may long continue and thrive.   The two papers are published weekly,

> When men rush out to buy these penny sheets,
> And con the news while passing through the streets;
> Then some atrocity or dreadful fire
> Arrests attention or awakes their ire;
> Or some event which keeps the world in awe,
> So stills the heart that breath they scarcely draw.

It must be understood that this section is not by any means of an exhaustive character.   We have in the briefest terms indicated the works which have occurred to our memory; and to have entered into full details of the various works, which we should have been glad to do, would have occupied more of our space than could be spared for the purpose.   Perhaps, also, strict chronological order may not have been observed, but this, however, is not of much consequence in brief notices which only attempt to preserve the names of some of the works which have appeared from time to time in our local history.

A RAMBLE THROUGH THE PRINCIPAL STREETS.

"Oft have I smiled the happy pride to see
Of modern tradesmen in their evening glee,
When of some pleasing, fancied good possessed,
Each grew alert, was busy, and was blest."

THE ancient shop-keepers of Rochdale, in character and physique, were of the true John Bull type, and their very appearance seemed to embody the favourite expression of the Miller of the Dee—"I care for nobody, no, not I, and nobody cares for me." When not engaged in serving customers, or in other employment connected with business, they were to be seen leaning over their (half) shop doors in a dreamy mood, with a long clay pipe in their mouth, and now and then complacently nodding and smiling at the passers by, or engaged in a chat, for in the days we refer to the shop-keeper knew nearly the whole of the population; but if an unfortunate stranger turned-up, all eyes were upon him, and whence he came, and for what purpose, were made the subject of conversation for some time. Most of the old streets were narrow and tortuous, and consisted either of quaint stone houses with mullioned windows, Gothic doors, and peaked gables, or of the white and black timber houses projecting over, first, a low-browed shop, then with an overhanging storey, containing often a wooden oriel, and higher a gabled storey whose bolder projection invaded the upper area of the street. The shops had a bay-window on each side of the doorway, and the merchandise mostly displayed was of varied character. For instance, a customer could buy at the same shop a yard of calico or a box of pills, a quartern of tea or a bunch of carrots, a red herring or a mince pie, a pair of boots or a pound of sausages. In the course of time shops of a better description were erected and the business was confined within the limits proper to that of a draper, a grocer, a chemist, or a green-grocer; and the shop-keepers became more cultivated in their tastes, better educated, and keen competition would not permit them to lounge and indulge in a smoke at their shop doors, for as the prices of goods were lowered, a larger quantity had to be sold in order to afford a fair profit on the capital invested. As soon as the railway was opened to Manchester, some of the inhabitants were pleased to entertain the idea that they could purchase goods cheaper and better in Manchester, and this fallacious impression lingers yet in the minds of some. Perhaps they are not aware, or do not remember, that the tradesmen of Rochdale buy their merchandise from exactly the same wholesale dealers as do the tradesmen of Manchester; that the latter have to pay higher rents, heavier rates, and larger salaries, and is it not more likely that inferior goods might be palmed off upon an entire stranger, as it might be thought there were ten chances to one whether he would visit them again? whereas, a Rochdale tradesman is intimately acquainted with his customers, and considers it highly discreditable and injurious to sell articles which may appropriately be termed "cheap and nasty," knowing that if he does so, it must, on the principle of "once bitten, twice shy," lead to the ultimate destruction of his business.

A mental stroll with an imaginary companion through the principal streets of Rochdale, and a description of the changes that have taken place, and a narration of interesting events may be acceptable to many of our readers.

> " This is the place, here let us stand
> While we review the scene,
> And summon from the shadowy past
> The things that once have been.
>
> The past and present here unite
> Beneath life's flowing tide,
> Like footprints on the sands of time
> Which serve us as a guide."

We will begin our brief description as the visitor emerges from the principal railway station into Oldham-road, and inform him that this road was constructed about 1823, and as he will, of course, infer it leads to the neighbouring town of Oldham. Speaking first of the top of Oldham-road, it may be stated that the canal crosses the road near to the shop of Mr. Wm. Kershaw, tailor and draper, Lockbridge, and that Crawford-street runs in an easterly direction. There are several mills in this street, and the tannery of Mr. Loversidge. Directing our footsteps towards the heart of the town along Oldham-road, it will be noticed that on the other side of the canal, and directly opposite to the shop of Mr. John Varty, pork butcher, stands the ruin of a once extensive flannel mill, formerly occupied by Mr. Morgan Brierley and Mr. L. Stott, which was burnt down about twelve months ago. Lower down the road,

in a southerly direction, opposite to the shop of Mr.
Harrison, saddler, runs Elbow-lane. As we proceed,
we reach Milnrow-road which leads to the thriving
village of Milnrow. Molesworth-street, so named after
Dr. Molesworth, the present vicar, branches out of
Milnrow-road, and at the corner stands conspicuously
the marble works of Mr. W. Holdsworth. Near to
Mr. Edward Kierby's elastic engine web packing manufactory on Milnrow-road, there has been erected, within
the last ten or twelve years, quite an extensive village,
which is rapidly increasing, and will soon fill up the
vacant land between there and Crawford-street. Retracing our steps to Oldham-road, brings us to Livsey-
street, which takes its name from the family of the late
Alderman Livsey having some property in this street.
Baron-street, in which are situated Mr. Charles
O'Doherty's engine packing works, was named after
the well-known drawing master, Jeffrey Baron, who
built houses in this street. In a short street named
Wet Rake, at the top of Drake-street, near the premises now occupied by Mr. J. Clegg, printer and
stationer, is the site of a once famous well, which con-
tributed to a rivulet which ran down Drake-street.
Wet Rake and its continuation, School-lane, sixty
years ago was a country lane, and all that thickly
populated locality was then the suburban part of the
town. School-lane was so named from the Old Grammar School which faced the premises now converted
into Turkish Baths, and stood near the present carriage
works of Mr. Lodge. The Turkish Baths, which were
established fifteen years ago, have undergone great
improvement lately; amongst other medical baths given

is the hydropathic treatment, which has been introduced by Mr. Thomas Brierley, the manager. The triangular plot of land in front of Mr. James Duckworth's whole-sale grocery establishment and Mr. Lister's shoe shop, between Oldham-road, Milnrow-road, and Drake-street, which is now filled up by a foundry, was once suggested as a suitable site for the Town Hall, and it is to be regretted that it was not left an open space. Drake-street was named after the Rev. Dr. Drake who formed that street about the year 1810, and it opened out the vicarage land for building purposes. As we proceed, a fine, lofty, and capacious building attracts our notice (nearly opposite to Mr. Renshaw's dentistry establish-ment), which was erected a few years ago by Mr. W. A. Scott, the spirited proprietor of the *Rochdale Observer*, a most ably-conducted Liberal paper, which has been established nineteen years, and which has a very ex-tensive circulation. Before Drake-street, which is a main artery to the town, was opened, the locality where at present stand the premises of Mr. William Shepherd, auctioneer, Mr. R. Sutcliffe, optician, etc., and the shop lately occupied by Mr. Councillor B. Butterworth was a deep valley, and the site upon which Mr. Daven-port's foundry is built was a knoll higher than St. Chad's Churchyard, and was called "The Heart Ache," on account of the difficulty of forming it into building land. A street on the right, in which Mr. R. Rothwell's flock bed manufactory is situate, and named Water-street, is so named from the fact that it runs down to the River bank. One of the first buildings erected in Drake-street was the "country" residence of the late William Chadwick, Esq., which has recently been con-

verted into a shop, and part of it is at present
occupied by Mr. Edwin Brownson, tailor and woollen
draper.   John Chadwick, Esq., a few years after, built
some neat private dwellings, which have also been
turned into shops, and Mr. Howarth, hatter, now carries
on business in one of them.   The street leading off to
the left, near the brush shop of Messrs. Bentley and
Shaw, and nearly opposite Messrs. Jones and Co.'s
sewing machine establishment, and Mr. John Goul-
burn's cabinet maker's shop, was named Nelson-
street, in commemoration of Nelson's victories.   Further
down Drake-street, on the right, at the corner of
which stands the stationer's shop of Messrs. Schofield
and Hoblyn, and opposite to Mr. Turner's stationer's
shop, runs River-street, in which Mr. William
Ashworth's emigration office is situated.   Near the
druggist's shop lately occupied by the late Mr.
Hamilton Rothwell, and now by Mr. John Jones,
stood a famous fish pond, where some of the present
inhabitants may remember having caught "jack
sharps" and "gold fish," and the small rivulet
from Wet Rake flowed into it.   The old road to Manchester was through the street now called Church-lane,
at the corner of which is the shop of Mr. Holt, tobacconist.
Church-lane is the oldest part of the town, and the
way to Manchester was along Church Stile, through
Milkstone-road (at the corner of which now stands Mr.
Buckley's dentistry establishment), and on the west
side of the new Board School, and came out at Castleton
Moor.   The old road to Oldham turned off at the east
side of the Board School, and through Lowerplace.
One of the principal coal depôts in the town is situated

on Milkstone-road, near to Messrs. Ingham, Hawks-
worth, and Co.'s livery stables, and Mr. James
Butterworth, coal merchant, does an extensive business
here, and so does also Mr. Thomas Schofield, as well as
at his Castleton siding. Cattle fairs have been held in
Church Stile and School-lane from time immemorial,
and they have increased from three fairs in the
year to monthly and fortnightly fairs. The Corporation has bought the manorial rights from the
Lord of the Manor, and the holding of fairs in
School-lane being found to be inconvenient, it is expected that they will be held elsewhere. Mr. Cheetham,
the assistant overseer of Castleton, has kindly given us
access to books containing the particulars of the rateable
value of property in the township of Castleton as far
back as could be got, and we find that in 1760 the poor
rate for six months of that year was twelve pence in
the pound, which produced a total of £106 19s. 11d.
The rateable value of the property was £2,140. In the
year 1860 the rateable value had increased to £67,317,
and in 1874 to £121,944 10s. 0d. In 1820 the Rev. W.
R. Hay paid a poor rate of 4s. 6d. in the pound, for
a half-year, upon the vicarage land and buildings,
which amounted to £5 8s. 0d. That year the poor rate
increased to 9s. in the pound, whereas at the present
time it is only 1s. 6d. in the pound, and the rate now
paid on the vicarage land and buildings for the whole
year amounts to £7 10s. In 1820 there were 1,040
assessments, but in 1874 they numbered 8,827. From
the Bottom-o'-th' Lane Corn Mill, behind the Wellington Hotel in Drake-street, there was formerly a goit
under the present hosier's shop of Mr. Rishton, in

Drake-street, Mr. W. G. Land's cabinet-maker's shop, South Parade (formerly New Wall), and Mr. Davies's dye establishment, and the water was delivered into the Roach at the south corner of the bridge. Up till the year 1819 there was an annual sport on the 7th of November of bull-baiting in the bed of the river, on the southerly side of the bridge, and it was witnessed by thousands of spectators who used to lean over the river wall. In that year, during the sport, the wall fell into the river, and with it a large number of the spectators, seven of whom were killed, and this lamentable occurrence ended the sport of bull-baiting in Rochdale. King-street, which branches off South Parade on the left, was formerly called Packer Meadow. Packer-street runs parallel, its etymology being apparent, as it was associated with the packing of the old pack-horses. This street was once the locality of the most respectable shops, and two of the leading hotels were situated here, namely, the "Golden Ball," which was kept by Mr. Daniel Nield, the parish clerk, and the "Flying Horse," the landlord of the latter for many years being Mr. James Whitehead, who was celebrated in an election song as "James o' Peters." For a considerable time the magistrates sat in Petty Sessions at this house. Packer-street was the main thoroughfare for the whole of Castleton, the road up the Church Steps being direct, and that up Sparrow Hill being long and circuitous. After the opening of Manchester-road and Drake-street the traffic was almost entirely withdrawn from Packer-street, and the property there was thus depreciated quite two-thirds in value.

The Iron Bridge leading to The Walk was erected
22

by Messrs. Vavasour, about the year 1825, to improve
their property in The Walk, which was built upon part of
the site of the Eagle Inn yard, which reached nearly from
Yorkshire-street as far back as Miss Meredith's book-
seller's shop. "Town Hall Chambers," in which are
the offices of Mr. William Beswick, mining engineer,
and of Mr. Hoyle, accountant, were, some few years
ago, used as a post office. At the bottom of Packer-
street there is a fine stone building, a branch bank of
the Manchester and Liverpool Banking Co. The
extensive cabinet and upholstery work rooms of Mr.
Snowdon are on the southern side of the Town Hall. The
fine, broad street in front of the Town Hall received
the name of " Esplanade " from Mr. Alderman Taylor,
on account of its width and inclining to the river side.
The "Old Bridge " has been widened six times, and
many years ago, on the north-east side, there was a
direct road to the river side. Passing over the bridge,
and turning to the left, leads to The Orchard, in which
may be noticed the office of Mr. Edward Hill, and the
insurance office of Mr. Samuel Brierley. This thoroughfare was formerly called The Walk, as a footpath ran
along the river side, which was a favourite resort for
lovers. Many of the present inhabitants remember
this "path by the river" as one of their favourite walks
in the days of their courtship, and, looking back upon
their love episodes, they cannot but agree with the asser-
tion that "All that has been written in song, or told in
story, of love and its effects, falls far short of its reality.
Its evils and its blessings, its impotence and its power,
its sin and its holiness, its weakness and its strength,
will continue the theme of nature and of art, until the

great pulse of the universe is still." Turning to the
right of the bridge, we are led to the Butts, an open
space, and the origin of its name was from the fact that
archery was formerly practised here, and many merry
and delightful scenes, no doubt, have been witnessed
on this plot of ground.

"May day games of archerie,
Pageants, wyth thyr gallant showe,
Towrnaments, wyth knyghtes a rowe."

Mr. W. Snowdon has a splendid shop in The Butts,
in which he displays his furniture. Messrs. Clement
Royds and Co.'s bank, which was established in 1819,
is situated here. Smith-street, is a continuation of the
Butts, and in January, 1854, a serious fire occurred at
Messrs. R. & J. Kelsall's mill, which stands at the
corner of Duncan-street and Smith-street, on which
occasion two women jumped out from an upper storey
and were killed. The fire commenced in the third
storey, near the staircase, which prevented the operatives making their escape by the stairs. Some men
slid down by the teagle rope, and Abraham Taylor
lowered a number of men and young women by the
means of flannel pieces. Henry Ratcliffe, of Smith-
street, saved the lives of fourteen persons by a rope,
which he fastened in the roof of the building, and after
they had slid down it he escaped by the same means.
A public subscription was made, and £200 presented to
Mr. Ratcliffe, and £100 to Mr. Taylor, for their presence
of mind and courage.

Commencing at the bridge again, it will be noticed
that the property opposite Mr. Robert Lawton's
stationer's shop is old, and the other buildings in the

neighbourhood have been rebuilt, with the exception of
the premises in which Mr. Hicks, sculptor, has his
offices. Messrs. J. and J. Fenton and Sons' Bank
adjoins. The cashier, Mr. Anthony Baldwin, is
agent for the Manchester Fire Assurance Company.
Mr. Peter Lee's wholesale and retail provision establishment, was built on the site of the Old Roebuck
Hotel, a famous coaching house. It was here an
admiring crowd used to assemble to watch the prancing
horses [and the coaches, under the command of
individuals buried in a multiplicity of coats, broad
brimmed hats, and huge rolls of coloured handkerchiefs
about their necks. These consequential personages had
commonly full faces, which had swelled into jolly
dimensions by frequent potations of malt liquor.
" It's a good sign to see the colour of health in a man's
face; it's a bad sign to see it all concentrated in his
nose." Mr. King's ironmonger's shop was formerly
called " Union Buildings," and was a noted hotel, and
afterwards a gentleman's residence. -

In the Stuart rebellion of 1745, a party of the rebels
visited Rochdale, on the 30th of November, and
demanded the " Militia Arms, Land Tax," etc., and
they made the Union Hotel and the Vicarage their
head quarters. The authorities at first determined to
repel the invaders, but when they had actually arrived
they found it no easy matter, and allowed them to be
quartered in various parts of the town. One of the
kilted highlanders went into the kitchen of the Union
Hotel, and asked the cook permission to dip his bread
into the dripping pan. The cook refused, but he threw
in a lump of black bannock, which she threw out with

the dripping spoon into the ashes. Upon this, " Sandy"
drew his sword, but the Lancashire lass laid hold of
her spoon and splashed his face and knees with hot
dripping, causing him to scream. At the same moment
the scullery maid let loose the dog, which chased him
out of the house, and tore a large piece out of the back
part of his kilt. The scalds proved serious, and he
was placed under the skill of Dr. Mott. Betty, the
cook, relented, and nursed him with great attention,
their hostile feelings changed to affection, and it ended
in a matrimonial union. He settled in the town,
became a successful tradesman, and his descendants are
at the present day respectable and prosperous.

> The cook worked her purpose by means of her grease,
> And the feud which existed was turned into peace;
> For the scalds she inflicted by means of hot dripping
> Set herself and the Scotchman a-kissing and clipping;
> The "Union" she left for a union more pleasing,
> And they loved with a love which was sweet and unceasing.

The inhabitants of Rochdale on the occasion remained
loyal, only one joining the rebel army. His name was
Valentine Holt, of Yorkshire-street, a noted poacher
and marksman. He was captured, found guilty of
high treason, and executed at Penrith, on the 28th of
October, 1746.

The shop opposite Lord-street, Mr. Henry Howorth's,
is the oldest printing office in the town, himself and his
family having been in this special trade for the last
hundred years. Part of the building occupied by Mr.
Henry Butterworth, jeweller, and watch and clock maker,
which is called Town Hall Buildings, was built on the
site of a large news-room belonging to the Market
Company. Lord-street runs out of Yorkshire-street on

the left, and it was formerly called Blackwater-street,
but the Commissioners decided that streets of one continuous line should only bear one name. In this street
the Flannel Market is held every Monday, and it is
still called the "Blackwater Market." At the junction
of Blackwater-street with Lord-street, before the year
1825, stood a house in Lord-street, at the right angle
with the King's Head, four yards. The opposite house
which is now occupied by Mr. Owen March, solicitor,
and that of Mr. Lawton's the maltster, used to be one
tenement, and bore the name of "the Manor House."
It is a very ancient building, and it is supposed to have
been once the property of the Byron family. The late
Alderman Livsey was born on the 17th of June, 1815,
at the Duke of Wellington Hotel, bottom of Blackwater-
street, and he was the son of Robert Livsey, the
landlord. The career of honest Tom Livsey is intimately connected with the history of progress in Rochdale and the innumerable advantages conferred upon
the working class—

> "A king can make a belted knight,
> A marquis, duke, and a' that ;
> But an honest man's aboon his might,
> Guid faith, he manna fa' that."

Baillie-street, which opens to the right of Yorkshire-
street, took its name from Colonel Baillie, who was the
owner of land in this street. The first shop on the
right, Messrs. John Pollitt & Sons, hair dressers, was
formerly the Branch Banking House of the Manchester
and Liverpool Bank. The Joint Stock Bank, a handsome structure, is a little further on the left, and it was
registered under the Companies' Act in March, 1872.

The registered capital of this bank is £500,000 in 2,500 shares of £20 each, £113,280 of which is subscribed at the date of the last balance sheet, September 30th, 1874.   The Lyceum, on the right, where the services of the Chapel for the Destitute are held, reminds us of our now lamented townsman, Mr. John Ashworth, who, since his name was mentioned in a previous part of this work, suffered intensely, his once robust frame being reduced by sheer starvation, from his inability to pass food of any kind,

> " Till pitying nature signed the last release,
>   And bade afflicted worth retire to peace."

He died on the 26th of January, 1875, and was followed to his burial place in the Rochdale Cemetery by hundreds of his sympathising friends belonging to Rochdale, and from neighbouring towns.   The good which John Ashworth has done will continue to benefit not only the present but many generations, and of him it may be said—

> " The actions of the just
>   Smell sweet and blossom in the dust."

The Public Hall is situated in this street, and has been the scene of many interesting and im portant meetings.   On the 5th of March, 1868, a serious riot occurred here on account of the Public Hall Company refusing to let Messrs. Houston and Mackey, followers of Murphy, the anti-Popery advocate, have the use of the hall.   Mackey shot at police officer David Halstead, but, fortunately, the bullet struck the officer's belt, and thus he escaped injury.   Mackey was imprisoned for sixteen months for the offence, and his partisans afterwards built a " Protestant Hall " in

Milkstone-road, in which to hold meetings and services. The first Board School was in Baillie-street, which was previously a British School, and it extends as far back as Portland-street, near to Mr. J. Schofield, the dentist's. Returning to Yorkshire-street, so named as it is the principal road to Yorkshire, has been very much improved and widened within the last fifty years. The portion of the street from the shop of Mr. A. Williamson, jeweller and silversmith, to the timbered building of Mr. Holt has been much improved, and the buildings themselves have been renovated. Mr. Holt's warehouse is perhaps one of the oldest buildings in Rochdale. There used to be an old-fashioned building where the shop of Mr. Joseph Handley, grocer, now stands, but the Market Company rebuilt the present structure, and all the shops as far as that of Mr. J. Muir's, clothier, extends in the Market Place. Mr. Wm. Swift's boot shop, and Mr. Clough's hat shop, in Yorkshire-street, are ancient buildings, and have been modernised. The old road to Yorkshire was down Church-lane, right across a ford into the Butts, up "Bull Brow," by the large and extensive building which is now occupied as the offices of the *Rochdale Times*, the newspaper which so ably advocates the Conservative cause in Rochdale, and into Yorkshire-street at the corner of Mr. Gilbert Haworth's stationer's shop. The respective premises occupied by Mr. Levi Clegg, woollen draper and cloth merchant ; Mr. William Wallace, boot and shoe manufacturer ; Mr. W. Brocklehurst, tailor and woollen draper ; Mr. A. Barraclough, tea dealer and grocer ; and Mr. Robinson, chemist, are all comparatively modern structures. Nearly opposite, the Baum turns off to the left, and in this narrow street or passage on the 15th of October, 1862, a shocking accident occurred in a building facing Messrs. Charles Walker & Son's skip manufactory and insurance offices. While a sale was proceeding in the top room of the building, part of the flooring gave way, and the whole contents of the room, audience, and auctioneer, fell through 'the lower storeys to the bottom, creating the greatest havoc and consternation. Mr. John Mattley, machine broker; Mr. John Turner, cotton spinner; and Mr. Abraham Knight, furniture broker, were killed on the spot, and a number of other persons were very seriously injured. Many persons providentially escaped unhurt, and the auctioneer declared "that though he had felt himself to be going he was extremely glad to find he was not gone." The shop of Mr. Thomas Reid, cloth merchant and woollen draper, which is opposite to Bell-street; Mr. David Oldfield's tailor and outfitter's shop, and that of Mr. Jas. Hamilton, ironmonger, etc., were formerly the front rooms of the Reed Hotel. This hotel now stands further back, having been rebuilt, and there are excellent livery stables connected with it, under the management of Mr. Joseph M. Hepworth. Hunter's-lane, in which the offices of Messrs. Schofield and Son, agents for the National Provident Insurance are situated, leads into Cheetham-street. Returning into Yorkshire-street, some of the oldest inhabitants remember the erection of the shops now occupied by Mr. J. Cleminson, grocer; Messrs. G. & T. Rushworth, drapers; Mr. Robert Adamson, tea and coffee merchant; Mr. Joseph Handley, family mourning establishment; Mr. Davis, boot and shoe manufacturer; Mr. J. Whipp,

watch maker; and Mr. Albert Wheeler, tailor; and
that formerly they were private dwellings. Acker-
street, in which Mr. J. H. Baskeyfield has his shop and
cooperage, and Mr. C. Renshaw his extensive carriage
works, leads to the Public Hall, to which we have
previously referred. Cheetham-street turns off on the
left of Yorkshire-street, and it derives its name from
Cheetham College, Manchester, as some of the land here
belongs to that college, but in old deeds the street is
named Northgate. The whole aspect of this now important thoroughfare has been completely changed by
the elevation of the level. From the shops of Mr. Wm.
Frost, general dealer; and Mr. Arthur Skelton, wholesale and retail tobacconist, there was formerly a decline
to a rivulet named the Lord-burn, which flowed across
the road down Cable-square, and into the Roach at the
Orchard. A few doors beyond the shop of Mr. James
Hadfield, druggist, some of the buildings are two storeys
below the present surface of the street. The street
turning off nearly opposite the shop of Mr. Lynch,
chemist, and near to Mr. John Whitehead's furniture
depôt, is Mill - street. On the right, nearly
opposite Mrs. Hanson's furniture shop, runs Redcross-
street. In 1868, Murphy, the anti-Popery lecturer,
lodged in a house within a few doors of Mr. Clegg's
dentistry in Cheetham-street, and on the evening of the
26th of March in that year an angry mob followed
Murphy, and a young woman named Ann Swift
assaulted him nearly opposite the shop which is now
occupied by Mr. Simeon Taylor, agent for the Singer
Sewing Machine. For this offence she was imprisoned
for fourteen days. Murphy, during his stay in

Rochdale, was the cause of riotous proceedings in various parts of the town, and instigated religious strife, which culminated in an attack upon St. John's Catholic Chapel, where the rioters smashed the windows and committed damage to the amount of several hundred pounds.   He visited other towns, carrying on his crusade against the Catholics, and a few years later he received blows which ultimately resulted in his death.   Toad-lane crosses the end of Cheetham-street, at right angles, and its name is supposed to have originated from the word "Tod," namely, 14 lbs. weight of wool, as here, in remote times, wool was largely dealt in, and where the shops of Mr. J. Grindrod, watch maker; Mr. E. Whiteley, tobacconist ; and the office of Mr. John Howe, auctioneer, now stand, was the site of the ancient wool warehouses. The flannel market, as before-mentioned, was held a little lower down near the famous dining-rooms of Mr. James Ashworth.   At the top of Toad-lane Falinge-road branches off, on the left, and on Greenhill Estate, in this road, as mentioned in a preceding page, the annual Rochdale Agricultural Show is held.   This show was formerly called the Whitworth and Rochdale Agricultural Show.   It originated at Whitworth in 1854, and its early success was partly attributable to the exertions of the late Mr. Robert Tweedale, of Healey. Heights-lane branches off Toad-lane to the right, and this was originally the old road to Bacup, passing through Shawclough and into the Whitworth-road at Ending.   Retracing our steps to the short street named St. Mary's Gate, the Hanging-road cotton mill, opposite the shop of Mr. Alexander Gillespie, tailor and outfitter, is one of the oldest mills in the town.   Continuing our

course we are brought to the end of Blackwater-street,
at the corner of which may be noticed a lofty building,
which site was at first intended for a Temperance Hall,
but it is now used for warehouses and offices, and Mr.
Sutcliffe Bridge, agent to Messrs. Boddington & Co.,
brewers, occupies part of the premises.

Spotland-road is a continuation of St. Mary's Gate,
and the houses in this locality cannot boast of much
antiquity. Bury-road leads off opposite the shop of
Mr. Benjamin Heywood, undertaker. About twelve
months ago a new road was opened out of Spotland-
road past the saw mills of Mr. James Grandidge into
Toad-lane, which has been of the greatest advantage in
relieving some of the narrow and busy streets hereabouts. Returning to Yorkshire-street, from which
we branched into Cheetham-street, it may not be unin-
teresting to state that where now stand the grocer's shop
of Mr. O. P. Bevan; the upholstery establishment of
Mr. Henry Shaw; the furniture shop of Mr. H. D.
Butterworth; the dentistry of Mr. Marlor; the drapery
establishment of Mr. Taylor, and Mr. G. H. Robinson's
grocery shop, the locality ninety years ago, was an
extensive nursery on both sides of the then lane, and
the only house then standing was the old police office
now occupied by Mr. James Schofield, dentist. John-
street turns off to the right near to St. James's church,
and leads to the railway station. The fine warehouse
near to the shop of Mr. William Adamson, tailor, John-
street, belongs to Messrs. Willans & Co., flannel
manufacturers. Whitworth-road is a continuation of
John-street, and some of the oldest inhabitants can
remember that this locality from the part where Mr.

Bamford Taylor's druggist shop, and Mr. Diggle's
bakery, Townhead, now stand, up to Healey, was laid
out in corn and potato fields. George-street runs down
out of Yorkshire-street, parallel with John-street, and
the large timber yard there situated, belongs to Mr. W.
A. Peters, builder and timber merchant. Roach-place,
leads out of George-street, and amongst other residents
there is Mr. George Hulme, machine agent and general
valuer. The Infirmary, is situated in Yorkshire-street,
near Mr. Wm. King's clothing establishment. Elliott-
street, turns off Yorkshire-street, nearly opposite to
Mr. A. Whitham's photographic studio. A building
once used as a chapel in this street has recently been
converted into the carriage works of Mr. H. Graul.
We now transport ourselves to the south west side of
Rochdale, where within the last twenty years, an
extensive range of land, named the Freehold, has
been laid out in a better class of dwellings, interspersed
with shops, and amongst the works are those of
Mr. George Harrison, joiner and builder, and Mr.
Butterworth, mason and builder.

Having now completed a rapid, and, we hope, a
pleasant perambulation through the principal streets
of the town, it may perhaps be agreeable to the reader
to have his attention turned to the chief attraction of
our neighbourhood—Hollingworth Lake.

HOLLINGWORTH LAKE AND BLACKSTONE EDGE.

ROMINENT amid the scenery of the district of which Rochdale is the centre, are the alternations of meadow, moorland, and hill, stretching between its confines and the boundaries of the West Riding. Less enchanting, perhaps, than the rocks and dells which dot the course of the Roach and its smaller confluents, and possessing few of the leaf-clad cloughs to be met with at almost every winding of the brawling little streamlets running through Spotland, Healey, and Whitworth, but with a marked distinctiveness and an artistic beauty all its own. This was the route followed by the legions of Rome in the construction of that Way which the effacing imprints of fifteen centuries have yet been compelled to spare, and which still crops out in sturdy squares of stone pavement as the foot passenger makes his journey into Yorkshire by way of Blackstone Edge. Those old Romans, utilitarian as they were in their policy, their life, and their conquests, had a fine eye for the picturesque, look you. With them, the straight road was always the best road, but they have managed to include in this magnificent highway over the ridge which divides the two counties, not only strategical positions, but also the chief points from which the country might be viewed. And the old Roman road which eschews the pass over Blackstone Edge, prefer-

HOLLINGWORTH LAKE

ring to take the shorter cut to Ripponden, over the
moors, still remains, the characteristic of a people who
warred, as Oliver Wendel Holmes, says, "not with
fifteen foot lances, but with swords as short as the
grace, and as pointed as the laws they gave to all the
world."

Starting from Rochdale, north eastwards, the Roman
road, when three miles out, skirts what is now the
western side of Hollingworth Lake, and as we now
light on a work of modern engineering, we may leave
the more ancient construction to the researches of
antiquarians, and give landmarks more in accordance
with the requirements of the ordinary railway passenger
and tourist.

HOLLINGWORTH LAKE

Is a sheet of water covering 90 acres, originally constructed by the Rochdale and Manchester Canal Co.
as a feeder to that channel of communication. Later
works, however, have rendered its existence no longer
necessary for that purpose, and within recent years it
has fallen into the hands of a company by whom it has
been transformed into a resort of pleasure. Lying
about three miles from Rochdale, its shores may be
gained either by highways from Smithy Bridge and
Littleborough Stations, or by following the windings of
two pleasant footpaths running from the town. One
passes out of the top of Yorkshire-street, by way of
Hamer Mill, and leads through the Hamlet of Clegg;
the other, by Milnrow road and over Uncouth Bridge.

The Lake cannot be called either "grand" or
"lovely." Its surroundings neither awe by their

frowning majesty, nor captivate by their fairy witcheries.
Here are no rugged mountains, snow-topped and grim ;
no far stretching forests of beech, and oak, and pine ;
the nightingale makes not her home upon its shores in
leafy bowers perfumed with odours of richest blossom,
nor does the sighing wind breathe sweetest music
through the groves.   In short, it is neither Loch
Lomond nor Lago Maggiore.   But one is not obliged
to be always viewing the bluest of blue skies of Italy,
or watching the descent of Highland squalls, with their
wonderful changes of light and shade, and Holling--
worth has merits of its own.   We do not expect to be
at Venice when we go to Greenwich, nor at Naples
when we voyage to Blackpool.   And so, though
Hollingworth is neither a Derwentwater nor a Killar-
ney, it may, and does possess attractions of a special
nature worth viewing.   It is homely ; it is pleasant,
and it is the Lake of south Lancashire and the Riding ;
the charming spot where on gala days gather thousands
of workers in this teeming district.   Leeds sends excur-
sions ; Manchester makes holiday here ; contingents
flock from Bradford, and Bury, and Oldham, and not a
district among the moors but is proud if its amateur
instrumentalists can score well at a Hollingworth brass
band contest.   On a summer afternoon, there is wonderful natural variety at Hollingworth.   Its elevated
position unfolds a wide panorama.   Over the sombre
hued Blackstone Edge and russet tinged moorlands of
Wardle, light and shade play strange antics.   The
heather on Whittaker moor is bathed in colours an
artist would give his eyes to catch, while, to the south-
west over the murky atmospheric tinge which tells.

where Rochdale is, the champaign country rolls towards
Manchester in undulating waves of meadowland,
absorbing the brilliant sunshine and throwing back hues
attuned in harmony with the amphitheatre of surrounding hills. Upon the Lake itself, float or dart craft of
every description—the racing skiff, the pleasure boat,
the fishing punt, and the snorting ferry steamer—glide
in every direction, leaving in their wakes long lines of
glittering sheen, while on the western bank linger
crowds for whose patronage numerous caterers of
sweets, and toys, and tea, clamour in no uncertain
voice. For those of more robust appetite, the many
hotels which fringe the lake offer every accommodation.

The lovers of aquatic sports have formed a rowing
club in connection with this lake, and the members
number about 50. Henry Newall, Esq., J.P., is the
president, and Mr. Wm. Lord, the secretary. They
have a boat-house on the north side of the lake neatly
fitted up. They possess eight and four-oared gigs;
four and pair-oared racing cutters, and skiffs, and
canoes.

The Beach Hotel is a commodious inn, built of brick,
and occupying a commanding site. Here are large
refreshment rooms, and overhanging the water, a
spacious dancing stage, capable of accommodating some
two thousand persons. This is brilliantly lighted with
gas, and at night presents a most lively and animating
appearance. Round the hotel are grounds fitted up
for *al fresco* sports.

Crossing the lake from one landing stage to another
by means of a paddle steamer, we reach the Lake
Hotel and pleasure grounds. The hotel is a picturesque

23

building, constructed somewhat after the fashion of a
Swiss chalet.   The neatness and excellence of its
accommodation have given it a name far beyond that of
mere local celebrity.   The Lake Hotel stands within
large and tastefully laid out pleasure grounds.   Drives,
lined with shrubbery will be found along the shores of
the lake, while at the back of the hotel is a well-kept
bowling green, and, beyond that again, flowery arcades
and summer houses, where one may ruralize at leisure.
Standing at the edge of the lake is a very handsome
building, the lower floor of which is used as a refreshment room, the upper floor forming a fine billiard
room, with commodious balcony, from which the sports
on the lake can be conveniently witnessed.   In front of
the veranda of the hotel is a dancing stage, a scene
of gaiety on summer evenings when the lake is
aglow with the setting sun, and joyous sounds of
laughter come rippling over the water.

   There have been temporary reverses to the picture,
for the lake has been the scene of several catastrophes.
About twenty-six years ago there was an accident on
the ice, and several persons were drowned.   On the
6th of April, 1861, a melancholy boat accident occurred.
It seems that on this occasion a great number of people
had come over from various parts of the country to
spend the day at Hollingworth.   There were about
forty small boats besides two steamers on the lake, all
of which were floating about in different directions,
when suddenly about four o'clock, two of the small
boats came into collision with each other near the
centre of the lake.   The collision was so violent as to
capsize both boats; some thirteen persons being pre-

cipitated into the lake, which at this place is sixteen or seventeen yards deep. Before assistance arrived, five of the party were drowned, namely, Ben. Taylor, John Tatham, Sydney Smith, Richmond Richardson, of Higher Crompton, and Henry Crossley, of Shaw.

It may be mentioned in connection with Hollingworth Lake, that its shores are in winter time not an infrequent resort of wild fowl, and that fair sport has been afforded in this direction.

HOLLINGWORTH LAKE BY MOONLIGHT.

The moon sheds down her mellow silver light
　Upon the placid waters, sweet and clear,
While all arouud, the stillness of the night,
　Gives grateful solace to the listening ear.

Mirror of beauty! with what splendour gleams
　The sheen which falls from yon resplendent orb
Upon thy waters, that one almost dreams
　Of magic powers which all her beams absorb!

On such a night as this we feel in love
　With all that nature's holy touch hath warmed;
And while our thoughts upsoar to One above
　We mourn that aught on earth should seem deformed.

Oh, that this peacefulness might long endure,
　This lovely scene continue, free from mist!
Who would not seek for what is true and pure?
　Who would in aught unbeautiful persist?

None but the gross and foul who make the earth
　A scene of terror, havoc, and distress.
O give us, gracious God, a second birth,
　And stem the tide of human wretchedness.

Give us to love thy works, so bright and fair;
　Give us to know where truest goodness lies;
Give, from on high, a living, freshening air,
　Before whose current all pollution flics.

CLEGG HALL.

Lying half or three-quarters of a mile to the south west of the lake, and between it and Rochdale, is the hamlet of Clegg. The principal object of interest here is the fine old mansion of Clegg Hall, a superb specimen of architecture of the days of James I. Although it has fallen sadly from its high estate, the excellent condition of preservation in which its external decoration has been maintained serves to afford a capital notion of the homes of our forefathers. A massive stone porch with steps, gives character to the building, throwing out in fine proportion the heavy carvings above the eight mullioned windows, each with their ten lights; and the sculptured monsters with which the front is further adorned, show the elaborate nature of the architecture. Many a time must the large and lofty rooms have resounded with the glee of deep potations; and, in looking at the wide open mantelpieces with their handsome carvings, one can picture up a scene in the olden time, when the walls were still relieved with dark wainscoting, and the ruddy blaze of the logs on the hearth-stone threw fanciful shadows over the floor and ceiling. The history of this mansion, which once did duty as a roadside public-house, and received its license in the name of "The Black Sloven," is carried back by tradition to the early part of the twelfth century, when it was in the hands of a family who drew their name from the estate. Down to the time of Henry VI., the Cleggs (veritable children of the soil since the meaning of the word in Saxon is "clay,") were possessors of Clegg Hall. It then passed into the hands of the

Ashtons, and from that family, in the reign of
the first Charles, to the keeping of the Howarths. It
requires no antiquary to test the tenure on which
possession in these times was gained. The Wars of the
Roses, and the Parliamentary struggle, being at their
fiercest when these transitions occurred, are a sufficient
reason for the change of proprietors. Since the Civil
War, the hall was bandied about from owner to owner
until it now rests in the possession of Mr. James Fenton,
and recently formed the roof-tree of a tavern, with spare
accommodation for separate dwellings behind.

It would not be fair to pass from a notice of this
place without an allusion to the "boggart" which
"Clegg Ho'" possessed in its palmy days in common
with every other well regulated and antiquated country
house. The legend is worth a short relation, and as
told in Roby's "Traditions of Lancashire," is to the
following effect:—About the middle of the 17th
century, the ghost being about that time so particularly
troublesome as to frighten all comers from approaching
the haunted chamber, Alice Howarth, sister to the
then head of the family, received a mystic summons to
repair to the ghost's apartment at the dead hour of
night under dread penalties to the house in case of
refusal. She goes; the door is bolted behind her and
she is conveyed by one whom she has before met and
shuddered at as a beggar-man, through vaults and
passages to the very foundations of the house. Here
she is met by a stranger who demands her hand in
marriage, and threatens to keep her imprisoned until
she is wearied into consenting. Meanwhile, Alice
is missed from her home, and strict search made. The

beggar-man is arrested on suspicion of complicity with
the crime. In reply, he declares himself one of the
Cleggs, the original owners of the estate, and the right-
ful heir. While undergoing further examination the
house is shaken by an explosion, and the beggar makes
his escape in the confusion. Afterwards, he emerges
from the ghost's apartment bearing the body of Alice,
who had fainted, and again leaves the hall, this time,
to return no more. It is subsequently found that he
was the chief of a gang of coiners, who had used the
ancient portion of the hall for their nefarious practices
(which explained the mysterious sounds), and that as a
means of bringing back the possession of the hall to
the Clegg family, he had abducted Alice in order to
force her into marriage with his son. Needless to add
that henceforward the "boggart" existed but in old
wives' tales, and the vivid imaginations of children.

BLACKSTONE EDGE.

The highroad from Rochdale into Yorkshire passes
over a ridge of hills which form a line of uplands
extending from the Cheviots to the Derbyshire Peak.
To prevent the otherwise unavoidable steep ascent, the
road, after leaving Littleborough runs in zig-zag lines
through a rugged country, where broom, and moss,
and dark ravines alternate with waste moors. This
was the road the mails travelled before the age of
railways, when the coaches were liable to be stopped
by highwaymen, and the young bloods of Littleborough
and the district formed outriding guards to convey the
vehicle to the White House; and doubtless recompensed
their labours when this renowned hostelry was reached

with vigorous application to strong liquors. The White House on Blackstone Edge is the most prominent mark in the whole district. From any point from which a glimpse of the hills may be obtained the inn· at the summit of the road is readily seen, its colour being in strong contrast with the rocks adjacent. This much said, the view obtainable from the hotel itself may be imagined. Standing at the doorway, or, better, on one of the projecting points of Blackstone, all the valley of the Roach is within sight, and the truth of the statement that Rochdale is cradled in hills is fully borne out. The view is charming. Hamlets and mills dot the valley, in the centre of which the winding course of the river which gives its name to the principal town is clearly discernible. In the distance to the south and west, are the chimneys and spires of Manchester, Bury, Oldham, Heywood, and busy centres of industry more far away still, while the knolls and hills stand out with pleasing distinctness. The moors adjacent are well stocked with game, strictly preserved. A little to the east of the White House is "Robin Hood's Bed," a knot of time-worn and weather-riven rocks, bearing no resemblance whatever to a resting place either for an outlaw or honest man. Still tradition has been good enough to couple them with the name of Sherwood's bold forester, and to associate with his wanderings this bleakest of the many bleak spots upon the Lancashire moors. There is here very little indeed of that placid scenery characterising the lower parts of the valley, and yet the wild waste is in admirable keeping with the diversified prospect. Altogether the country side of which Hollingworth and the moors running thence to

Blackstone Edge form a part is not the least beautiful,
nor is it in any whit less interesting than the other spots
to which the attention of the visitor is directed in
other portions of this volume. Both to the antiquary
and the artist, this district presents attractions which
have only to be made known to be taken advantage of
in their fullest extent.

Our views of Hollingworth Lake are from photographs taken by Mr. A. Whitham, and the remainder
of the illustrations are from photographs executed by
Mr. J. Jackson.

L'ENVOI.

And now we pause, our task at length is done,
The goal is reached, and breathing space is won;
None know but they who've trod the rugged way,
How bright the scene is when the heavens display
Their radiant beauties to the grateful eye
Of travellers who have reached the summit high
Of some vast mountain from the plain below,
Where nature's charms in all their splendour glow.
Thus we have upward toiled, and back we cast
Our eyes in retrospect on what we've passed;
Labour is sweet if only friends approve,
And sure 'tis pleasant to dispense one's love.
One only purpose has sustained us still,
The purpose to do good and nothing ill;
It seemed to us that it were well to aim
To keep on record somewhat of the fame
Of our good town of Rochdale, proud and old,
Whereof so much has been and can be told.
Aided by friends whom we full well esteem,
We place before our readers what we deem
An offering not unworthy their regard,
Unseeking thence mere personal reward;
Honest in aim, we make our final bow,
Our book shows ROCHDALE PAST and ROCHDALE NOW.

THE END.

ESTABLISHED 1854.

NOTICE OF REMOVAL.

J. SCHOFIELD, DENTIST,

HAS REMOVED TO

NO. 103, YORKSHIRE STREET, ROCHDALE.

And takes this opportunity to inform the public that he possesses every New and Improved Patent in the practice of Dental Surgery.

He warrants all Artificial Teeth, made by himself to be light, strong, and durable, and worn with the greatest ease and comfort. For mastication and articulation they are equal to natural teeth, being warranted for perfect workmanship.

SUPERIOR TOOTH POWDER.

HIGHLY RECOMMENDED.

Prepared by

J. SCHOFIELD,

DENTIST,

103, Yorkshire-street, Rochdale.

DECAYED TEETH FILLED

Teeth Cleaned and Extracted

On the most approved principles.

Teeth Stopping in all its Branches.

Children's Teeth carefully regulated.

Observe the Address :—J. SCHOFIELD, Dentist, 103, Yorkshire Street

(Late Borough Police Office), ROCHDALE. ATTENDANCE DAILY.—CHARGES MODERATE.

W_{M.} BROCKLEHURST,

TAILOR

AND

WOOLLEN DRAPER,

49, YORKSHIRE STREET.

DAVID OLDFIELD,

TAILOR & OUTFITTER,

65, YORKSHIRE STREET,

ROCHDALE.

SKILLED WORKMANSHIP.

FIRST-CLASS MATERIALS.

CAREFUL OPERATORS.

Mr. J. Renshaw,

Surgeon Dentist,

61, Drake Street,

Rochdale.

REASONABLE CHARGES.

HENRY DEAN BUTTERWORTH,

AUCTIONEER,

Valuer, Estate, & Patent Agent,

99, YORKSHIRE STREET

(NEARLY OPPOSITE THE WHITE LION INN),

ROCHDALE,

Licensed to take Valuations for obtaining Probate of
Wills, Letters of Administration, for Transfer of Hotels,
Public Houses, Beerhouses, Machinery of every description, Farming Stock, Stocks-in-Trade, Furniture, and
every other kind of Property; also Agent for obtaining
Patents and Registrations of Inventions. First cost of
a Patent about £10 10s. of an average.

N.B.—H. D. B. served a Seven Years' Apprenticeship
with the late Mr. Richard Clegg, Auctioneer, &c., since
when he has taken out Eighteen Auctioneers' and
Valuers' Licences in his own name; he therefore trusts
that the practical experience he has gained, during the
last twenty-five years he has been in the business, will
entitle him to a fair share of public patronage and
support.

**Cash to any amount Advanced, at a moment's notice, on
Goods of any description consigned to him, at his Auction
Rooms, for Absolute Sale.**

Valuations undertaken, and any other business entrusted
to him will be attended to with promptitude and despatch.

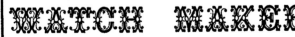

Henry Boddington and Company,

BREWERS,

AND

BURTON-ON-TRENT,

STRANGEWAYS, MANCHESTER.

ESTABLISHED 1786.

Agent for Rochdale:--Sutcliffe Bridge, White Swan Hotel.

Stores: 24, Blackwater-street, Rochdale.

i

NOTICE OF REMOVAL.

———:-o-:———

B. BUTTERWORTH,

TAILOR AND DRAPER,

From 68, Drake Street,

To 83, SPOTLAND ROAD.

JAMES BUTTERWORTH,

Coal Merchant,

HOUSE, ENGINE, SMITHY,

AND

GAS COAL,

CANNEL, &c.,

MILKSTONE RAILWAY SIDING,

ROCHDALE.

JOHN BARKER,

𝔇𝔯𝔞𝔭𝔢𝔯 𝔞𝔫𝔡 𝔊𝔢𝔫𝔢𝔯𝔞𝔩 𝔇𝔢𝔞𝔩𝔢𝔯,

35, MILKSTONE ROAD,

ROCHDALE.